Maiden,

Maiden, Mother and Queen

Mary in the Anglican Tradition

Roger Greenacre

Edited by
Colin Podmore

CANTERBURY PRESS
Norwich

Copyright in this volume © The Estate of Roger Greenacre, 2013

First published in 2013 by the Canterbury Press Norwich
Editorial office
3rd Floor, Invicta House,
108–114 Golden Lane,
London EC1Y 0TG

Canterbury Press is an imprint of Hymns Ancient & Modern Ltd
(a registered charity)
13A Hellesdon Park Road, Norwich,
Norfolk, NR6 5DR, UK

www.canterburypress.co.uk

All rights reserved. No part of this publication may be reproduced, stored in a retrieval system, or transmitted, in any form or by any means, electronic, mechanical, photocopying or otherwise, without the prior permission of the publisher, Canterbury Press.

The Author has asserted his right under the Copyright, Designs and Patents Act, 1988, to be identified as the Author of this Work

British Library Cataloguing in Publication data

A catalogue record for this book is available
from the British Library

978 1 84825 278 3

Typeset by Regent Typesetting, London
Printed and bound in Great Britain by
CPI Group (UK) Ltd, Croydon

Contents

Acknowledgements	vii
Foreword by the Bishop of Chichester	ix
Introduction by Colin Podmore	xi

Part 1 Roger Greenacre — 1

1 Roger Tagent Greenacre *by Colin Podmore*	3
2 Address at the Funeral Requiem *by Jeremy Haselock*	21
3 Sermon at the Requiem Mass in Chichester *by Bishop John Hind*	26
4 Tribute at the Requiem Mass in Chichester *by Cardinal Jean-Louis Tauran*	30

Part 2 Homilies on the Blessed Virgin Mary — 35

Contents	35
5 Introduction to the Homilies *by Colin Podmore*	37
6 Mother of God Incarnate	41
7 Blessed Among Women	62
8 Queen of Heaven	75
9 St Joseph	90

Part 3 The Blessed Virgin Mary in the Anglican Tradition   93

10 An Anglican Witness   95
11 I Sing of a Maiden: Devotion to the Blessed Virgin in the Middle Ages   106
12 Mother Out of Sight: Anglican Devotion to Mary   115
13 Mark Frank (1613–64): A Caroline Preacher   132
14 The Virgin Mary in the Liturgical Texts of the Anglican Communion   157

Part 4 The Blessed Virgin Mary in Ecumenical Dialogue   181

15 Mary and the Church: The Ecumenical Dialogue and Our Lady (1964)   183
16 Mother of All Christians (1998)   189
17 An Ecumenical Pilgrimage in Honour of Mary, Mother of Our Lord (1998)   193
18 Our Lady, Chosen by God (1999)   200
19 Mary: Grace and Hope in Christ (2005)   205

Publications by Roger Greenacre: A Select Bibliography   219
Index   226

Acknowledgements

Chapters 2, 3 and 4 are included by kind permission of the Revd Canon Jeremy Haselock, the Rt Revd Dr John Hind and His Eminence Cardinal Jean-Louis Tauran respectively.

Italicized texts in Chapter 10 first appeared in the *Walsingham Review*, 130 (Assumptiontide 2002) and Chapter 15 first appeared in the *Walsingham Review*, 13 (September 1964); they are reproduced by kind permission of the Administrator of the Shrine of Our Lady of Walsingham.

Chapters 12 and 13 were first published as pamphlets by the Ecumenical Society of the Blessed Virgin Mary and are reproduced by kind permission of the General Secretary of the Society.

Chapter 14 was first published in *De Cultu Mariano Saeculo XX: Acta of the International Mariological-Marian Congress*, Częstochowa, 1996 (Vatican City: Pontificia Academia Mariana Internationalis, 1999) and is reproduced by kind permission of the Secretary of the Pontifical Academy.

Chapter 16 first appeared in *The Tablet* for 24 January 1998 and is reproduced with permission of the Publisher (www.thetablet.co.uk).

The French text translated in Chapter 19 first appeared in *Je suis l'Immaculée: Colloque organisé par les Sanctuaires Notre-Dame de Lourdes et la Société Française d'Études Mariales* (Editions Parole et Silence, 2006); the translation is published by kind permission of Editions Parole et Silence.

Foreword
by the Bishop of Chichester

Maiden, Mother and Queen: Mary in the Anglican Tradition is an affectionate and important collection of material. It pays fitting tribute to Roger Greenacre, a much-loved and respected priest of the Church of England whose international ministry in France and England spanned more than half a century. His sermons, lectures, and published articles on the place of Mary in the Anglican tradition provide us with a lens through which to understand and interpret significant shifts in our ecumenical and devotional life.

Here is evidence that regard for the indispensible role of Mary in the economy of salvation has never been fully erased from the Church in this land. It lived on in the sixteenth and seventeenth centuries in sermons, hymns, and poetry. Latterly, it has flowered again in the visual arts and in the restoration of places of pilgrimage, such as Walsingham, where Anglican, Roman Catholic, and Orthodox Christians, together with those of the reformed tradition, all have a home.

At Roger's golden jubilee of priestly ordination, a long-standing friend, Cardinal Jean-Louis Tauran, spoke of the need for Christians to be 'artisans of reconciliation'. That striking phrase was quoted by Bishop John Hind at Roger's Requiem Mass in Chichester Cathedral.

Attention to Mary's example of self-offering led Roger to describe the Church as 'a womb-community'. This is the context in which we, as artisans, co-operate in the work of redemption, uniquely inspired by the Holy Spirit. It is a joyful undertaking by priest and people alike, in 'bearing', 'making present', 'bringing forth', and 'preaching'.

Roger is also remembered for describing and practising with consummate skill this public work of co-operation. It is done, quite simply, through the liturgy – the transformative work of sacred worship in which glory is given to God alone.

Roger's choice of Colin Podmore as his literary executor is an example of Roger's genial perspicacity. We owe a huge debt of gratitude to Colin for editing these papers so adroitly and thus producing a timely contribution to our self-understanding.

This volume invites us to breathe more deeply and to enjoy more fully the richer, broader vision of our inheritance. May it also prompt us to magnify the Lord with greater hope. With Mary, let us rejoice in God our Father, and give thanks to him through Jesus Christ, the word made flesh, by whom unity and reconciliation have been won for the whole human race.

✠ *Martin Cicestr:*
The Rt Revd Dr Martin Warner
Bishop of Chichester

3 July 2012
St Thomas the Apostle

Introduction
by Colin Podmore

When Roger Greenacre was planning his final retirement to the London Charterhouse in 2010, he thought of two or three retirement projects on which he hoped to work. One of these was a book on the Blessed Virgin Mary, drawing together and building on his earlier work. Sadly, the cancer that had first struck in 2008 returned within weeks of his arrival in London. He gave what energy he still had to beginning another writing project and was never able to embark upon this one. As his literary executor, charged with the stewardship of his publications and papers, I was aware that many of his friends wished his writings to achieve a wider audience in a publication which would also honour his memory. It seemed to me that fulfilling – in part, at least – Roger's own intention by collecting into a book his work on the Blessed Virgin Mary would be the best way to set about discharging my responsibility.

The citation which Archbishop Carey read when conferring the degree of Doctor of Divinity on Roger at Lambeth Palace in 2001 identified three themes of his life: Christian unity (and in particular relations between the Churches of England and France), Christian liturgy, and devotion to the Blessed Virgin Mary:

> It is striking that most of these publications are concerned with one of these three themes – Christian unity, liturgy and Our Lady – an indication of the consistency which has been a feature of Roger's life.[1]

---

[1] The citation was printed in full in the *Church Observer* for November 2001, p. 10.

The first two of these themes found expression in Roger's books: *The Sacrament of Easter* (1965), of which later editions, written with Jeremy Haselock, appeared in 1989, 1991 and 1995, and *The Catholic Church in France: An Introduction* (1996), on which I had the privilege of collaborating with him. That makes it fitting that this book should concentrate on the third theme. But they are in fact inseparable: most of the articles and papers brought together in this book either presented the Anglican tradition of devotion to Our Lady to an ecumenical audience or presented the results of ecumenical dialogue about Mary; and one of them looks at the Blessed Virgin in the liturgies of the Anglican Communion.

Roger Greenacre and Walsingham

For this book to focus on Roger's writings about Our Lady is also appropriate because his very first solo publication was an account of a pilgrimage to Walsingham, published in the *Church Observer* in July 1957. Aged 27 and in his second year as a priest, he had – as in the previous year – taken ten teenage schoolboys from All Saints, Hanworth, where he was serving his title, on a week-long cycling pilgrimage to the Shrine of Our Lady. They set out on Easter Monday and arrived back on the Saturday. Roger and eight boys cycled the 130 miles, carrying sleeping bags and food, over two days, staying the night in a church hall in Cambridge. Two other boys made the whole journey in a single day. (One wonders what risk assessments, disclaimers and precautions might now be necessary were this idea to be repeated 55 years later.) Roger concluded his article as follows:

> It is possibly worth adding that All Saints' is not at all an 'extreme' parish: our Sunday worship centres on a simple Parish Eucharist, and we do not use incense. Yet the boys have felt the great attraction of Walsingham and the holiness of Our Lady's Shrine, and there is no other place I feel I can

INTRODUCTION

take them – I am afraid they would be bored. Where else can one find everything as it is in Walsingham, where else, above all, a real consciousness of meeting with Our Lady and the saints, and where else the converting power of an atmosphere so tangibly supernatural?[2]

It was also in 1957, the year before the death of Fr Alfred Hope Patten, the restorer of the Shrine, that Roger became a priest associate of the Holy House. At this time, the Shrine was still perceived by many as 'extreme', and Roger's identification with it is significant. In 1960 he worked at the Shrine for some months as Assistant Priest to Fr Patten's successor, Fr Colin Stephenson.

Overview of the Book

The book begins with a biographical account, which sets Roger's writings in the context of his life and experiences. Also included in Part 1 are the addresses given at his funeral requiem in Charterhouse and at the requiem mass in Chichester Cathedral which preceded the interment of his ashes, by Canon Jeremy Haselock (Vice-Dean and Precentor of Norwich Cathedral), Bishop John Hind (then Bishop of Chichester) and Cardinal Jean-Louis Tauran, the Cardinal Proto-Deacon of the Holy Roman Church.

Then follow an Introduction to the Homilies (Chapter 5) and fifteen homilies, selected from those which Roger gave on the Blessed Virgin Mary between 1988 and 2008, together with one on St Joseph, which he gave at the Abbey of Notre-Dame du Bec in 2007 when celebrating the 25th anniversary of his becoming an oblate. These show how Roger's study of the Anglican tradition and his experience of ecumenical dialogue enriched his preaching, both to his regular congregations in Chichester Cathedral and St Michael's, Beaulieu-sur-Mer,

---

2 'By Bicycle to the Shrine of Our Lady', *Church Observer*, 115 (July 1957), p. 5.

and as a guest preacher elsewhere. They are grouped into four chapters. Those in Chapter 6 focus on the Annunciation and on Our Lady as 'Mother of God Incarnate'. Chapter 7 ('Blessed Among Women') brings together three homilies on the Visitation with another relating to Pentecost. In Chapter 8 ('Queen of Heaven') the focus is on the Assumption and on Our Lady in heaven.

The rest of the book is divided into two parts which represent, in a sense, the 'iceberg' of Roger's scholarship regarding the Blessed Virgin Mary, of which the homilies that his congregations heard displayed merely the tip.

The Blessed Virgin Mary in the Anglican Tradition

Part 3, which looks at the Blessed Virgin Mary in the Anglican tradition, begins with Chapter 10, which indicates how Roger presented the place of Mary in Anglican life and worship to French-speaking audiences, linking it with modern ecumenical dialogue. This piece thus serves to give an overview of the territory that is explored in greater detail in the rest of the book.

After a brief introductory review of the mediaeval background to later Anglican devotion to Our Lady (Chapter 11), Chapters 12 and 13 focus on the writings of the Anglican divines of the seventeenth century, who were so important to Roger. They first appeared as pamphlets published by the Ecumenical Society of the Blessed Virgin Mary (ESBVM), on the Council of which Roger served for many years.[3] Chapter 12 surveys the seventeenth-century writers in general and considers John Keble, whose poem 'Mother Out of Sight' inaugurated the nineteenth-century revival of Anglican Marian devotion. Chapter 13 looks in detail at the Caroline preacher Mark Frank. This paper served to introduce to a wider audience one of the more obscure of the Caroline Divines, who figured neither in *The Oxford Dictionary of the Christian Church* nor in More

---

[3] Further information about the Ecumenical Society of the Blessed Virgin Mary may be found on its website, www.esbvm.org.uk.

and Cross's anthology *Anglicanism*. As Roger mentions, it was he who had drawn Frank's sermons to the attention of Donald Allchin, who, he comments, 'has done most to make Frank better known again' – notably in his book *The Joy of All Creation* (1984/1993). It is fitting that Allchin's book and Roger's paper are the two modern sources that were cited by the late Bishop Kenneth Stevenson in his entry on Frank for the *Oxford National Dictionary of Biography* (2004).

Chapter 14 presents to an ecumenical audience the place of the Blessed Virgin in successive Anglican liturgies from the first English Litany of 1544 to what became the Common Worship Calendar, Lectionary and Collects, which had just been approved by the General Synod when this paper was given in 1996. It includes historical sections which summarize or repeat some of the material covered in Chapter 12 in particular, but this overlap has been retained so that both chapters can stand alone.

The Blessed Virgin Mary in Ecumenical Dialogue

The fourth and final part of the book brings together a number of pieces in which Roger looked at ecumenical dialogue about the Blessed Virgin Mary.

The first (Chapter 15), a review article from the *Walsingham Review* for September 1964, presented the Marian teaching of the Second Vatican Council (then still in progress) and reviewed the English translation of a book by Max Thurian of the Taizé community, *Mary: Mother of the Lord, Figure of the Church*.

Then follow three pieces from 1998 to 1999. In the first (Chapter 16), published as part of a series in the *Tablet* in January 1998, Roger warned that if Mary were to be infallibly proclaimed 'Co-Redeemer' that would be 'the end of ecumenism for the Catholic Church'. Chapter 17 is a sermon preached at an ecumenical pilgrimage to Durham Cathedral 'in honour of Mary, the Mother of Our Lord' in May 1998, in which he reflected on the place of Mary in ecumenical dialogue. In Chapter 18, his address to the Society of Our Lady of Pew at

Westminster Abbey in February 1999, Roger gave his English audience an overview of the report by the French ecumenical *Groupe des Dombes* 'Mary in God's Plan and in the Communion of the Saints'.

In a paper given in French at a colloquy held in Lourdes in November 2005, when Roger was already 75, he presented the ARCIC II Agreed Statement *Mary: Grace and Hope in Christ* to a French audience, locating it in the context of almost forty years of Anglican–Roman Catholic dialogue and offering his own reflections upon it. That paper forms Chapter 19 (the final chapter of the book). The book concludes with a Select Bibliography of Roger's publications.

Mary: Grace and Hope in Christ

One disappointment about *Mary: Grace and Hope in Christ* is that it has very little to say about the Anglican tradition between the sixteenth and twenty-first centuries. Para. 44 of the Agreed Statement considers the Reformation in general and para. 45 the English Reformers. Para. 46, which begins by looking at the Prayer Book Calendar in the form it took from 1561 and summarizing the references to Mary in the liturgy, continues thus:

> In spite of diminution of devotion to Mary in the sixteenth century, reverence for her endured in the continued use of the *Magnificat* in Evening Prayer, and the unchanged dedication of ancient churches and Lady Chapels. In the seventeenth century writers such as Lancelot Andrewes, Jeremy Taylor, and Thomas Ken re-appropriated from patristic tradition a fuller appreciation of the place of Mary in the prayers of the believer and of the Church. For example, Andrewes in his *Preces Privatae* borrowed from Eastern liturgies when he showed a warmth of Marian devotion 'Commemorating the allholy, immaculate, more than blessed mother of God and evervirgin Mary.' This re-appropriation can be traced

INTRODUCTION

into the next century, and into the Oxford Movement of the nineteenth century.[4]

On the flowering of devotion to the Blessed Virgin Mary in the twentieth century, on the growth of pilgrimage to Marian shrines, and in particular on the significance of Walsingham for the Church of England and the Anglican Communion in the second half of the century, the Agreed Statement is silent.

Surprisingly, the Study Guide published with the Agreed Statement has even less to say about the Anglican tradition between the sixteenth and twenty-first centuries than the Statement itself. The 'Anglican Commentary' says only that 'Mary's great psalm of praise, the Magnificat, is part and parcel of the Anglican service of Evening Prayer';[5] the rest of the book leaves the Anglican tradition unmentioned.

Only in the volume of ARCIC working papers can one find an account of 'The Virgin Mary in the Anglican tradition of the sixteenth and seventeenth centuries', by two Anglican members of the Commission, Michael Nazir-Ali and Nicholas Sagovsky. This looks briefly at James I, Lancelot Andrewes, George Herbert, Mark Frank, John Pearson, Jeremy Taylor, Thomas Ken and George Hickes.[6] Amazingly, this 277-page book of 'Reflections on the Virgin Mary in Anglican and Roman Catholic Theology and Devotion' mentions John Henry Newman and the Oxford Movement only in passing and Walsingham only in the context of the sixteenth century. Its index does not include the names of John Keble, John Mason Neale or Alfred Hope Patten. All of these and more ought surely to feature in

---

4 Anglican–Roman Catholic International Commission, *Mary: Grace and Hope in Christ. An Agreed Statement* (Harrisburg and London: Morehouse, 2005), pp. 43–4, para. 46.

5 T. Bradshaw, 'The Anglican Commentary', in D. Bolen and G. Cameron (eds), *Mary: Grace and Hope in Christ. The Seattle Statement of the Anglican–Roman Catholic International Commission. The Text with Commentaries and Study Guide* (London: Continuum, 2006), pp. 133–65 at p. 150.

6 M. Nazir-Ali and N. Sagovsky, 'The Virgin Mary in the Anglican tradition of the sixteenth and seventeenth centuries', in A. Denaux and N. Sagovsky (eds), *Studying Mary: Reflections on the Virgin Mary in Anglican and Roman Catholic Theology and Devotion* (London: T&T Clark, 2007), pp. 131–46 at pp. 139–44.

any balanced account of 'the Virgin Mary in Anglican Theology and Devotion'. One cannot help wondering whether the absence of traditional Anglo-Catholics from ARCIC II (over-compensating for the problematic inclusion of only one Anglican Evangelical in ARCIC I) may not have contributed to the Commission's rather partial engagement with the Anglican tradition of devotion to the Blessed Virgin Mary.

A briefing paper on the report, prepared by the Church of England's Faith and Order Advisory Group (FOAG) for the General Synod, noted: 'A widely expressed concern has been whether the report does justice to the range of Anglican teaching and practice with regard to Mary.' On the one hand, it 'was not clear' that the view of those who are critical of invocation of Mary and the saints 'has been adequately represented in the report'. At the same time,

> Wider knowledge and understanding amongst Anglicans of the resources within Anglicanism, which might form the basis for moving towards an ecumenical agreement about Mary, could place the historic disagreement about the status of the Marian dogmas in a new and more helpful context.

FOAG therefore recommended 'further study of the theology and practice with regard to the Blessed Virgin Mary within Anglicanism, taking the full range of Anglican perspectives into account'.[7] In this context, Roger Greenacre's presentation of the Blessed Virgin Mary in the Anglican tradition, in the papers that are brought together in this volume, seems to deserve the wider audience which this publication should give it.

---

7 *Briefing Paper by the Faith and Order Advisory Group (FOAG) on the Anglican–Roman Catholic International Commission (ARCIC) report Mary: Grace and Hope in Christ* (GS 1818) (London: General Synod, 2010), p. 7.

INTRODUCTION

Conclusion

The publication of this book honours Roger Greenacre's contribution to the life and worship of the Church of England in England and in France, at the parish and diocesan levels, nationally and internationally, and presents it to a wider audience. It also honours what he represented: as an Anglican priest who, though not an academic theologian, historian or liturgist, was certainly a scholar; as a Canon Chancellor who saw it as part of his remit to write and to teach, in the cathedral, in the diocese, in its theological college, and more widely; as a representative of a catholicism that was reasonable, restrained and quintessentially Anglican, while at the same time unswervingly orthodox and fully open to the life and thinking of the wider Church. May it also inspire younger generations of Anglican priests to imitation.

PART I

Roger Greenacre

I

Roger Tagent Greenacre

COLIN PODMORE

Canon Roger Tagent Greenacre was born on 17 November 1930 and died on 30 July 2011, aged 80. For over forty years he was the pre-eminent English interpreter of the Church of England to the French Church – and vice versa.[1] His mother's French descent (he had Tagent cousins in the Beaujolais) inspired a 'love affair with France', where he lived a quarter of his life. Teenage exchanges with a Belgian family kindled his love of the French language, and their devout Catholicism made a profound impression.[2]

His own family was, as he explained in an interview three years before his death, 'une famille anglicane traditionelle mais peu practiquante'.[3] However, at the age of thirteen he went to Aldenham School in Hertfordshire as a boarder. Though the school chapel was no more high-church than his parents' parish church had been, its chaplain, Mervyn Sweet, was an Anglo-Catholic. Looking back almost sixty years later, Roger described him as 'a remarkable man': 'To him I owe my conversion to the catholic faith, the faith of the undivided Church,

---

[1] Parts of this account have appeared in earlier appreciations of Roger Greenacre's life and thought by the present author: the obituary in the *Church Times* (12 August 2011), p. 27; 'Roger Greenacre's Anglican Catholicism', *New Directions* (September 2011), pp. 13–14; and 'A Memorable Michaelmas Day', *St Michael's Messenger* (Winter 2006: Golden Jubilee Supplement), pp. 12–13.

[2] C. Aubé-Elie, 'Le chanoine Roger Greenacre' [interview], *Unité des Chrétiens*, 152 (October 2008), pp. 29–31 at p. 29.

[3] Aubé-Elie, 'Le chanoine Roger Greenacre', p. 29.

one, holy, catholic and apostolic.'[4] It is clear that Mervyn Sweet had an influence on Roger that set the course of his life (and demonstrates the importance of school chaplaincy):

> Humanly speaking, I owe my vocation to the priesthood to Mervyn Sweet, Chaplain of Aldenham at the time of my confirmation in 1946. He heard my first confession and made me a full-blooded Catholic Anglican before I had ever seen Eucharistic vestments or sniffed the heady scent of incense. He also inspired in me a love of the theatre and of the art of Eric Gill. He was a grammar-school educated Welshman, a Socialist and an Anglo-Catholic (everything the school was not!).[5]

It is significant that for Roger the catholic faith and catholic ecclesiology came first; its expression in Anglo-Catholic worship was always secondary.

Roger went on to read history and divinity at Clare College, Cambridge, and trained for ordination at the College of the Resurrection, Mirfield: history, theology and monasticism remained powerful interests. At Cambridge Roger would have encountered a liberal (in the sense of reasonable) Anglican catholicism. Among those who taught him at Cambridge were Michael Ramsey (Regius Professor of Divinity in Roger's second and third year) and Henry Chadwick (Dean of Queens' College and a future member of the Anglican–Roman Catholic International Commission).[6] Writing to the Dean of Clare on the death of the liberal evangelical theologian Charles Moule in 2007, Roger commented, 'He was Dean when I came up in 1949 and was wonderfully kind, understanding and encouraging to the rather aggressive young Anglo-Catholic undergraduate I then was.'

---

4 Translated from an address given at the Nice diocesan seminary in Laghet, 16 March 2004.
5 *Aldenhamia*, 32 (February 2006), p. 14.
6 Aubé-Elie, 'Le chanoine Roger Greenacre', p. 29.

Graduating in June 1952, Roger spent a fortnight touring Northern France with a friend, drawn by its Benedictine abbeys. Having visited Chartres, Solesmes and many of the Loire abbeys and castles, it was, he later recalled, 'quite by chance' that they went on 1 July to the Abbey of Notre-Dame du Bec in Normandy, to which Benedictine monks had returned just four years earlier: 'We had heard about Bec but we knew very little. Not being sure where the Abbey was, we were not able to give notice of our arrival, so we just presented ourselves on that summer evening.' In the courtyard of the still rather dilapidated Abbey buildings they found the abbot, Dom Paul Grammont, and the prior, Dom Philibert Zobel, sitting on two old wicker chairs. This two-night stay when Roger was twenty-one was to be the first of many visits. His diary for the summer of 1952 testifies to the broader interest in monasticism that he was to retain, recording visits to Nashdom in June and July and Quarr in August.

While at Mirfield, he read contemporary French theologians such as Louis Bouyer and Henri de Lubac and travelled in France, learning about the liturgical movement and other developments. The Mirfield regime was 'austere', but the liturgy was 'rich and solemn, with much plainsong'. The tombs of the Founders, on either side of the High Altar in the Community Church, were an inspiration: both Gore and Frere had participated in the Malines Conversations of the 1920s, whose goal of corporate reunion between the Church of England and the Roman Catholic Church the Belgian liturgist and ecumenist Dom Lambert Beauduin had expressed as 'L'église anglicane unie, mais non absorbée'. It was above all to Anglican–Roman Catholic ecumenism that Roger gave his life.

Roger was ordained to the diaconate at St Paul's Cathedral on Michaelmas Day 1954. A five-year curacy at All Saints, Hanworth, in London and two years of college and school chaplaincy followed. As a priest at Hanworth, Roger took groups of teenage boys on pilgrimage to Walsingham, and in 1957 (the year before Fr Hope Patten's death), he became a Priest Associate of the Holy House. In 1960 he spent some months there as Assistant Priest to Fr Patten's successor, Fr Colin Stephenson.

Belgium

Roger spent the academic year 1961–62 at the Catholic University of Louvain, as the Archbishop of Canterbury's Priest Student. Following the announcement of the Second Vatican Council in 1959, the Louvain theology faculty had invited the Archbishop to send a series of priests to study for a year. Of the eight who went, four in particular – Martin Reardon, Roger, John Halliburton and Hugh Wybrew – repaid the investment by contributing significantly to ecumenical relationships. Already widely read in contemporary French theology, in Louvain Roger encountered many of the Belgian theologians who were working in the preparatory commissions for the Council and would have such great influence upon it after it opened in October 1962. He also visited Chevetogne, the Benedictine monastery founded by Beauduin, whose vocation was ecumenical and liturgical – as his own would be.

Holy Week and Easter

Back in England, Roger moved to Central London as curate of St Mark's, North Audley Street, and then Chaplain of Liddon House, ministering to the William Temple Association (for intelligent young professional people starting work in London). In 1963 he preached a series of Lent sermons at the Annunciation, Marble Arch, and St Mary's, Bourne Street, giving the biblical, theological and spiritual background to the celebration of Holy Week and Easter. These were informed by Roger's knowledge of Continental liturgical scholarship and practice. Eric Mascall, who heard them, persuaded him to publish them. *The Sacrament of Easter* (1965) was influential and of lasting significance. Later editions, written with Jeremy Haselock, appeared in 1989, 1991 and 1995. In 2008 Roger was still the obvious person to introduce the season in the relevant *Using Common Worship* volume.[7]

St George's, Paris

In 1965 Roger became Chaplain of St George's, Paris. When he arrived, St George's was still a rather conservative Anglo-Catholic church. There were no women at all on the church council and it was unthinkable that a woman should read the lesson. He immediately began to change both the church's worship and its life. In line with the fashion of the mid-1960s he had the altar moved out into the chancel and started celebrating mass in the westward position. (It was 'a happy coincidence' that an architect had declared the top step of the old high altar unsafe.) The 'fiddle-back' chasubles were packed away; clergy and servers began wearing modern-style chasubles and albs. Wine and cheese were served every Sunday after mass, and a year or two later a simple lunch of home-made soup, bread and cheese, fruit and wine began to be offered. The inadequacy of the church hall meant that lunch had to be served in Roger's sitting room, the cooking and washing up being done in his kitchen, but he was happy to open his home to his people in this way.[8]

St George's is the Church of England's 'flagship' in France, and in the heady days of ecumenism following the Second Vatican Council (which concluded in December 1965) Roger became the pre-eminent English interpreter of the Church of England to the French Church. That role he retained, through lecturing and writing, for over forty years.

---

[7] R. T. Greenacre, 'Introduction', in D. Kennedy with J. Haselock, *Using Common Worship: Times and Seasons, Lent to Embertide: A Practical Guide* (London: Church House Publishing, 2008), pp. 1–11.

[8] P. Lake, 'Memories of St George's', *Newsletter of St George's Anglican Church*, 101 (November 2011), pp. 5–7; M. Harrison, *An Anglican Adventure: The History of Saint George's Anglican Church, Paris* (Paris: St George's Anglican Church, 2005), p. 73.

In 1967 he guided Archbishop Ramsey through a visit to the French churches. In 1969 the French Anglican–Roman Catholic Committee (ARC) got underway, with Roger as Co-Chairman. He attended the French bishops' annual assemblies as the Anglican observer, and travelled widely, lecturing and addressing ecumenical gatherings. Lecturing at the Institut supérieur d'études oecuméniques of the Institut catholique de Paris from its inception in 1967, a generation of future bishops sat at his feet. He became Rural Dean of France in 1970.

Chichester

In 1975 Bishop Eric Kemp brought Roger to Chichester as a residentiary canon (Chancellor until 1997, then Precentor). Jeremy Haselock has commented, 'Roger was not entirely unhappy to move out of the ramshackle Presbytère in the rue Auguste-Vacquerie into a house in Vicars' Close, Chichester, which combined the characterfulness of the fifteenth century at the front with the elegance of the eighteenth century at the back. Here he made a comfortable home where his hospitality rapidly became legendary.'[9]

During his time in Chichester Roger lectured at catholic universities across Europe, but the focus now was on trying to make the Church of England less insular and more closely linked with the European main. As Diocesan Ecumenical Officer (1976–88) and Chairman of the European Ecumenical Committee (1989–99), he developed and maintained a flourishing cathedral and diocesan twinning with Chartres. As Chancellor he gave an annual lecture series. From 1976 to 1988 he lectured in church history at Chichester Theological College; one former student recalls him reducing a whole class to tears by his account of the fall of Constantinople to Muslim forces in 1453.

---

9 J. Haselock, 'A Personal Recollection of Father Roger's Ministry', *St Michael's Messenger* (Winter 2006: Golden Jubilee Supplement), p. 4.

During his twenty-five years in Chichester Roger brought into the Church of England insights gleaned from his knowledge of the Church in France and Belgium and his experience of ecumenical dialogue. Immersion in the thought-world of French-speaking Catholicism enabled Roger to place the Anglican tradition in a wider European perspective which highlighted its essential catholicity. Comparison with what befell the French Church during the Revolution brought out its continuity: France has nothing comparable with an English cathedral of the old foundation such as Chichester. Intensive ecumenical experience tends to make one less starry-eyed about other churches and somewhat more sanguine about one's own.

As a member of English ARC (1981–96), Roger was Anglican co-author of its *Study Guide* to ARCIC I's Final Report (1982) and played a key part – with the French ecumenist Suzanne Martineau – in the genesis of *Twinnings and Exchanges* (1990), the important agreement with the French Bishops' Conference on eucharistic hospitality. His book *The Catholic Church in France: An Introduction* (1996) presented the French Church and its relations with the Church of England. Roger brought his ecumenical insights to bear on the General Synod (1980–85, 1987–95), its Board for Mission and Unity (1981–85), the Archbishops' Group which produced *Episcopal Ministry* (1990), and the Liturgical Commission (1991–96). From 1979 to 1991 he chaired the Church Union Theological Committee, contributing to its occasional papers and books. He served on the Council of the Ecumenical Society of the Blessed Virgin Mary.

In 1982 Roger sealed his relationship with Bec (thirty years after his first visit) by becoming an oblate. He explained his decision thus:

> My step is inspired by the historic links that once united the Abbey of Bec and the Church of England and by the ecumenical vocation of the Abbey today, which is to pray and work for the unity of all Christians and – more particularly – for the reconciliation of the Roman Catholic Church and

the Anglican Communion. I desire, in becoming an oblate of Bec, to place a concrete sign of this coming unity in a spirit of confidence and hope.

As an Englishman, I want to manifest my love of France. As an Anglican, I want to manifest my love of the Roman Catholic Church. As a priest, exercising a ministry in the world, I want to manifest the spiritual need which I feel to be sustained by the prayer and the life of a monastic community and to know that I can live in communion with it.

I desire to take the name Lambert in witness of my great veneration for a monk who was an authentic precursor, pioneer and prophet of Christian unity, Dom Lambert Beauduin.

Thus Roger's oblation brought his interests in monasticism, history and ecumenism together with his love of France, its language and its church.

The Ordination of Women to the Priesthood and Episcopate

Roger loved the Anglican tradition, rejoicing in its catholicity. He remained agnostic about whether women could in principle be priests – a common stance among Anglo-Catholics then but now probably a minority view among those who are opposed, especially younger generations. He was unable to accept the 1992 decision not for reasons concerned with Christian anthropology or the nature of priesthood, but on two other related but distinct grounds: he saw it as damaging not only ecumenically but also ecclesiologically – jeopardizing not only the ARCIC process but also the Church of England's self-understanding as 'a fragment of a divided Church' that 'does not have the right to act as if it were the whole'.[10]

In his powerful and still topical '*Epistola ad Romanos*', published in the Jesuit periodical *The Month* in March 1993,

---

10 *The Chronicle of Convocation, being a Record of the Proceedings of the Convocation of Canterbury*: 11 July 1992, p. 35.

Roger set out the multi-stranded dilemma he now faced. One strand concerned the Anglican tradition:

> I [have] always valued and lived fully within the Anglican tradition and would miss it terribly ... In Anglicanism there has always been a mutual interaction between theology and liturgy and the formation of a spirituality, *pietas anglicana*, which has been both profoundly theological and profoundly liturgical ... It is no use preserving artificially an Eastern rite unless there is a genuinely Eastern character to the theology and spirituality which accompany it. If nothing of Anglicanism is to survive within the Roman Communion but some elements of its liturgy, then some of the most tragic and divisive features of 'Uniatism' will be perpetuated and the lessons of history ignored.[11]

In the Synod debate on what became the Episcopal Ministry Act of Synod 1993 Roger contrasted two ecclesiologies. According to one, 'The Church of England is a sovereign and independent Church and can decide all issues which affect its life without having to defer to any other Christian body' and 'When it has made a decision it ... has the right, even the duty, to demand compliance ... from all its members.' This was 'basically, perhaps unconsciously, a Roman Catholic ecclesiology'. According to the other,

> The Church of England ... only constitute[s] part of the universal Church. There is, therefore, an inevitable fragility or provisionality about decisions that it may make which affect more than its own domestic life ... 'To make provision' (to quote the preamble to the Act of Synod) 'for the continuing diversity of opinion in the Church of England' is not a measure of generosity nor a concession but a necessary consequence of this second model of Anglican self-understanding.

---

11 R. T. Greenacre, '*Epistola ad Romanos*: An open letter to some Roman Catholic friends', *The Month* (March 1993), pp. 88–96 at pp. 94–5.

What was at stake in debating the Act of Synod, therefore, was 'Our whole understanding of the place of the Church of England within the One, Holy, Catholic and Apostolic Church of Christ.'[12]

The Episcopal Ministry Act of Synod enabled Roger to remain in the Church of England, but the ordination of women to the priesthood remained a cause of sadness. From 1961, when he was thirty, he had spent a year getting to know the Roman Catholic Church in Belgium. He had followed with interest the Second Vatican Council, which opened in October 1962, on which Belgian theologians whom he had met had significant influence. In 1965, as the Council, which had brought the Roman Catholic Church into the ecumenical movement, drew towards its close, Roger moved to Paris where he was for ten years at the forefront of the development of Anglican–Roman Catholic relations in France. There and in Chichester he had followed closely the work of the first and second Anglican–Roman Catholic International Commissions, and – both as a member of the French and English Anglican–Roman Catholic Committees and as an individual ecumenist – had helped to promote interest in and understanding of their work. Now, in his sixties, he saw the ordination of women to the priesthood in the Church of England place a new and grave obstacle in the way of the ecumenical vision to which he had devoted much of his energy in the best years of his life.[13] Not surprisingly, his sadness and disappointment, to which Bishop John Hind referred in his sermon at the requiem for Roger in Chichester Cathedral (Chapter 3 of this book) can be detected in those chapters of the book which were written in an ecumenical context or reflected on the progress of ecumenical dialogue. What is remarkable is not that this was mentioned but that it did not

---

12 General Synod, *Report of Proceedings*, 9 November 1993, pp. 725–36.

13 Already in their Common Declaration of 2 October 1989 Archbishop Runcie and Pope John Paul II had said: 'The question and practice of the admission of women to the ministerial priesthood in some Provinces of the Anglican Communion prevents reconciliation between us' and described it as 'this obstacle' on the path to unity: www.vatican.va/holy_father/john_paul_ii/speeches/1989/october/documents/hf_jp-ii_spe_19891002_dichiaraz-comune_en.html.

dominate Roger's writing and thinking or discourage him from continuing his ecumenical work.

St Michael's, Beaulieu-sur-Mer

Roger's life's work was recognized when he became an Officer of the French Order of Merit (in 1998) and a Lambeth DD (2001). In November 2000 he retired from his Chichester canonry after twenty-five years, aged seventy. He bought a house in Chichester but went first to the French Riviera as Chaplain of St Michael's, Beaulieu-sur-Mer – for two or three years, which eventually became ten.

During this Indian summer Roger continued to make connections. He and his Roman Catholic counterpart, Père Jean-Marie Tschann, organized ecumenical services, including joint prayers for Christian unity each Good Friday. The ecumenical high-point of these years was a joint celebration in 2003 of the centenaries of the opening for worship of the Roman Catholic church and the consecration of St Michael's. For this Roger brought to Beaulieu the then Archbishop of York, David Hope, whose predecessor had consecrated St Michael's 100 years earlier. Perhaps the most notable event was an ecumenical procession from St Michael's to the Roman Catholic church, the Bishop of Nice walking with the Archbishop. The centenary celebrations included a music festival, of which Roger was one of the promoters, which was repeated in succeeding years.

Roger's genius for spotting connections was demonstrated again when he discovered that Queen Victoria's third son, Prince Arthur, Duke of Connaught (1850–1942), who lived at Bagshot Park in Surrey, had been a regular worshipper at St Michael's. The third son of the present Queen, Prince Edward, Earl of Wessex, who lives at Bagshot Park, was accordingly invited to visit Beaulieu with the Countess of Wessex in 2006. He unveiled a plaque in honour of the Duke, naming the area in front of St Michael's (writing in the *St Michael's Messenger*, Roger dignified it into 'the square in which St Michael's is situated')[14] 'Place Duc de Connaught'. As the Danish Church on the French Riviera worships at St Michael's each month, the fact that the Duke of Connaught was the great-grandfather of the present Queen of Denmark and her sister Princess Benedikte offered yet another connection. Princess Benedikte duly visited St Michael's in 2008 and unveiled a memorial inscription on the occasion of the blessing of a new font cover in commemoration of the Duke. Such events strengthened community relations.

Michaelmas 2005

Roger's life, thought and liturgical style were summed up in the Eucharist in Chichester Cathedral on Michaelmas Day 2005 which celebrated the golden jubilee of his priesting. Roger concelebrated with a number of fellow-priests; Bishop John Hind, as diocesan bishop, presided at the Liturgy of the Word and gave the Blessing; and Cardinal Jean-Louis Tauran (who had been the Holy See's Secretary for Relations with States and was then Archivist and Librarian of the Holy Roman Church) preached – surely the first curial cardinal to fly to England from the Vatican to preach at a celebration of Anglican priestly ministry? Cardinal Tauran spoke – in exquisite English – not about Roger but about three convictions that were central to his priesthood. Each concerned 'encounter' – the importance of the Liturgy as the place of encounter with God, of pastoral encounter with our contemporaries and engagement with the questions that concern them, and of encounter in dialogue with our fellow Christians of other churches – crossing boundaries for the sake of unity.

The most memorable moment came towards the end. The congregation stood while the choir sang John Tavener's ethereal Magnificat and Roger, accompanied by his Deacon (the Revd Elizabeth Carver), walked down into the nave and censed

---

14 R. T. Greenacre, 'Her Majesty's Third Son', *St Michael's Messenger*, 21 (Autumn 2006), p. 17.

an image of Our Lady of Walsingham. Nothing was said: it didn't need to be. Six times Tavener punctuates Mary's song with the refrain

> Greater in honour than the cherubim,
> and glorious incomparably more than the seraphim;
> thou who inviolate didst bring forth God the Word,
> and art indeed the Mother of God:
> thee do we magnify.

Roger, for whom we had come to give thanks, gave honour to Our Lady, who in turn points us to her Son, the incarnate Word of God.

In a warm personal greeting read just before the Dismissal, the Archbishop of Canterbury, Dr Rowan Williams, recalled first meeting Roger in Paris in 1973 and working with him in different contexts, including the Church Union Theological Committee, since then. He praised Roger as representing 'a particular style of Catholic Anglicanism that is deeply rooted in liturgy and personal prayer, critical and generous all at once', and added, 'For what he is, and for what he has done unobtrusively for so long to enrich our ecumenical work, I am profoundly grateful.' The importance of Roger's ecumenical work was underlined in a message from the Abbot of Bec, and in a hand-written letter the Bishop of Gibraltar in Europe, Dr Geoffrey Rowell spoke of Roger as 'a devoted priest and servant of the Church, a tireless worker for Christian unity, and an interpreter particularly of the Church of England to the Church of France and *vice versa*'.

One of the things that made the occasion special were the people. For example, turning round to exchange the Peace to those in the row behind me, I found myself shaking hands with Roger's friend Patricia Routledge (TV's Hyacinth Bucket). The congregation of 350 included numerous people from St Michael's, Beaulieu. Among the representatives of other churches were Père Tschann from Beaulieu and many Roman Catholic priests. There were several retired bishops, including Bishop Eric Kemp (then aged ninety), who had brought Roger to Chichester in 1975 and was still Bishop when he left in 2000. At the party afterwards, this comment was overheard: 'What a wonderful idea to have your memorial service before you die. That way you can really enjoy it.'

Retirement and Death

In September 2008, I visited Roger in Beaulieu as I did every year during his time there. It was while I was staying with him that he was rushed to hospital in consequence of what turned out to be a cancerous growth. At his request I presided at a Liturgy of the Word on Sunday 7 September and preached, as he had intended to, on the Blessed Virgin Mary, drawing on his paper 'Mother Out of Sight' which is printed in this volume. He recovered and was hopeful that the cancer had been defeated, but it was not to be.

Against the background of his earlier reflections on the ordination of women to the priesthood, Roger contemplated the possibility of women bishops two decades later 'with a great sadness'. In 2006 the then President of the Pontifical Council for Promoting Christian Unity, Cardinal Kasper, had told a meeting of bishops of the Church of England:

> Ecumenical dialogue in the true sense of the word has as its goal the restoration of full church communion. That has been the presupposition of our dialogue until now. That presupposition would realistically no longer exist following the introduction of the ordination of women to episcopal office.[15]

The restoration of communion between Rome and Canterbury for which Roger had worked and prayed for fifty years would definitively recede over the horizon. Furthermore, Roger's

---

15 *Women in the Episcopate? An Anglican–Roman Catholic Dialogue* (GS Misc 885) (London: General Synod, 2008), p. 21.

position as an Anglican would again come under question. He had never served under a bishop who ordained women to the priesthood, and perhaps rarely needed to make the sort of principled compromise to which many have become accustomed. After a life in the mainstream, for much of which Anglo-Catholics were in the ascendant in the Church of England or at least in the dioceses in which he served, the counter-cultural or even nonjuring situation familiar to earlier generations would have been difficult. Roger might have faced a choice comparable with that which the Act of Synod had spared him back in 1993. As he approached his eightieth year, he commented more than once, 'If the Lord is kind, he will take me before the first woman bishop is consecrated in the Church of England.'

Roger retired for a second time in 2010 and returned to England. He spent his last year as a Brother of the London Charterhouse, whose history and traditions he relished. At his funeral requiem the then Master of Charterhouse, Dr James Thomson, recalled:

> It was in September 2002, when attending a gathering for Holders of Lambeth Degrees, that the Reverend Canon Dr Roger Greenacre first set foot in Charterhouse. From that moment he felt he would eventually like to become a Brother and the process began in early 2004. It was therefore splendid that we were able to welcome him on 10 August last year after a long wait while he was Chaplain at Beaulieu-sur-Mer. He had been here only a very short time when he was taken ill and that illness shaped his very short time as a member of this community. We all admired the way he coped with his increasing problems and kept alive his participation in the life of this house, especially in this our 400th anniversary year. He faithfully attended Mass and was present the Sunday before he died. He was assisted in these achievements by many of the community, happy to help and to whom he was always most grateful. Brothers of Charterhouse have a nominated Governor and the three Royal Governors take part in this. Roger's Governor was His Royal Highness The

Prince Philip. It was so good that he was able to take lunch next to him when His Royal Highness visited in June to mark our Quatercentenary.

Roger celebrated his eightieth birthday with a party for his friends in the Great Chamber of Charterhouse in November 2010. The cancer had returned not long after his arrival in Charterhouse – possibly triggered by the stress involved in moving from France to a much smaller set of rooms in London, while also trying to clear and sell his house in Chichester. At first he hoped for some further remission, but it soon became clear that that was not to be. I shall always remember his exemplary preparation for his death and his acceptance of it: in all our conversations there was never a note of complaint. On Good Friday 2011 he joined me for the Liturgy of the Day at All Saints, Margaret Street, and, though already weak, stood throughout the Passion Gospel. Supporting a dying man as he walked up to venerate the cross and again to receive communion was a moving experience.

When I visited him on Friday 22 July he was still able to walk with support and to chat with his brethren at a reception for the Lord Mayor of London, who in accordance with tradition had come to be presented with mulberries from the Charterhouse mulberry trees. A week later I was sitting with him in St John's Hospice in St John's Wood, for much of the time just holding his hand in silence as he was unable to sustain a conversation. As it turned out, I was the last of his friends to see him: he died that night, having been anointed by the hospice's Anglican chaplain.

His funeral requiem was celebrated by Canon Jeremy Haselock in the Chapel of the London Charterhouse on 12 August 2011, just two days after the anniversary of his arrival there. On 23 September his ashes were interred in the Paradise lawn within the cloisters of Chichester Cathedral, following a requiem mass celebrated by the Bishop of Chichester, Dr John Hind, at which Cardinal Tauran, now Cardinal Proto-Deacon of the Holy Roman Church, gave a tribute (Chapter 4 of this book). Those present included monks from Bec and Chevetogne, and the service booklet included this message from the Archbishop of Canterbury, Dr Rowan Williams:

> I am grateful for this opportunity to contribute to this celebration of the life of a priest of rare quality.
>
> Canon Roger Greenacre's importance in building bridges between Anglicans and Roman Catholics, especially on the Continent of Europe, can hardly be exaggerated. His patient, intelligent and sympathetic engagement with the Church in France in particular helped to set the tone for a relationship that has been especially constructive in recent decades.
>
> But he also had a highly significant role in the Church of England – as a liturgist and ecumenical theologian who faithfully served a number of bodies, formal and not so formal, in these areas. Not least of these was the Church Union Theological Committee, whose deliberations he guided with a particularly steady hand, defending the theological integrity of tradition without ever becoming reactive or reactionary.
>
> His personal kindness, wit and graciousness made his company a delight to all who encountered him. His death will be deeply felt by all who knew and loved him.
>
> ✠ ROWAN CANTUAR:

Appreciation

Roger's liturgical style was post-conciliar and Anglican, characterized by both a 'noble simplicity' and high aesthetical standards. For the sacraments he wore a monastic-style cassock alb, for the offices a full English surplice, scarf and hood. Privately he joined in the daily prayer of the Western Church (in French or Latin), but in public worship he was scrupulous in using the rites of the Church to which he owed allegiance – with only the most minimal and necessary emendation.

Roger wrote many articles, in English and French, on Christian unity, liturgy, and the Blessed Virgin Mary, all composed (as a self-proclaimed 'technophobe') in his clear, attractive handwriting. (A select bibliography concludes this book.) But he was first foremost a faithful priest and pastor, whose scholarly lectures and writing formed part of a ministry of teaching and spiritual guidance. As Jeremy Haselock said in his funeral address, Roger's sermons, delivered in a clear, precise voice, presented very good basic catholic teaching stylishly and attractively; they nurtured and nourished a generation of worshippers in Paris, Chichester and Beaulieu.

Conviviality – drinks, dinners, parties – was similarly prominent in Roger's ministry. As I myself experienced in the last two decades of Roger's life, the celibacy which he embraced as 'what's right for me' gave space for faithful friendships and generous hospitality. He entertained his friends with (oft-repeated) anecdotes, curious facts and amusing turns of phrase, and was much loved.

2

Address at the Funeral Requiem in the Chapel of Sutton's Hospital in Charterhouse Friday 12 August 2011

CANON JEREMY HASELOCK
Vice-Dean and Precentor of Norwich Cathedral

Soli Deo Gloria +

Dear Roger, we have known one another for over forty years – I was an undergraduate at York when we first met. I had heard a great deal about you from my flatmate, your friend Derek Jennings, and was eager to meet you. We met in Paris, at St George's in the rue Auguste Vacquerie. I came to the Sunday Mass with a group of youngsters from the Minster Song School which, at the invitation of the Headmaster, the wonderfully named Fr Wardrobe, I was helping to escort round the city. I loved the liturgy you had devised and the way the old St George's had been re-ordered to provide a seemly setting for it. Most vividly I remember the Pax – rather a daring feature in those days. You announced to the congregation, 'Let us now offer one another the kiss of peace, either with Gallic exuberance or English reticence', and the regulars in that most friendly of congregations each turned to their neighbour and kissed him or her warmly on both cheeks. How shocked we were – this did not happen at the Solemn Eucharist in York

Minster where nothing much had changed since Milner-White's day. Leaving the Minster schoolboys to their fate, I remember responding to your generous and hospitable invitation to join you and what seemed an enormous group of others for lunch in the ramshackle presbytère you inhabited, once the 'thirst after righteousness' had been quenched.

Looking back, I learned a number of things about you on that day, qualities that I was to discover far more about later when we became firm friends. I learned how good you were at the ordering of worship: unlike, alas, so many clergy, you knew about the liturgy – not just an academic knowledge of the history and origins of rites, Eastern and Western, but how to put on a beautiful act of worship that made the necessary connections with the community you served. Your liturgical sensibilities had been fashioned first by the austere splendours of the Office and Mass at Mirfield, then by your first-hand experience of the fruits of the Liturgical Movement in Belgium when you were the Archbishop of Canterbury's Priest-Student at the Université Catholique in Louvain. You knew what influences were going to shape *Sacrosanctum Concilium*, the Constitution on the Sacred Liturgy, because before the Council issued it in 1963 you had studied with the Belgian *periti* who helped in its drafting. The liturgical style you adopted at this time you maintained to the end and St George's Paris, Chichester Cathedral and St Michael's Beaulieu-sur-Mer all benefitted from its outworking in public worship.

I discovered that Sunday in St George's what a gifted preacher you were and I enjoyed and benefitted from your sermon. You were often invited to be a visiting preacher at all the best places and I felt privileged to have you preach at my First Mass back in 1984. You delivered your sermons in that clear, precise voice, which we all remember and which none but the deeply deaf could fail to hear. Technophobe that you were, even the typewriter defeated you and so, invariably, you wrote the sermons out longhand on sheets of Basildon Bond of the same size – looking through a stack of them the other day I noticed how few crossings-out there were. The handwriting also so clear and distinctive: I remember you saying – more than once – 'The only things of which I can boast are an audible voice and a legible hand.' The sermons always contained good, basic, catholic teaching, stylishly and attractively presented, and your friends gathered here today will bear witness that they nurtured and nourished a generation of worshippers. I hope the best of them may one day gain a wider circulation for the Church still has need of that teaching.

Some of your early sermons that did gain wide circulation were on the rites and ceremonies of Holy Week and Easter. At Professor Mascall's suggestion you worked them up and published them in 1965 shortly before you moved to Paris. I have the copy you gave to Derek Jennings – *The Sacrament of Easter*, Faith Press, 8s 6d. Years later, once new liturgical provision for the celebration of Lent, Holy Week, and Easter in the Church of England had appeared, you invited me to help you with producing a new and expanded edition. I contributed very little save typing and computer skills and perhaps a very small amount of new material, but with characteristic generosity you insisted I shared the billing on the title page. 'Greenacre and Haselock' went through three editions and is still in print in America.

Over a fifty-year period you wrote and published a large number of articles, reviews and contributions to *festschrifts, symposia* and learned journals in France, Belgium and Germany. There was also a second book, *The Catholic Church in France*, in 1996, which confirmed you as the foremost interpreter of the French Church to Anglicans as you were already the foremost apologist for Anglicanism to the French. Altogether these writings constitute a significant and lasting contribution to Christian learning in the fields of Ecumenism, Mariology, Anglican Identity and Ecclesiology. So many of us have been glad of the breadth of your perspective, the depth of your knowledge and insight, and the clarity and supreme elegance of expression revealed in this corpus. I know just how much material there was because through a stratagem I got you to update a list of all your published articles. I then smuggled it out of 4 Vicars' Close and gave it to Colin Podmore to help promote your cause with Archbishop Carey who was keen to award you a Lambeth degree. The Archbishop and his advisers were impressed by the bibliography and the degree awarded in 2001 was a well-deserved DD. How amused we all were in our happiness at this long-delayed recognition, to see you, a Cambridge man to the core, arrayed in the doctoral robes of the University of Oxford.

On that well-remembered Sunday in Paris, I discovered exactly how hospitable and generous a man you were. The Presbytère was always filled with people, fascinating people. Some lodgers and frequent visitors have gone on to great things: you gave a penniless American harpsichordist room and board in return for cooking you a dinner once a week – he is now a world-famous conductor and interpreter of the music of your favourite French Baroque. A young priest from Bordeaux whom you befriended and with whom you shared the riches of the Anglican spiritual tradition is now the Cardinal Proto-Deacon of the Roman Church.

Your lovely house in Chichester was home from home for so many people because you loved sharing. With the overflowing generosity you learned from our Lord's first miracle at Cana of Galilee, you shared your home, your friends, your life, your resources. You used to say that in order to be invited to stay at 4 Vicars' Close one had 'to be intelligent, or good looking, or able to cook'. Thankfully, I fell into the last of these categories and what wonderful times we had around your dining table, Roger, in the company of the intelligent and the beautiful. I remember wonderful holidays – the Chancellor's Reading Parties, you called them – in that spacious villa with its glorious swimming pool, at Montauroux in the Var. How you loved our September pilgrimages to the wayside chapel of Notre Dame du Cyprès, below the village of Fayence. They would involve that potent mixture of the sacred and the secular in which you revelled: Mass in the morning, a vin d'honneur afterwards with local vermouth and particularly delicious marinated olives, a procession with Bravadiers noisily discharging their ancient muskets, Benediction in the parish church and then dancing in the village square!

ADDRESS AT THE FUNERAL REQUIEM

Roger you were – and still are – a friend of God, and because of this deep and lasting friendship within, you were profligate with your friendships with others. Hard to say this when you were gifted in so many ways, but for me this was your greatest gift. You shared friendships, enabled friendships, encouraged friendships to flourish and were never jealous of friendships. At one level your ecumenical friendships went, as they say today, 'viral'. Friendships begat friendships and a network of Christian mutual understanding and love spread wider and wider through your influence. These friendships not only benefitted those who enjoyed them but have contributed significantly over the years to the unity of Christ's Church. At every international event at which you represented the Church of England you made lasting friendships. Some of them are represented here and other friends doubtless will come to Chichester. Many of the friendships represented here today were begun through you or have lasted because of your wise counsel and support. How we all enjoyed your friendship! How genially you put up with all our teasing. Thank you, Roger, for your patient, forgiving friendship.

Well, this last year which should have been a rest from your labours and a time to enjoy this place, your Club and the society of your friends has turned out to be a sore trial. But you, being the man you are, have borne everything with great patience, faith in God and confidence in the prayers of his Blessed Mother. We have heard no word of complaint, irritation or frustration, only a calm acceptance of the inevitable. Like St Paul, your life has been poured out as a libation. You have fought the good fight, run the race, kept the faith. We your friends, we who love you, will surely miss your company in this life, but the memories of all that was true, all that was honourable, all that was just, pleasing and commendable and always such FUN, will be with us until, please God, we will meet right merrily in heaven.

3

Sermon at the Requiem Mass in Chichester Cathedral Friday 23 September 2011

THE RT REVD DR JOHN HIND
Bishop of Chichester, 2001–12

When Roger Greenacre was ordained to the priesthood on Michaelmas Day 1955, one of the questions the Bishop put to him was:

> Will you maintain and set forwards, as much as lieth in you, quietness, peace, and love, among all Christian people, and especially among them that are or shall be committed to your charge?

Roger dutifully answered, 'I will do so, the Lord being my helper.'

Both as a pastor and as an ecumenist, Fr Roger always sought to live that promise out. He knew the intimate connection between being a priest and being a minister of unity – of unity in Christ of course, a unity that is inseparable from the sacrifice of Christ by which the wall of separation has been demolished and from the Eucharist in which 'what he never can repeat, he shows forth day by day'.[1]

---

1 William Bright, 'Once, only once and once for all' (1866): *New English Hymnal* (London: Canterbury Press, 1986), hymn 304.

As Cardinal Tauran will be giving a personal tribute at the end of this liturgy, I do not need in this sermon to say much about Roger himself, but rather to speak about our Christian hope.

I recall with appreciation some of His Eminence's words at the mass here for Roger's Jubilee as a priest just a few years ago:

> There is one thing that is certain, the divided and violent world that we have built for ourselves has never had more need for united and consistent Christians, artisans of reconciliation. We Christians can contribute to changing the world. A celebration such as [this] tells us that there is no reason to be discouraged; rather there is reason to continue our journey, hand in hand, so that the world may believe and have reason to hope.

Those words are a double challenge. United Christians may help change the world for the better. Divided Christians probably change it for the worse.

In the life and ministry of Roger Greenacre personal discipleship, priesthood, theological understanding and commitment to unity were of a piece; in this respect, he certainly was 'a consistent Christian'. Standing here in the cathedral church at whose altar Roger himself over so many years devoutly offered the Eucharist, the Sacrament of Unity, I thank God for his faithfulness to the vision of full visible communion as the ecumenical goal.

The lifetime of the Revd Canon Dr Roger Greenacre spanned the heights and the depths of expectation. He knew the heady days of the Second Vatican Council and the hopes that sustained the early years of the Anglican–Roman Catholic International Commission, during which he enthused generations of theological students and fellow journeyers on the pilgrimage to unity, including me. And he also knew what now feels like the 'serious and long-lasting chill' predicted by one of the greatest modern ecumenists.[2] In the face of this 'chill' some people

---

2 Cardinal Walter Kasper, in *Women in the Episcopate? An Anglican–Roman Catholic Dialogue* (GS Misc 885) (London: General Synod, 2008), p. 20.

conclude that peaceful coexistence and collaboration are the best that can be hoped for. That simply will not do of course for the followers of Jesus, who himself prayed for his disciples and for those who would believe in their words 'that they may all be one' (John 17.21).

I know how deeply disappointed Roger Greenacre was by the cooling of relations in the last decade of his earthly life between the Church of England and the Roman Catholic Church. I share that disappointment. But, to quote again from Cardinal Tauran's address here in 2005, Roger himself demonstrated, in his justly famous book *The Sacrament of Easter*, that 'The only event that matters is the resurrection.' That being the case, we must *not* despair. God's ways are not our ways, nor his thoughts our thoughts. Nor for that matter is God's timing ours.

So enough of the despondency many of us feel. If Roger Greenacre taught us anything, it is to trust that God knows what he is doing. 'The only event that matters is the resurrection.' Is that true or is it not? It is no accident that, like so many other 'artisans of reconciliation', Roger Greenacre's ecumenical zeal was matched by his love for the Eucharist, by his concern for liturgical renewal and his special interest in the mysteries of Holy Week and Easter. It is only the resurrection of Jesus that makes sense of our present situation and gives us hope for the future.

So today is not an occasion either to enthuse about the heady enthusiasm of the past or to bewail the sorry depths to which the vision of our predecessors has declined, but rather to thank God both for *their* vision and for *his* promise. Roger Greenacre believed in that promise – and so too do I, who stand only on the lowly foothills of the ecumenical work to which he devoted so much of his life.

I finish with a personal reminiscence. When, on 18 November 2000, I instituted Fr Roger as Chaplain of St Michael, Beaulieu-sur-Mer[3] I took as my text the closing words of the Gospel read

---

3 Bishop John Hind was Bishop of Gibraltar in Europe from 1993 to 2001.

at that mass: 'I am giving you these commands so that you may love one another' (John 15.17). These words come from the instructions given by Jesus, the Lord of the Church, to his disciples at the Last Supper. They provide a sort of charter for the Church at both the local and the universal level. If we are called into unity with Jesus and love for each other by God himself, it follows that the way we must be united with Jesus and the way we must love each other are equally determined by God. The Church is not a 'members' club' which can make up its own faith, nor are individual Christians, churches or ecclesial communities independent, autonomous beings with the right to try to shape the Church or even their own way of life according to their own will.

In a lecture on the long history of attempts to repair the breach between the Church of England and Rome, Roger once quoted a letter from William Wake, the Archbishop of Canterbury in the early years of the eighteenth century, to the French Catholic theologian Du Pin, as one of a number of unity initiatives was coming to grief. He wrote:

> May it suffice to have designed something in so great a task; and perhaps to have cast some seeds in the ground which at length will bear manifold fruit. Meanwhile let us (for this none can deny us) embrace each other as members and brethren of the same mystical body.

That is not of course to suggest that there is an invisible unity, which simply has to be made visible, but rather to underline the mystery of our unity in Christ whose manifestation involves real changes and real repentance. May the life and example, the teaching (and indeed the prayers) of Fr Roger Greenacre sustain our mutual love, the faith it informs and the hope it engenders – and, of course, may he rest in peace and enjoy the fulfilment of Christ's promise of unity with himself and the Father in the communion of the Holy Spirit.

4

Tribute at the Requiem Mass in Chichester Cathedral Friday 23 September 2011

HIS EMINENCE CARDINAL JEAN-LOUIS TAURAN

Cardinal Proto-Deacon of the Holy Roman Church

The last time I saw Roger was on July the 20th last, in his little apartment at Charterhouse. Jonathan Goodall, who was accompanying me, delivered to Roger a personal message from the Archbishop of Canterbury. Roger was moved by the solidarity of his Archbishop and also, of course, by my presence. I found him serene. He knew he was going to die, but if his body was frail, his gaze remained vivid and full of bounty as usual. His intelligence was alert: he said, 'Let us speak in French; I don't want to lose my French!'

Of course, he was preparing himself for the great encounter with God with lucidity and calm. Before I left, he asked me to bless him, which I did, and I could feel in the strength of the hand he extended to me, a sign of gratitude, the intensity of his faith and the value he attached to our friendship. Both of us knew it was our last encounter on this earth. His asking me to preach at his funeral service gives you an idea of the depth of our friendship. As a matter of fact, when we last met, we did not talk much; it was not necessary. Our communion of ideas and convictions was so obvious.

I received many gifts from Roger. The pectoral cross I am wearing was the gift of all my Anglican friends, co-ordinated by Roger, on the occasion of my Episcopal ordination on 6 January 1991. This Episcopal ring I am wearing today belonged to Bishop Leonard, an Anglican Bishop who was one of the finest representatives of the great Catholic tradition of the Anglican Communion, who wanted that his ring go to a Roman Catholic bishop. I received it from a friend of Roger. And finally this little book, *The Catholic Church in France: An Introduction* – a country he loved so much. On the first page you can read the dedication he wrote: 'For Jean-Louis from whom I learned so much and with whom I shared so much.'

To learn and to share: these two words give an exact picture of Roger's humanity and spirituality. To learn: history was his subject. He knew perfectly well that you cannot preach the Gospel if you are not formed – and informed – because no dialogue can be built upon ambiguity. Roger was eager to transmit to the younger generation the beauty, the coherence and the intelligence of the Christian message.

To learn is also to accept that we are not in possession of all the truth. So we have to multiply encounters with persons of other beliefs and philosophies and opinions in order to see what we can do together to better the society in which we live. Roger met many different people: intellectuals, political leaders, artists, remembering always he was first a priest. But he was also attentive to the dignity of the ones who do not count and whose names are not on the agenda of the important persons. As a matter of fact, I remember from when he was the pastor of the Anglican parish in Paris the kindness he showed to ordinary people.

But the great spiritual adventure of his life would have been his ecumenical engagement, where he gave the best of himself. Ecumenism for him was not a fashionable subject; it was a necessity for the credibility of the Gospel. He practised with great sincerity the dialogue of love and the dialogue of truth. He knew that if the Church remembers the past, the same Church, in spite of her divisions, has to find her place in our societies. Not because of ambition or some hidden strategy but because all Christians must be in a position to say, 'We have come to know and believe in the love God has for us.' God is love, and whoever remains in love, remains in God and God in him' (1 John 4.16–17).

To learn but also to share. Of course, when you have the grace to be a Christian, to know who you are and where you go, you cannot keep for yourself only such a treasure. That is why Father Greenacre was curious to know what the other thinks, in order to see what our divided Church can proclaim and offer to the world.

Roger never practised the spirituality of the besieged city. He was open-minded. He had a great sense of human relations. And he was convinced that the Christian communities have a role to play in our secular societies.

Today our consolation is to know that, as Jesus said:

> In my Father's house, there are many dwelling places. If there were not, would I have gone and prepared a place for you? So that where I am going, you also may.

Roger has only changed address. He is now in a new dwelling where the Father was waiting for him. His new home is not made by human hands but it is an everlasting home, which is a part of the greatest home, our Father's house, which can be the dwelling of so many people, says Jesus in the Gospel we have heard.

The place where Roger is, he has built gradually during his lifetime, by his gifts, his personal qualities and even his limitations. As a matter of fact, death is not only the end of the human adventure, it is also the beginning of our heavenly adventure. There is always a danger when you celebrate funerals to transform the homily into an academic speech. There is also a danger to speak much about earth and not enough about heaven. We look at the past but rarely do we try to look at the future when human life is over – because, of course, it is impossible for the human mind to imagine heaven. Blessed

TRIBUTE AT THE REQUIEM MASS

John Henry Newman wrote that when we die we come before God. We have to stand before his righteous presence and one-by-one we shall have to endure his holy and searching eye: 'Then I say that first appearance will be nothing less than a personal intercourse between the creator and every creature. He will look on us while we look on him.'

We must be convinced anyway that nothing can cancel God's project, who wants each of us to be fully realized. I remember an old friend of mine who was going to die from cancer and who some hours before passing away asked his daughter, 'How shall I know when I am dead?' And she answered, 'Darling, it is when you know and feel you are completely better.'

At the very last stage of his human pilgrimage, Roger found the way and the strength to teach and to share. His behaviour in the face of disease and death has been exemplary. Death is inevitable, disease is a cross to bear, to be dependent on the other can be sometimes a great humiliation: Roger faced all these difficult aspects of life with faith, because he knew that after his awaking 'God will set him close to Him ... From my flesh I shall look on God. He whom I shall see will take my part: these eyes will gaze on him and find him not aloof' (Job 19.27).

Today Roger reminds us that death is not just an event but Someone who is coming to meet us. When you leave this earthly home, you know that 'having died with Christ we shall return to life with Him'. Let us all pray together with the psalmist: 'O Lord, teach us to count our days aright, that we may gain wisdom of heart' (Psalm 90).

Roger, our companion in humanity and faith, was faithful to his friends on earth and I am sure he will continue to be the same in heaven. He will be for each one of us a precious intercessor.

For the time being, let us commend him to God's mercy. When you have been a minister in the Christian community you cannot but be afraid by the inadequacy of what you preached and what you lived. We received so many of God's gifts and we gave back so little. At the end of your life, you realize that your bag of good deeds is very light. But there is a sentence in the New Testament which is astonishing and extraordinarily inspiring. St John in his first letter wrote: '... whatever our hearts condemn ... God is greater than our hearts and knows everything.' Our hope rests on this.

May the example of our friend help us to prepare ourselves for the day when we shall not argue anymore, but we shall look at this unveiled face of God, and in the light and the joy of it, we shall not reason any more, we shall adore, or to say in St Augustine's words:

> We shall rest and we shall see;
> we shall see and we shall love;
> we shall love and we shall praise;
> in the end that is no end.

PART 2

Homilies on the Blessed Virgin Mary

Contents

5	Introduction *by Colin Podmore*	37
6	Mother of God Incarnate	41
	Ark of the Covenant	41
	(Chichester Cathedral, Advent IV 1989; Boxgrove Priory, Advent IV 1993)	
	Bearer of the Word-made-Flesh	45
	(Chichester Cathedral, Advent IV 1995)	
	The God-Bearer	49
	(Chichester Cathedral, Advent IV 1997)	
	Tabernacle of God	51
	(Beaulieu-sur-Mer, Advent IV 2004)	
	The Angelus	54
	(Beaulieu-sur-Mer, Advent IV 2005)	
	Bernard of Clairvaux and Mary's *Yes*	57
	(Beaulieu-sur-Mer, Advent IV 2008)	
7	Blessed Among Women	62
	Two Grounds of Blessedness	62
	(Little St Mary's, Cambridge, 31 May 1997)	
	The Grace of God is in Courtesy	65
	(Westminster Abbey, 27 July 1990)	
	All Generations will call her Blessed	69
	(Beaulieu-sur-Mer, Advent IV 2003)	

Waiting for Pentecost 71
(Holy Redeemer, Clerkenwell, May 1989)

8 Queen of Heaven 75

The Assumption 75
(SS Peter and Paul, Chichester, 15 August 1988)
Taken up into Heaven 78
(Holy Trinity, Bath, 15 August 1993)
Crowned with Glory 82
(Chichester Cathedral, 15 August 2000)
Mary: Grace and Hope in Christ 84
(Ufford, 14 August 2005)
The Prayers of the Saints 87
(Beaulieu-sur-Mer, 7 September 2003)

9 St Joseph 90

St Joseph 90
(Notre-Dame du Bec, 19 March 2007)

5

Introduction to the Homilies

COLIN PODMORE

Roger Greenacre's sermons were never preached *ex tempore* and only very occasionally did he speak from notes rather than a full text. Only rarely – before periods of illness towards the end of his time in Beaulieu – was a sermon repeated. Among his papers are all the sermons that he preached from 1965, when he became Chaplain of St George's, Paris, at the age of 35, until 2010, when he finally retired, in his eightieth year, to London. This collection of sermons, preached over forty-five years, will give future generations an interesting insight into catholic Anglican theology and devotion in the last third of the twentieth century and the first decade of the present century.

In his address at Roger's funeral in the Chapel of the London Charterhouse on Friday 12 August 2011 (Chapter 2 of this book), his friend and executor Canon Jeremy Haselock evoked Roger's preaching style and underlined the quality and importance of his sermons:

> You delivered your sermons in that clear, precise voice, which we all remember and which none but the deeply deaf could fail to hear. Technophobe that you were, even the typewriter defeated you and so, invariably, you wrote the sermons out longhand on sheets of Basildon Bond of the same size – looking through a stack of them the other day I noticed how few crossings-out there were. The handwriting also so clear and distinctive: I remember you saying – more than once – 'The only things of which I can boast are an audible voice and

a legible hand.' The sermons always contained good, basic, catholic teaching, stylishly and attractively presented, and your friends gathered here today will bear witness that they nurtured and nourished a generation of worshippers. I hope the best of them may one day gain a wider circulation for the Church still has need of that teaching.

For this publication I have chosen fifteen of Roger's sermons about Our Lady, and one about St Joseph, preached between 1988 and 2008. I have given each a title that gives an indication of its subject. Inevitably there is some repetition of ideas, phrases and quotations (though never of whole paragraphs), but each homily has important points to make in building up the overall body of teaching that, taken together, they represent. To retain the repetitions is also to reflect Roger's own style, for in life as in his preaching Roger was given to repeating important ideas, quotations and telling phrases. In one of the earlier sermons included here, preached at Clerkenwell in May 1989, he said of one of his points that 'it cannot be too often or too energetically affirmed' and, as this collection demonstrates, he duly repeated it on several occasions over the next twenty years. In the same sermon, he introduced a saying of the Fathers with the phrase, 'as the Fathers loved to repeat ...': Roger loved to repeat it too, and often did so, always with the same introductory remark. Of course, these repetitions occurred over two decades, and often in preaching to different congregations, but as a teacher Roger knew the value of repetition – especially when the ideas and phrases are striking and memorable.

In preparing these homilies for publication, I have been struck by their literary quality. As Jeremy Haselock noted, there are very few crossings-out, and these were mostly made in order to improve the literary style. Some may have been fair copies, but it is still significant that only the most minimal copy-editing in respect of punctuation and capitalization has been needed, and only very rarely indeed has it seemed desirable to add a word or two to make the meaning crystal clear. One of the most remarkable things about these homilies, therefore, is that Roger wrote them in longhand in publishable prose. The word-processing that Roger never embraced makes it so easy to edit and re-edit texts that fluency in prose composition has become much rarer than it once was. In this, as in other aspects of his life, Roger's younger friends gained through their acquaintance with him insight into a world that was passing away.

As Jeremy Haselock remarked, Roger's sermons always contained 'good, basic, catholic teaching, stylishly and attractively presented'. It was catholic teaching that was deeply rooted in the Anglican tradition: it is noticeable how often Roger quotes seventeenth-century Anglican divines – in this collection, John Donne, William Laud, Jeremy Taylor and Thomas Ken. He quotes too from the *Book of Common Prayer* and from the *New English Hymnal* (a Latin hymn translated by John Mason Neale and a hymn written by George Timms) and refers to the history of the English Church. He also quotes earlier Anglo-Catholics (here, Gregory Dix, Anselm Hughes and Eric Mascall) and expresses his loyalty to Anglo-Catholicism. These sermons are not only thoroughly catholic but also distinctively Anglican.

Roger's catholicism was Anglican but never insular. (Any would-be 'catholicism' that is isolated from, and uninterested in, the broad, catholic, main does not merit the description 'catholic'.) In these sermons Roger's knowledge of the Church in Belgium and France, as of the history and culture of France more generally, is apparent. Roger's catholicism was, like that of the Church of England, both firmly rooted in the western catholic tradition and also open to the east, as represented here by repeated reference to the Orthodox icon known as *Platytera ton Ouranon*.

It was the authentic Anglicanism of Roger's catholicism that enabled him to contribute to ecumenical dialogue, notably between the English and French Churches, as he did. Part of his contribution was in publicizing and disseminating the work of the Anglican–Roman Catholic International Commission, and the Church of England's responses to it, as he did in some of the sermons reproduced here.

This small collection of some of Roger's sermons that relate to the theme of this book will begin to give his teaching and writing a wider circulation, and in doing so will rightly honour a priest and friend to whom many were devoted. It is important, therefore, to recall that the text of every sermon that Roger ever wrote began with a cross and the words 'Soli Deo Gloria': 'to God alone be the glory'. These words were never spoken, and on the rare occasions when Roger's sermons were subsequently typed up they were not included, for they were addressed to himself. Roger had them printed on the back of the memento card which was distributed at his Golden Jubilee Eucharist in 2005, however, and they are included here as a reminder of the humility that always underlay Roger's proper pride in his honours and achievements.

   Sometimes, when the text did not conclude at the foot of a page, Roger traced a larger cross beneath it. Such a cross has been added to each sermon, not only to separate them, but also as a concluding reminder that they were given not to display the preacher's ability but to point his hearers to Christ and his blessed Mother.

6

Mother of God Incarnate

Ark of the Covenant

+ Soli Deo Gloria: Advent IV (24.xii.89):
Chichester Cathedral at 11.00; (19.xii.93): Boxgrove Priory

Many of you will know our magnificent sister cathedral in our twinned City of Chartres; some will have been there on one of our Chichester pilgrimages led by our bishop and will therefore have been to the prayerful crypt chapel of *Notre-Dame de Sous-terre* (Our Lady Undercroft). You may remember seeing there the pre-Christian Gallo-Roman well and the nearby foundations of what seems to have been a pagan temple. A persistent legend recounts that this temple housed an image bearing the inscription '*Virgini Pariturae*' – 'To the Virgin about to give birth'. If that was so, then there are two ways of interpreting the continuity between the pagan *cultus* of a virgin mother goddess and the later Christian *cultus* of the virginal Mother of God. To some it simply confirms their belief that Catholicism is basically pagan and the veneration of Our Lady and the saints an uncritical takeover from the pagan worship of many gods and goddesses. Others, however, will remember the wise advice given by Pope Gregory I to St Augustine of Canterbury. He was told not to destroy the pagan temples but only the idols, and having purged the temples with holy water to convert them to Christian churches and consecrate altars in them. He was told too to keep the old feasting that accompanied the pagan rites; they were no longer to sacrifice oxen to idols but they could kill them for food. More profoundly, the mainstream Christian tradition has always affirmed that although God has spoken in a unique and privileged way through his covenant with Israel, yet even in paganism there have been confused intimations of truth, which find their fulfilment too in Jesus Christ. So any pagan cult of a virgin mother would require very radical transformation, but transformation rather than destruction.

On this Sunday before Christmas the prayers and readings of the liturgy direct our attention to the Blessed Virgin Mary – to a waiting, expectant, pregnant Virgin, who has conceived in her womb, at the message of the Angel and by the overshadowing of the Holy Spirit, the Word of God and is about to give birth to him.

Familiar passages of Scripture take on a new light according to the liturgical context in which they are read.[1] The story of the Annunciation is very familiar; we hear it, for example, on Lady Day, but today's context does shed a particular kind of spotlight on it. In particular, our first reading, which tells the story of Nathan's prophetic word to King David, who wanted to build a house for the Ark of God, the Ark of the Covenant, invites a comparison with the Gospel story of the Annunciation. Nathan tells David that it is not for him to build a house for the Ark of God: God will build a house for David and the House of David will endure for ever. And in the Gospel this prophecy is fulfilled: Gabriel speaks to Mary, betrothed to a man of the House of David, promising her a Son to whom God will give 'the throne of his Father David'. And as Mary gives her consent, she becomes in her own person the Ark of the Covenant – the precious shrine which houses the presence of God.

So Israel's destiny finds its fulfilment in this moment when Our Lady conceives the Son of God. Israel was 'the womb-community' (a striking if inelegant phrase), which only existed in order to bring forth the Messiah. Israel had kept a long vigil, a centuries-long Advent, a watch on behalf of the whole human

---

[1] This paragraph and the next were added when the sermon was preached at Boxgrove Priory in 1993, when the first reading (in Year B of the three-year lectionary) was 2 Samuel 7.1–11, 16.

family, until this moment when salvation dawns in Christ, the glory of Israel and the light of the Gentiles.

So as we fix the eyes of the imagination on the mental icon of the Expectant Virgin, we draw from that contemplation at least three lessons.

First, any truly Christian reflection on Mary does not lead us away from her Son; on the contrary, it deepens our understanding of the Incarnation and strengthens our faith in the God-Man Jesus Christ, Son of God and Son of Mary. The title *Theotokos*, normally translated into English as 'Mother of God' but literally in the Greek 'God-bearer', was solemnly defined by the fifth-century Council of Ephesus (the third of those first four General Councils of the Church to which the Church of England assigns particular authority), not so much to give honour to the Blessed Virgin as to strengthen and protect orthodox Christian faith in the Incarnation, to make it clearer that there is only one Person in Christ, who is both fully human and fully divine, and that Mary is the human Mother of the Word of God incarnate. Perhaps we cannot really grasp the full and earthy reality of the Incarnation 'unless' – to quote Dr Eric Mascall – 'we reflect calmly and reverently upon the fact that for nine months Mary carried God incarnate within her as she went about her work'. The icon of the Expectant Virgin – the *Virgo Paritura* of Chartres, *la Vierge qui devait enfanter* – points us to this truth. So does this morning's final hymn:

> The Lord whom earth and sea and sky
> Adore and praise and magnify,
> Who o'er their threefold fabric reigns,
> The Virgin's spotless womb contains.[2]

Second, Mary's motherhood of the Incarnate Word is unique and unrepeatable. But she is not honoured simply for her physical – her biological – role in the mystery of redemption but for

---

2 Venantius Fortunatus (530–609), 'Quem terra, pontus, aethera', tr. J. M. Neale (1818–66) and editors: *New English Hymnal*, hymn 181.

her exemplary faith and humble obedience. God does not force us to co-operate with him against our will, and in this case the divine purpose of redemption which had come to maturity after so many long centuries of preparation waited in suspense for one awe-inspiring moment while Mary, having heard the angel's message, made her risky leap of faith and trust: 'Behold I am the handmaid of the Lord; let it be to me according to your word.' The receptivity of motherhood is not purely physical; as the Fathers loved to repeat of Mary, this Son, the Word of God, she conceived in her heart and mind by faith before she conceived him in her womb. 'Blessed are those who hear the word of God and keep it,' said Our Lord to a woman who had praised his mother. This is indeed her greatest blessedness and one in which all Christians can and must imitate her.

Thirdly and lastly: it is, however, too much of an oversimplification to say of Mary's two great privileges that though we cannot imitate the divine motherhood yet we can imitate her faith. Physical motherhood is a privilege which is ruled out for at least half of the human race, and yet the Church, of which all the baptized are members, exercises a spiritual motherhood of which Mary is the type and figure. The Church is a 'womb-community', bearing the incarnate Lord within her, making him present in the world and bringing forth new brothers and sisters for the first-born of all Creation, through the faithful preaching of the Gospel and through the maternal womb of the baptismal font. So the Church is the Christ-bearer and we are all Christ-bearers; in a sense therefore the Church (and we as her members) fulfils the role of *Theotokos*, the God-bearer. In this sense, therefore, we can make our own the prayer of one of the greatest of the Anglican divines of the seventeenth century, Jeremy Taylor, Bishop of Down and Connor, a prayer of preparation for Christmas communion:

> O Holy and ever blessed spirit, who didst overshadow the holy Virgin-Mother of our Lord, and causedst her to conceive by a miraculous and mysterious manner: be pleased to overshadow my soul, and enlighten my spirit, that I may

conceive the holy Jesus in my heart, and may bear him in my minde, and may grow up to the fulnesse of the stature of Christ, to be a perfect man in Christ Jesus.[3]
Amen.

+

Bearer of the Word-made-Flesh

+ Soli Deo Gloria: Advent IV (24.xii.95):
Chichester Cathedral at 11.00

In a charming and informative but very dated and rather triumphalist account of the Catholic Movement in the Church of England, *The Rivers of the Flood*, Dom Anselm Hughes presents a piquant contrast by means of two photographs reproduced together on the same page.[4] One is of St John's Church, Chichester (the Chapel of St John the Evangelist, St John Street); the other is of a church in London of which the Precentor[5] was once the assistant priest and of which I am a trustee: Our Most Holy Redeemer, Clerkenwell. I don't know how many of you have managed to get *inside* St John's; it is handsome enough from the outside, but nobody could call the interior beautiful or inspiring. Dom Anselm reproduced a photograph of its unutterably dreary interior, with its unchanged early nineteenth-century arrangement of a three-decker pulpit in the centre of the east end and an invisible Communion Table tucked away out of sight behind the pulpit, in order first of all to induce a shiver of horror in his readers at the

---

3 J. Taylor, *The Rule and Exercises of Holy Living* (1650), Ch. 4, section 10: modern edition: J. Taylor, *Holy Living and Holy Dying*, ed. P. G. Stanwood (Oxford: Clarendon Press, 1989), Vol. 1, p. 283.

4 A Hughes, *The Rivers of the Flood: A Personal Account of the Catholic Revival in England in the Twentieth Century* (2nd edn: London: Faith Press, 1963), opposite p. 47.

5 Canon John Hester (1927–2008).

realization that before the Oxford Movement many churches had identical furnishings and secondly to induce a feeling of relief, pride and gratitude that those dark days were now no more and that the hope of the future was represented by Our Most Holy Redeemer, Clerkenwell, with its Italianate High Altar with tabernacle, crucifix, and a forest of very tall candles under an imposing Renaissance ciborium or baldacchino, an ornate canopy set on four columns.

Liturgical taste has moved on since 1961, but although Our Most Holy Redeemer can no longer be seen as an exemplary model of liturgical ordering,[6] at least the model of St John's, Chichester, is one which nearly everyone agrees should be avoided at all costs. In their determination to remove pulpits from the centre of the east end (where the Altar should be) to a more modest position to the side of the Altar, our nineteenth-century forebears were not innovating. They were simply taking up a theme that Archbishop Laud had developed in the seventeenth century, when in the course of a speech he reminded those among his distinguished audience who were Knights of the Garter that by the rules of their Order they were enjoined to reverence the Altar:

> You do your reverence ... to Almighty God, I doubt not; but yet it is *versus altare*, 'towards His Altar', as the greatest place of God's residence upon earth. I say the greatest, yea greater than the pulpit; for there it is *Hoc est corpus meum*, 'This is My Body'; but in the pulpit it is at most but *Hoc est verbum meum*, 'This is My Word'. And a greater reverence, no doubt, is due to the Body than to the Word of Our Lord.[7]

By now you are probably saying to yourselves, 'What is the poor old Chancellor wittering on about? Has he forgotten that

---

[6] In the sixteen years since this was written, liturgical taste has changed again, so that this comment itself now sounds outdated.

[7] From a speech delivered in the Star Chamber on 14 June 1637, quoted in P. E. More and F. L. Cross (eds), *Anglicanism: The Thought and Practice of the Church of England, illustrated from the Religious Literature of the Seventeenth Century* (London: SPCK, 1951), p. 608.

it is Christmas – well, not quite, Christmas only begins this afternoon – but has he forgotten that this is the Fourth Sunday of Advent and only hours away from Christmas?'

But in fact I have now – at last – come to the point. Last Sunday was dominated by the figure of St John the Baptist; this Sunday is dominated by the figure of Our Lady. The contrast between them and between their respective vocations (complementary not opposing) is mirrored in the contrast (complementary not opposing) between the Pulpit and the Altar, between the Word and the Body, the Word as word and the Word-made-flesh. John has a voice: you could even say he *is* a voice – a loud, clear, resonant, urgent, demanding trumpet of a voice; he has a message and he is essentially a messenger, a herald, of the Lord's coming. Mary *says* very little, but she has a womb and in that womb the Eternal Word of God is becoming flesh, is taking to himself a Body. John points to a mystery outside himself, Mary to a mystery which is growing and taking shape within her. Both John the Baptist and Our Lady are in their different ways fulfilments of the Old Testament and bridges between the Old and New Covenants; John the Baptist fulfils the prophetic tradition, Mary the vocation of Israel to be a womb-community (a striking if not very elegant phrase), the community within which the Messiah is conceived, nurtured and in the fullness of time brought to birth; the daughter of Zion with whom the Lord makes his dwelling in this morning's first reading.

In churches of the Byzantine tradition the apse over the sanctuary is often decorated by a fresco of a woman shewn with arms outstretched in the traditional posture of prayer (which the priest at the altar still maintains); below her breast is a circle and within that circle is shewn her Child – this particular icon, incidentally, has become the logo of one of the fastest growing of the new communities in the French Church, the Emmanuel Community, Communauté de l'Emmanuel. In the first place, of course, it represents Our Lady, *virgo orans*, the praying virgin, and the mystery of the Word-made-flesh in her womb. But in the second place, it represents the Church, virgin Bride and Mother, which has in every place and for every generation to bring forth Christ into the world and in the womb of the font to give birth to new children.[8] By baptism we are all brothers and sisters of Christ and members of his Body; in conceiving and giving birth to Christ, Mary in a sense conceived and gave birth to us all, which explains why, in the prayer we said together at the lighting of the fourth Advent candle, we acknowledge Mary as '[Christ's] mother and ours'.

But lastly, there is a sense in which that icon of the virgin, prayerful, expectant, and pregnant, represents each and every one of us – man, woman, and child. Listen to St Ambrose, Bishop of Milan at the end of the fourth century:

> 'Blessed are you,' said Elizabeth to Mary, 'who believed.' But you too, who have heard and believed, are blessed. Every soul who has believed both conceives and generates the Word of God and recognizes his works.

Listen too to Jeremy Taylor, Bishop of Down and Connor in the seventeenth century:

> O Holy and ever blessed spirit, who didst overshadow the holy Virgin Mother of Our Lord ...; be pleased to overshadow my soul, and enlighten my spirit, that I may conceive ... Jesus in my heart, and ... bear him in my minde.

Listen finally to the author of that well-known Christmas hymn 'O Little Town of Bethlehem', the nineteenth-century Bishop of Massachusetts, Phillips Brooks; listen again to these well-known words and ponder them as you return from the Altar, bearing Christ within you as Mary did as she waited to give him birth:

---

[8] In a sermon preached in Chichester Cathedral on Advent IV 1983 (and again at Boxgrove Priory on Advent III 1992), Roger had observed that the font's 'function as a maternal womb is signified in the unashamedly phallic ceremony at the Easter Vigil when the paschal candle is plunged into it three times': R. T. Greenacre, 'Theotókos', *Studies and Commentaries* 1984 (Society of Mary/ American Region), pp. 1–4 at p. 3.

O holy Child of Bethlehem,
Descend to us, we pray:
Cast out our sin, and enter in,
Be born in us today ...

O come to us, abide with us, our Lord Emmanuel!

+

The God-Bearer

+ Soli Deo Gloria: Advent IV (21.xii.97):
Chichester Cathedral at Morning Prayer

Go into a typical Eastern Orthodox church – Greek, Russian, Balkan or Arab – and what will strike you most is the profusion of icons, even in the simplest wayside chapel. These icons may be painted on wooden panels (sometimes with a gilded covering hiding all but the hands and faces) or they may be mosaics or frescoes. Within a certain strictly limited range of freedom there will be some constants: an icon of Christ and an icon of the Mother of God on each side of the royal doors in the centre of the iconostasis or screen that separates the nave from the sanctuary, and over the apse, which enshrines the altar, a fresco of the Mother and Child.

In most cases this fresco follows a strict rule of composition; its name is *Platytera ton Ouranon* – She whose womb is more spacious than the heavens. (In his sonnet 'Annunciation', from that sequence of seven called *La Corona*, that extraordinary genius of the seventeenth century, the poet-priest John Donne, spoke of 'Immensity cloysterd in thy deare wombe'.)[9] She is represented with her arms held outstretched in prayer (in

---

9 Roger's script included only, inserted as an afterthought, the quotation and the word 'Donne'. The introductory phrases here are taken from a sermon delivered in the Cathedral at Mattins on Sunday 17 August of the same year, in which he quoted the whole sonnet.

a gesture often referred to in the Bible and repeated today by the celebrant at the Altar), and in a *mandorla* (the Italian word for an almond), an oval frame below her breast, is a figure of Christ, but – surprisingly perhaps – shown with adult features and holding a scroll. This is not, of course, a representation of the Virgin holding her new-born Son in her arms; this is, rather, the Expectant Virgin bearing within her Womb one who is both her Child and her Lord – Emmanuel, God-with-us. For the Word was made flesh in the womb of Mary.

In the recently published response of the House of Bishops of the Church of England to the Pope's Encyclical on Christian Unity, a very strong affirmation is made:

> Therefore, in continuity with the faith of the ancient Church, and with the support of the Third Ecumenical Council, Anglicans acclaim Mary as Theotokos ...[10]

Theotokos: why use a Greek word? Perhaps because the familiar translation 'Mother of God' *can* give rise to misconceptions. The word means literally 'The God-bearer', she who bore and brought to birth him who was God, and the title was proclaimed at the Council of Ephesus in 431 not so much to give honour to Our Lady but rather to make unmistakeably clear the inseparable union from the beginning of full humanity and full divinity in the one Lord Jesus Christ. Perhaps even today we cannot really grasp the full and earthy reality of the Incarnation unless, to quote Dr Eric Mascall, 'we reflect calmly and reverently upon the fact that for nine months Mary carried God incarnate within her as she went about her work'. This is the faith of the Church; this – I hope – is our faith too.

But there is more in the icon *Platytera ton Ouranon* than that. The woman portrayed is, of course, Mary; but she is also the Daughter of Sion – the People of Israel, the community

---

[10] *May They All Be One: A Response of the House of Bishops of the Church of England to Ut Unum Sint* (GS Misc 495) (London: Church House Publishing, 1997), p. 12, para. 32.

from whose womb after a centuries-long Advent of hope and vigil and expectancy the promised Messiah was to emerge. She is also Mother Church, lifting up her hands in prayer and bearing within her her Lord and Saviour whom she must bring forth afresh for every generation and in every place.

No man and not every woman will experience the pain and the joy and the deep mystery of childbirth. It is the faith and obedience of Mary we must imitate, rather than her unique privilege of divine motherhood.

And yet. And yet. There is a kind of spiritual pregnancy – a passivity and receptivity – that is proper to every Christian, male and female. And we can all make our own, especially on this final Sunday of Advent, as we look to our Christmas communion, the fine prayer of one of the greatest of the seventeenth-century Anglican divines, Bishop Jeremy Taylor:

> O Holy and ever blessed spirit, who didst overshadow the holy Virgin-Mother of our Lord, and causedst her to conceive by a miraculous and mysterious manner: be pleased to overshadow my soul, and enlighten my spirit, that I may conceive the holy Jesus in my heart, and may bear him in my minde, and may grow up to the fulnesse of the stature of Christ, to be a perfect man in Christ Jesus.
> Amen.

✟

The Tabernacle of God

✟ Soli Deo Gloria: Advent IV (19.xii.04):
St Michael's, Beaulieu-sur-Mer

'Look, the virgin shall conceive and bear a son, and they shall name him Emmanuel, which means "God is with us".'

The proper name of Mary's Son – given by the angel to Joseph, is, of course, Jesus. Emmanuel is therefore not so much a name as a title. It tells us that God is not a distant God, remote and unknowable, but a God who is with us and among us and alongside us. It sums up the message of the Incarnation – a word which means 'Enfleshing' – God taking on our human nature, body, mind and spirit. John expounds it in the majestic prologue to his Gospel, which we shall hear tonight in our Carol Service and again on Christmas morning, when he writes: 'The Word was made flesh and dwelt among us.' The title Emmanuel is, if you like, a one-word résumé of that message.

In the liturgy of Common Worship and the ecumenical three-year lectionary the Fourth and last Sunday of Advent invites us to contemplate Mary as a pregnant mother, pregnant with the Son of God, Emmanuel, God with us. During Mary's pregnancy Emmanuel was present in our world in the womb of our Blessed Lady – 'Immensity cloysterd in thy deare wombe', as the seventeenth-century Anglican poet-priest John Donne put it. In Year A (this year) the Gospel tells us Joseph's side of the story; next year, Year B, the Gospel tells us of the Annunciation (Gabriel announcing to Mary that she is to conceive the Son of God); the third year, Year C, the Gospel tells us of the Visitation, that encounter between two pregnant women, Mary and her cousin Elizabeth, mother of John the Baptist.

All three invite us to contemplate Mary as the God-bearer (the ancient Greek title *Theotokos*, normally translated 'Mother of God', actually means 'God-bearer'), as the Shrine, the Temple, the Tabernacle of God. I think I have already mentioned in a previous sermon the icon (fresco, mosaic) that traditionally decorates the apse of an Orthodox church (as in the Russian Cathedral in Nice) – a woman standing with outstretched arms and with the Christ portrayed as it were in her womb. I will come back to that image in a moment. Just now I want to concentrate on the word 'Tabernacle' or Tent. 'The Word was made flesh', says the Prologue to the Fourth Gospel, 'and dwelt among us' – pitched his tent among us. In their formative period as a pilgrim people travelling towards the Promised Land the children of Israel had no permanent building for worship –

either Temple or Synagogue – but only a travelling Tabernacle, the Tent of Meeting set up wherever they happened to halt on their journey, and they believed that God's glory and God's presence were made known to them in that Tabernacle. That, incidentally, is why the safe on our High Altar, in which the Blessed Sacrament is perpetually reserved, is called a 'tabernacle'.

But let us return to Mary as pregnant Mother, as God-bearer waiting for the moment to bring forth for the world the Son of God, Jesus the Saviour. If there was blessedness in her physical motherhood, there was even greater blessedness – as Jesus himself testified – in the fact that she heard the word of God and kept it. She was prepared by God's Holy Spirit for her unique vocation, but she was still free. She could have said No to the angel's message (for the risk she was taking is made clear in today's Gospel) but in faith and obedience she said Yes: 'Behold I am the handmaid of the Lord: be it unto me according to your word.' In a play on words our Latin-speaking forebears who called her the second Eve liked to point out how the angel's greeting *Ave* (Hail) is *Eva* (Eve) spelt backwards.

But if Mary is a Tabernacle bearing within her the Real Presence of Christ, then so is the Church. The Church, the whole Body of Christ, bears within her the Word made flesh (that is why we can talk of 'Mother Church') and the Church has to respond, like Mary, to God's call in faith, humility and obedience, and the Church has to bring forth Jesus Christ in the here and now of a heedless, cynical and unbelieving world.

And if the Church is a Tabernacle, a Shrine of Christ's Presence (and the figure in the Russian Orthodox Cathedral apse of the praying woman with Christ inside her body is both Mother Mary and Mother Church), then every Christian is also called upon to be a Tabernacle, a Shrine of Christ's Presence, bearing Christ within ourself and bringing him forth to the heedless, cynical, unbelieving world in which we live. We too need to be purified and prepared to be shrines of the Most Holy and to imitate the faith and obedience of Mary, Handmaid of the Lord. And when we return from the Altar, having received into ourselves the Body and Blood of Christ, are we not particularly at that moment living temples of Christ's presence? Christians have not only to be like John the Baptist, pointing beyond ourselves with a prophetic finger to the Lamb of God, but like Mary to welcome into our own hearts, souls and bodies the mystery of Emmanuel, God with us.

As we sing on Christmas morning (and indeed tonight),

O holy Child of Bethlehem,
Descend to us, we pray;
Cast out our sin, and enter in,
Be born in us today.

✝

The Angelus

+ Soli Deo Gloria: Advent IV (18.xii.05):
St Michael's, Beaulieu-sur-Mer

Do you ever ask the question: 'What is it that makes Christianity so revolutionary, so radically different from all other religions, even those close to us (in worshipping one God, the Creator of the universe) – Judaism and Islam?' And if *you* are asked that question, perhaps in the slightly more sceptical form: 'Is Christianity really – in the last resort – fundamentally different from all other religions?', then how would you try to answer?

I would put it this way. Jesus is more than a rabbi, a teacher, and his Gospel more than a collection of moral and spiritual precepts. For the human race is in a desperate plight and cannot pick itself up from the mess it has fallen into by its own efforts, so deeply engrained in us and in our world is evil. Humanity needs a saviour more than it needs a teacher – simply to be reminded of what we ought to be is no great help; it can even deepen our sense of impotence and frustration. So God's answer to the problem of human evil is not to preach at us or give us a code of law; it is to come among us as a man, sharing our human condition, and so to heal and renew humanity not from the outside but from within. God's answer to human need is the person and saving work of Jesus Christ – a teacher, yes; a model, yes; but more than that, a saviour.

The mystery of this coming of God into his own creation as man is called the Incarnation, from the Latin word for flesh: 'The Word was made flesh' (cf. the Nicene Creed – 'and was incarnate by the Holy Ghost of the Virgin Mary and was made man').

Now if there can be said to be a 'moment' of the Incarnation – a moment when the Eternal Son and Word of God became man – it was not so much Christmas Day but that day nine months earlier which we call in England 'Lady Day', 25 March, when the event recorded in today's Gospel took place. Between Lady Day and Christmas Day Mary carried the Word of God incarnate in her womb, she was the Ark of the Covenant, the Temple of God.

If you live anywhere near a church in this country (where ancient Catholic traditions still persist even if they are not understood or not even noticed by so many), you will be aware of the tradition of ringing the Angelus in the morning, at midday and in the evening. The bell rings three times and there is a pause, three times again and another pause, and then three times again and a third pause, followed by nine or more strokes. The Angelus is a call to recollection and to prayer three times a day – you will probably be familiar with Millet's painting 'The Angelus', shewing peasants pausing from their work in the field, taking off their hats and responding to the bell's call to prayer.

Perhaps you don't know the content of the Angelus. It is this:

3 strokes: V The angel of the Lord brought tidings to Mary,
            R And she conceived by the Holy Ghost.
               Hail Mary, full of grace, the Lord is with thee.
               Blessed art thou among women,
               and blessed is the fruit of thy womb, Jesus.
               Holy Mary, Mother of God,
               pray for us sinners now
               and at the hour of our death. Amen.

3 strokes: V Behold the handmaid of the Lord.
            R Be it unto me according to thy word.
               Hail Mary ...

3 strokes: V And the Word was made flesh,
            R And dwelt among us.
               Hail Mary ...

9 or more   V Pray for us, O holy Mother of God:
strokes: R That we may be made worthy of the promises of Christ.
               Let us pray. (The Collect for Lady Day)
               We beseech thee, O Lord, pour thy grace
               into our hearts; that, as we have known the
               incarnation of thy Son Jesus Christ our Lord
               by the message of an angel, so by his cross
               and passion we may be brought unto the glory
               of his resurrection; through the same Jesus
               Christ our Lord. Amen.

This devotion, Franciscan in origin, sums up admirably and precisely the message of today's Gospel.

The first versicle and response start where we need to start – with God's initiative. God's plan, prepared and matured over centuries and particularly in the history of Israel, God's chosen people – the 'womb community', comes at last to fruition today. God speaks through the message of an angel; God acts through the overshadowing of the Holy Spirit.

The second versicle and response bring us to Mary's response. God respects human freedom – even the freedom to say No to his invitation; none of us is forced to say Yes. But Mary acts in total freedom and with total faith and trust.

The third versicle and response bring us to the result of this creative dialogue between the God who calls and invites and the woman who says Yes. The Word was made flesh.

The *Hail Mary* itself conflates the angel's greeting to Mary, recorded in today's Gospel, with Elizabeth's, recorded a little later by Luke. And it concludes with the Church's prayer, 'Pray for us ...' Not 'Save us' or 'Have mercy on us', petitions which can only be addressed to God, but 'Pray for us and with us' – a request we make to all our Christian brothers and sisters, living and departed, for we are all knit together in the communion of saints.

And then finally we remind ourselves of the purpose of the Incarnation of the Son of God – by his Cross and Passion may we be brought to the glory of his resurrection.

I commend this devotion to you.

☩

Bernard of Clairvaux and Mary's *Yes*

+ Soli Deo Gloria: Advent IV (21.xii.08):
St Michael's, Beaulieu-sur-Mer

It was said of only two people in the whole history of France that, when they came to a town, frightened mothers would lock up their teenage sons for fear that, overwhelmed by the eloquent appeals of the man in question, they would abandon everything and leave home to follow this leader in an adventure that was hard and risky. One of these two men was Napoleon

Bonaparte, and we can well understand the anxiety of French mothers, fearful that their sons would die on the battlefields of Europe or perish in the snows of Russia or drown in conflict with the Royal Navy.

Who was the other? He was St Bernard of Clairvaux, born in 1090, one of the six brilliant sons of a Burgundian nobleman. After wavering for a time he decided in 1113 to join the new monastery of Cîteaux in Burgundy – an experiment in a very strict application of the Rule of St Benedict that looked as though it would fail completely until Bernard arrived with four of his own brothers and twenty-seven other friends to join it. Though not the founder of the Cistercian Order (which some of us have got to know through the Abbey of Lérins off the coast of Cannes), he was almost its re-founder. After two years at Cîteaux he was sent to establish a new monastery at Clairvaux, which prospered so much that it founded 68 daughter houses including Rievaulx and Fountains in England. Of his personal magnetism and eloquence there can be no doubt; no wonder mothers tried to prevent their sons listening to his preaching and joining his Order. He was known in the Middle Ages as *Doctor mellifluous*, the honey-tongued teacher, and I want to quote you an extract from one of his sermons that – in spite of the gap between the twelfth and the twenty-first centuries – can give us a hint of his extraordinary gifts.

He is preaching on the story of the Annunciation to Mary – the Gospel we have just heard this morning – and in imagination he is present at the scene waiting anxiously in that moment of silence between the Angel's message and Mary's response:

> You have heard that you shall conceive and bear a Son; you have heard that you shall conceive, not of man, but of the Holy Spirit. The angel is waiting for your answer: it is time for him to return to God who sent him. We too are waiting, O Lady, for the word of pity, even we who are overwhelmed in wretchedness by the sentence of damnation.
>
> And behold, to you the price of our salvation is offered. If you consent, straightway shall we be freed. In the eternal

Word of God were we all made, and lo! we die; by one little word of yours in answer shall we all be made alive.

Adam asks this of you, O loving Virgin, poor Adam, exiled as he is from paradise with all his poor wretched children; Abraham begs this of you, and David; this all the holy fathers implore, even your fathers, who themselves are dwelling in the valley of the shadow of death; this the whole world is waiting for, kneeling at your feet.

And rightly so, for on your lips is hanging the consolation of the wretched, the redemption of the captive, the speedy deliverance of all who otherwise are lost; in a word, the salvation of all Adam's children, of all your race.

Answer, O Virgin, answer the angel speedily; rather, through the angel, answer your Lord. Speak the word, and receive the Word; offer what is yours, and conceive what is of God; give what is temporal, and embrace what is eternal.

Why delay? Why tremble? Believe, speak, receive! Let your humility put on boldness, and your modesty be clothed with trust. Not now should your virginal simplicity forget prudence! In this one thing alone, O prudent Virgin, fear not presumption; for although modesty that is silent is pleasing, more needful now is the loving-kindness of your word.

Open, O Blessed Virgin, your heart to faith; open your lips to speak; open your bosom to your Maker. Behold! the Desired of all nations is outside, knocking at your door. Oh! if by your delay he should pass by, and again in sorrow you should have to begin to seek for him whom your soul loves! Arise, then, run and open. Arise by faith, run by the devotion of your heart, open by your word. And Mary said: 'Behold the handmaid of the Lord: be it done to me according to your word.'[11]

Bernard is trying to help his hearers to understand that here – at this moment and in this place – is one of the most crucial and

---

[11] Bernard of Clairvaux, *Homilies*, 4.8–9, quoted in *The Divine Office: the liturgy of the hours according to the Roman rite* (London: Collins, 1974), Vol. I, pp. 141–2.

decisive turning points in human history. 'Behold the handmaid of the Lord: be it done to me according to your word.' This is Mary's *Yes*, Mary's *Amen* to the project of God. The long history of Israel has come to this culminating point, and God wills to enter into human history and the human race in the Person of his Son. But in that moment of silence, while Mary ponders the Angel's message and glimpses all the risks and dangers that it brings, *God is waiting*; God is waiting for a human response, for the opening of a door, for that living, joyful and obedient Yes that will bring his plan into operation.

Christmas is sometimes called 'the Feast of the Incarnation', but perhaps that title belongs more precisely to Lady Day, the Feast of the Annunciation, when the Word was made flesh (*incarnatus est*) in the womb of the Blessed Virgin Mary. It was only in the eighteenth century when England accepted the Gregorian Calendar that the New Year was dated from 1 January. Before that the New Year (Anno Domini – the Year of our Salvation) began on 25 March, Lady Day. So, for example, contemporary prints of the execution of King Charles I on 30 January 1649 actually give the date as 1648.

Today's Gospel not only tells the story of how Mary conceived 'the Son of the Most High' in her womb, but also tells the story of her response of trust and faith (contrasted in St Luke's Gospel with the scepticism of John the Baptist's father Zechariah on receiving a similar message – a story which immediately precedes this one in his Gospel). The key point here (which has a lesson for us all today), is that Mary's response was *free*; she was free to say No and she was free to say Yes. Some Christians have tried totally to deny human freewill for fear that affirming human freewill somehow weakens or destroys the omnipotence of God. But to say that Mary made a free and willing acceptance in response to the Angel's message does not deny that she was only enabled to do so by the grace of God which had prepared her for this crucial moment. That is why the Angel describes her as highly favoured, graced by God, 'one who has been and remains endowed with grace', full of grace. St Paul could be speaking of Mary – he is speaking of all God's chosen – when in his Letter to the Romans he writes, 'Those whom he predestined he also called, and those whom he called he also justified, and those whom he justified he also glorified.'

But why do I say that here is a lesson for us all today? Let me quote from the Anglican–Roman Catholic agreed statement on Mary of 2004:

> Her response was not made without profound questioning, and it issued in a life of joy intermingled with sorrow, taking her even to the foot of her son's cross. When Christians join in Mary's 'Amen' ..., they commit themselves to an obedient response to the Word of God, which leads to a life of prayer and service.[12]

As we approach the Feast of Christmas (celebrating God's precious and unconditional gift of his Son to humanity), and as we approach a New Year (which we cannot be sure will be less threatening than 2008 has proved to be for most of us), let us prepare to make our response to God's purpose for us and to say with Mary,

'Here am I, the servant of the Lord: let it be with me according to your word.'

☦

---

[12] Anglican–Roman Catholic International Commission, *Mary: Grace and Hope in Christ. An Agreed Statement* (Harrisburg and London: Moorhouse, 2005), p. 7, para. 5.

7

Blessed Among Women

Two Grounds of Blessedness

+ Soli Deo Gloria: The Visitation of Our Lady (31.v.97): Little St Mary's, Cambridge

Before I begin, I would like to make two introductory remarks:

First, to express my gratitude to Fr Greany for his invitation to be here this morning. When I was an undergraduate at Clare in the early 50s,[1] Little St Mary's had a profound influence on me and I shall always be grateful to Fr Hugh Maycock,[2] Bishop Michael Ramsey (a frequent preacher here in those days)[3] and Dr Arthur Peck,[4] among others, for what I learned from them in this place.

Second, to greet the group from the Church of Notre-Dame-des-Grâces, Chant D'Oiseau, Brussels. Before I served for ten years at St George's Anglican Church, Paris, I did my apprenticeship in Anglican–Roman Catholic dialogue at the Université Catholique de Louvain and at the Monastery of Chevetogne. This was during the year which immediately preceded the opening of the Second Vatican Council and I was able to appreciate the immense contribution of the

---

[1] Roger was at Clare College, Cambridge, 1949–52.

[2] Fr Hugh Maycock (1903–80) was Vicar of Little St Mary's, 1944–52, and Principal of Pusey House, Oxford, 1952–70.

[3] Michael Ramsey was Regius Professor of Divinity in the University of Cambridge, 1950–52, and then became Bishop of Durham.

[4] Dr Arthur Peck was Vice-Master and Librarian of Christ's College, Cambridge, in the 1950s.

theologians of Louvain and the monks of Chevetogne to the opening up of the Roman Catholic Church to ecumenism put into operation by the Council.

In today's Gospel narrative Elizabeth twice acclaims Our Lady as 'Blessed'. As soon as Mary appears and greets her and Elizabeth realizes that her cousin too is pregnant, the babe in her own womb leaps for joy and she exclaims, filled with the Holy Spirit, 'Blessed are you among women and blessed is the fruit of your womb.' This attribution of blessedness brings together Mother and Child; Mary is blessed because the fruit of her womb is blessed, because she is – as Elizabeth goes on to say – 'the mother of my Lord', because she has received the amazing and unique grace of being Mother of the Messiah, Mother of the Redeemer, Mother of the Word Incarnate, *Theotokos*, Mother of God.

But later in the same acclamation Elizabeth continues by attributing to Our Lady a second title of blessedness: 'Blessed is she who believed ... that there would be a fulfilment (or, Blessed is she who believed, for there will be a fulfilment) of what was spoken to her from the Lord.' Mary is here greeted as a woman of faith, as a model of faith (perhaps in explicit contrast to Elizabeth's husband Zechariah, since he was temporarily dumb because of his failure to respond in faith, trust and commitment to the Angel's word). As the Fathers of the Early Church loved to repeat, 'Before she conceived the Word in her womb, she conceived it in her heart.' God treats his sons and daughters with immense courtesy. He always takes the initiative; his grace is sovereign, but he respects our human freedom and waits for our free response, as he did in the case of Mary: 'Behold, I am the handmaid of the Lord; let it be to me according to your word.' She was no passive, impersonal instrument, no surrogate lending her womb; because she was destined to be Mother in the fullest sense (psychological and spiritual as well as physical), her full and willing acceptance and co-operation in faith were necessary. But if we cannot imitate her unique Motherhood of the Word Incarnate, we can and should imitate her response of faith. Notre-Dame-*des-Grâces* in the plural; yet these two graces, these two grounds of blessedness, are in the end but one. She is indeed blessed in her womb and in her paps, but Jesus prefers to call her blessed (and ourselves blessed with her) insofar as she – and we with her – 'hear the word of God and keep it' (Luke 11.28).

Mary's response to Elizabeth is one of exultation but not of exaltation; she exults in magnifying God in a song of joy and thanksgiving but there is nothing of pride and self-exaltation in her hymn, though the lyrical tone of her cousin's greeting might well have turned her head. The humble, modest and lowly 'Daughter of Zion' gives all the glory to God, whom she acknowledges as her Saviour and as the one who has had regard for her and done great things for her, in her, and through her. 'Holy is his name', she proclaims, and in like manner our praise, and the Church's praise, modelled on her Magnificat, must turn away from self – even in the very act of acknowledging that God has done great things for and in us – and give all the glory to God alone. The Lord has indeed exalted her – is she not the Queen of Heaven? – but only because he has seen her humility and meekness.

Finally, there is a particular lesson in today's Gospel for the visit of Notre-Dame-des-Grâces in Brussels to Little St Mary's in Cambridge, even though Cambridge cannot by any stretch of the imagination be called 'hill country'!

In God's plan, because our humanity is meant to be a shared humanity lived in fellowship with one another, and because our redeemed humanity is lived within the fellowship of the Body of Christ, we all mediate and minister grace to one another within the common life of the Body. Pilgrimage – like Our Lady's pilgrimage to her cousin Elizabeth – is an expression of that mutual encouragement which builds up the life of the Body. Mary and Elizabeth ministered to each other; their faith, their joy, their trust in God were strengthened by their encounter and their dialogue. So we all need our friends – (even perhaps our relations!) – to be with us and alongside us in moments of joy and sorrow. In like manner our parishes can be strengthened in commitment to their Christian mission by contacts such as these. Our two Communions, Anglican and Roman Catholic, can also be strengthened in their difficult but necessary commitment to Christian Unity by such contacts, which help us to learn both from each other's weaknesses and from each other's strengths.

+

The Grace of God is in Courtesy

+ Soli Deo Gloria: Mass of Our Lady of Pew: 27.vii.90: Westminster Abbey

There was an interesting exchange of letters recently in that admirable Roman Catholic weekly, *The Tablet*, read by so many discerning Anglicans. I am having to rely on my memory, since a frantic search in my house this morning for the relevant copies was conducted in vain. An Irish Catholic had begun by comparing Irish and English attitudes to pilgrimage, greatly to the detriment of the English, you will be surprised to hear! He spoke of the penances and austerities which accompany Irish pilgrimages to – it may have been – Our Lady of Knock and spoke rather disparagingly of the rather low-key, relaxed attitudes displayed in pilgrimages to Walsingham – and here he had the Roman Catholic Shrine in view. An English Roman Catholic took up this provocative gauntlet and described how each nation, in colouring its devotion to Our Lady with the particular elements of its own national culture, temperament or psychology, was able to shed light on an aspect of Mary's personality and of her vocation.

Perhaps we should not be over-defensive. Perhaps the Irish have something to teach us. It is lovely – and very English – to end a pilgrimage with a garden party, but how did we begin?[5] Were all the Canons of Westminster called out to man the Abbey's confessional boxes for an hour or so before this Mass? Yet there *are* strains in the English tradition that give a particular colour to English Marian devotion; warmth and tenderness but without sentimentality or exaggeration, and a sense of reticence and discretion that exactly matches Our Lady's own refusal to take centre stage or to dramatize her person or her role. These qualities are marvellously expressed in that familiar fifteenth-century poem:

> I sing of a maiden
> That is makeless,[6]
> King of all kingès
> To her son she ches.[7]
> He came all so stillè
> There his mother was
> As dew in Aprillè
> That falleth on the grass.

Stillness, yes, and also quiet courtesy. May I take you at one leap from the fifteenth century to the twentieth century and to that very English though largely French writer, the Sussex poet, writer and controversialist Hilaire Belloc? An outrageously rude and belligerent man himself, he could yet write:

> Of Courtesy, it is much less
> Than Courage of Heart or Holiness,
> Yet in my walks it seems to me
> That the Grace of God is in Courtesy.

And a little farther on:

> Our Lady out of Nazareth rode –
> It was her month of heavy load;

---

5 The Society of Our Lady of Pew looks after the Pew Chapel in Westminster Abbey. The Society's Solemn Eucharist, at which this sermon was preached, was followed by a garden party.
6 Matchless.
7 For her son she chose.

Yet was her face both great and kind,
For Courtesy was in her mind.

If we turn now to our Gospel reading, we will see exemplified that same quality of courtesy. The Visitation follows on at once from the Annunciation: 'Mary arose and went with haste ... and entered the house of Zechariah and greeted Elizabeth.' The immediate context is therefore the infinite courtesy of God, who, respecting the freedom he himself has conferred upon humanity, proposes through his messenger the Archangel Gabriel that Mary should become *Theotokos*, the Mother of God. It is all done so gently, without threats or bullying, without thunder or lightning, and Mary responds with a firm but undemonstrative and undramatic act of faith and obedience.

And now, already 'Bearer of the Eternal Word' in her womb as well as in her heart and mind and will, she visits her cousin Elizabeth, who has also been favoured by God. That the two women are able to strengthen, reassure and comfort one another and rejoice in God together is shewn by the dialogue between them.

Elizabeth's greeting to Mary points to the double blessedness of Our Lady: 'Blessed are you among women, and blessed is the fruit of your womb! And why is this granted me, that the mother of my Lord should come to me?' Mary is indeed blessed on account of the fruit of her womb, because she is the mother of Our Lord. But Elizabeth continues: 'And blessed is she who believed ...' Mary is the Woman of Faith and it is only because, as the Fathers loved to repeat, she first conceived the Word of God in her mind that she was enabled to conceive the Word in her womb. Elizabeth here anticipates Our Lord's own blessing of his mother, and it must be seen of course as a blessing and not as a disparagement. To the woman in the crowd who called out, 'Blessed is the womb that bore you and the breasts that you sucked', he replied, 'Blessed rather are those who hear the word of God and keep it.' Who indeed kept God's word, pondering it in her heart, more faithfully than Mary? The vocation of Israel was to be through faith and obedience a womb community, a community that would bring forth for all nations the Messiah; the whole people of Israel is addressed as 'Daughter of Zion' but that role, that destiny and that title are personified in Mary when the Lord says to her what he has said to his people, 'Lo, I come and I will dwell in the midst of you.'

But how does Mary respond to the greeting of Elizabeth, that greeting of great courtesy and great prophetic insight? She responds with the greatest of the Gospel Canticles. In it she does indeed acknowledge what God has done for her and even that from henceforth all generations will call her blessed. But that is not the main thrust of her hymn of praise. She has two preoccupations: first of all to magnify the Lord and to rejoice in him as her Saviour; secondly, to identify herself with the poor, the weak, the hungry and the lowly of the Lord, who confidently look to God to be exalted and filled with good things. Her concern is for God and for the People of God, and as the Model of Faith for all Christians she calls us to share those concerns and gives a single but clear injunction as she points to her Son: 'Do whatever he tells you.'

'Of courtesy, it is much less than courage of heart or holiness ...' True enough, but there is no lack either of courage or of holiness in Mary, whose faith and obedience were to be so cruelly tested. So as we rejoice in this most English of devotions to Our Lady of Pew in this great national shrine of Westminster Abbey, let us not forget that touch of steel that must characterize all authentic Marian devotion and which lies underneath the happiness, the fun and the rejoicing; that touch of steel that calls not perhaps for exceptional austerities but for an obedience that can never be without pain.

> 'Behold, I am the handmaid of the Lord: let it be to me according to your word.'
> 'A sword will pierce through your own soul also.'
> 'Do whatever he tells you.'

+

All Generations will call her Blessed

+ Soli Deo Gloria: Advent IV (21.xii.03):
St Michael's, Beaulieu-sur-Mer

From the Magnificat: 'From this day all generations will call me blessed.'

If you were here two Sundays ago and endured my usual wearisome discourse without falling asleep, you may remember that I spoke about the three songs or canticles which St Luke (and Luke alone) records in the first two chapters of his Gospel:

- ❖ the Song of Zechariah (father of St John the Baptist) – Benedictus, which replaces the psalm after the first reading on Advent II,
- ❖ the Song of Mary – Magnificat, which replaces the psalm this Sunday, and
- ❖ the Song of Simeon – Nunc dimittis, which will dominate the liturgy on the last day of the Christmas season on 2 February, the Feast of Candlemas.

You may remember too that I reminded you that just as the Benedictus, the Song of Zechariah, forms the climax of the Church's office of Morning Prayer (Matins[8] or Lauds), so the Magnificat, the Song of Mary, forms the climax of the office of Evening Prayer (Evensong or Vespers). So every day, wherever Evensong is sung or said, the Church reminds itself of Mary's prophecy: 'Behold, from henceforth all generations shall call me blessed.' It is also highly significant that in the Anglican tradition, in the office of Evensong, the Magnificat forms a bridge between the Old Testament (the psalms and first reading) and the New Testament.[9] For Mary is in a sense the climax

---

8 The Prayer Book office.

9 In a sermon preached in Chichester Cathedral on Advent IV 1983 (and again at Boxgrove Priory on Advent III 1992), Roger commented, 'It was a stroke of genius on the part of Archbishop Cranmer to make the Magnificat the point of transition, the bridge, between the Old and New Testament at Evening Prayer': R. T. Greenacre, 'Theotókos', *Studies and Commentaries 1984* (Society of Mary/American Region), pp. 1–4 at p. 2.

of God's long work of formation and preparation in the Old Testament. Israel is the womb-people on whom God lavished so much care: it was destined to bring forth the Messiah, and Mary is the daughter of Zion, chosen to be the means whereby the Son of God would assume a human nature and come into the world as Messiah (Christ) and Saviour.

But why do we call Mary blessed? The answer is twofold and this twofold answer is given to us in the words of Elizabeth, Mary's cousin, recorded in today's Gospel.

First, 'Blessed are you among women and blessed is the fruit of your womb.' Mary's vocation was absolutely unique and mind-bogglingly paradoxical in its implications. Since the fifth century AD the Church has recognized Mary as *Theotokos*, sometimes translated as Mother of God but, more precisely, as the one who bore and brought into the world him who was God, the God-bearer. Her only glory is that of her Son – blessed is the fruit of your womb, the one who, God from all eternity, entered into our world and took his human nature from her, so that now he is not only Son of God but also Son of Man and Son of Mary, Emmanuel, 'God-with-us'.

But, secondly, Elizabeth went on to say, 'Blessed is she who believed.' God respects our freewill, though we so often use it to make wrong decisions. God waits upon our free assent to the initiative of his grace. We are free to say No, even though God wills us and gives us the grace to say Yes. So when Mary heard that terrifying message from the Angel Gabriel nothing happened – even though the salvation of the world depended upon it – until Mary had given her Yes to God: 'Here am I, the servant of the Lord; let it be with me according to your word.' It was Mary's faith, her humility, her obedience, her total openness to God and to God's will that made possible that Amen, that Yes: 'Here am I, the servant of the Lord.' God knocks at the door of her heart; God knocks at our doors, but he does not force the door: only we can open the latch from the inside.

So it was that, when one day a woman in the crowd cried out to Jesus, 'Blessed is the womb that bore you and the breasts that nursed you!', Jesus replied, 'Blessed rather are those who hear the word of God and obey it.' He was in no way turning honour away from his Mother: on the contrary, he was pointing out that quality in her that does not separate her from us but is a model that we can and must imitate. St Luke points out over and over again that Mary heard and pondered and meditated on the word of God, kept it in her heart and obeyed it willingly and totally. 'Before she conceived the Word of God in her womb, she harboured it in her mind and heart.'

So as we hear this second word of Elizabeth, 'Blessed is she who believed', let us set before us as a model Mary's faith and her obedience. And when we hear the first word, 'Blessed are you among women and blessed is the fruit of your womb', let us reflect that although there was only one Mother of God, yet the whole Church and every baptized Christian is called upon to be *Theotokos*, to carry Christ our God within us and to bring him forth to the world in which we live. So it is that for both these things, her motherhood and her faith, all generations will indeed called her blessed.

+

Waiting for Pentecost

+ Soli Deo Gloria: Sunday after Ascension (7.v.89):
May Procession, Our Most Holy Redeemer, Clerkenwell

One of the authentic marks of the Catholic Christian – whether he or she is Eastern Orthodox, Oriental Orthodox, Roman Catholic or Anglican; whether he or she is Ethiopian, Armenian, Greek, Russian, Polish, Italian, Irish, or English, Nigerian or Korean; whether he or she is a pope, an archbishop, a merchant seaman, a shopkeeper or a housewife – is a great love and devotion for the Mother of Our Lord and a natural desire to celebrate that love and devotion in a joyful and colourful way, in a way that many of our puritan and protestant neighbours find disconcerting and even repugnant. But if a note of sheer exuberant enjoyment is absolutely appropriate for our celebration tonight, that does not exclude a little serious reflection on the meaning of what we were doing. If it did, why bother with a sermon at all?

Catholic Christians honour Our Lady for two reasons, because of two great mysteries which are the foundations of their faith. The first is the Incarnation, the truth that God himself has taken to himself our human nature through being born of a human Mother; the second is the Church, that is, the People of God, the Communion of Saints, the Body of Christ.

The third Ecumenical Council of the Undivided Church, the Council of Ephesus in 431, proclaimed that Mary is *Theotokos*, literally the God-bearer, that is, the one who gave birth to the Word of God incarnate. It is a high and glorious title, but it cannot be too often or too energetically affirmed that it was not coined and it was not adopted for the purpose of giving honour to Mary but in order to make unequivocally clear the Church's teaching about the Incarnation of our Lord, one Person wholly divine and wholly human. To deny that Mary is *Theotokos* is either to deny that her Son is divine or so to separate his divinity and his humanity as to deny the oneness of the Person of Christ. Of course, the title *Theotokos* does give honour to Mary, but that is strictly secondary. She was and she is the Mother of God incarnate, for since her Son retains his humanity she remains for ever his Mother. Catholic Christianity takes seriously the earthy and the physical, because it has a high doctrine of Creation, a high doctrine of the Incarnation, a high doctrine of the Resurrection and a high doctrine of the Sacraments. The spiritual is not the opposite of the bodily; body and spirit belong together and fulfil and complement one another.

Catholic spirituality therefore delights to dwell on the full physical and psychical and spiritual reality of Mary's motherhood; she is the real Mother of a real man, with all that that implies and more. Jesus loved his Mother because she was his Mother, or rather, Jesus *loves* his Mother because she *is* his Mother, and that may seem good enough reason for us to love her too.

But there is another reason, and perhaps the best way for us to approach it today during these nine days that separate Ascension Day from the Day of Pentecost is to look for a moment at that scene in the Upper Room. In response to the command of the Ascending Christ the disciples had returned to Jerusalem from the Mount of Olives to wait for the gift of the promised Spirit. There, according to the Acts of the Apostles, they 'with one accord devoted themselves to prayer, together with the women and Mary, the Mother of Jesus, and with his brothers'. To understand the significance of Mary's presence there in the Upper Room we need to go back a bit.

Mary was never simply a passive instrument, used by God against her will. God, in his infinite courtesy, waited for her free consent to his plan that she should be the Mother of God. Her *Yes*, her 'Behold, I am the handmaid of the Lord, let it be to me according to your word', made possible the Incarnation. So we honour in Our Lady a woman of faith, the one who believed, the one who, as the Fathers loved to repeat, 'before she conceived the Word in her womb conceived him in her heart', the one who heard God's word, kept it, pondered it in her heart and did it. You may remember that there are some apparently rather hard words addressed by Jesus to his Mother in the Gospels – but all are designed to test and strengthen her faith, to help her to pass from the Mother-child relationship to the Believer-Redeemer relationship. It is therefore in her role as the first Christian that Jesus confides her to the Beloved Disciple at the foot of the Cross and says to him, 'Behold your Mother.' Mary is a model of faith, obedience and surrender, a model *to* the Church and a model *of* the Church, a Mother *in* the Church and even Mother *of* the Church, Mother of the faithful. Mother's role of motherhood is not finished; it finds a new expression in the Church.

And so in a sense it is inevitable and necessary that Mary should be there in the midst of the waiting expectant community of the disciples, prayerfully awaiting the miracle of Pentecost. For nine months she had been pregnant, expectant, waiting to give birth to Jesus Christ, the Head of the Church, quickened in her womb by the overshadowing of the Holy Spirit. Now for nine days she is, as it were, pregnant once again, waiting for that same overshadowing Holy Spirit to bring forth the Church, the Body of her Son.

So we honour Our Blessed Mary because of our devotion and commitment to the Incarnation; we honour her as the Mother of Christ. But we honour her too because of our devotion and commitment to the Catholic Church; we honour her as the Mother of all Christians, Mother of the Church – we know her as the one who was overshadowed by the Spirit at the moment of the Incarnation and as the one who was overshadowed by that same Spirit once again on the first Day of Pentecost. Blessed be the Holy Spirit who made her both Christ's Mother and ours!

Amen.

✢

8

Queen of Heaven

The Assumption

+ Soli Deo Gloria: The Assumption of the BVM (15.viii.88): SS Peter and Paul, Chichester

Tonight is the celebration of a homecoming, the loving welcome given by Our Lord to his Mother 'when her life on earth had run its course'[1] and the joy of Mary at being reunited with one who is both her Son and her Redeemer. We normally celebrate the feast of a saint on his or her 'heavenly birthday', the traditional term in the Christian vocabulary for the day of a saint's death: and 15 August is indeed the heavenly birthday of Mary, Mother of God Incarnate and spiritual mother of all faithful Christians. Mary has a number of feasts; her Nativity is also celebrated, as is John the Baptist's, and even her Conception is celebrated, alone of all the saints, because she was marked out by God and prepared from the first moment of her existence in the womb of her own mother. But the Presentation of Christ in the Temple and the Annunciation are really more feasts of Our Lord than feasts of Our Lady, though we can never separate Mary from her Son or Christ from his Mother. Today is, therefore, the Principal Feast of Our Lady according

---

1 The reference is to the Apostolic Constitution *Munificentissimus Deus* of 1 November 1950, in which Pope Pius XII defined it to be a divinely revealed dogma 'that the Immaculate Mother of God, the ever Virgin Mary, *having completed the course of her earthly life* [expleto terrestris vitae cursu], was assumed body and soul into heavenly glory'.

to an ancient and (until the sixteenth century) universal tradition of East and West.[2]

In the Church of England, unhappily, there is an element of controversy about this feast, and I shall have to ask you to turn your attention with me to that in a moment, but let us first of all emphasize what surely all Christians can agree upon; that Mary, whom all generations call Blessed, is enjoying the eternal happiness of heaven and that it is good for us to celebrate that. This homecoming has been celebrated in hymns which are dear to Anglicans, two of them written by very Anglican Anglicans – Thomas Ken, Bishop of Bath and Wells in the reigns of Charles II and James II, and George Timms, former Archdeacon of Hackney and still alive today, one of the founding fathers of the Ecumenical Society of the Blessed Virgin Mary.[3] This is the last verse of Ken's hymn ('Her virgin eyes ...': *New English Hymnal*, hymn 182):

Heaven with transcendent joys her entrance graced,
Next to his throne her Son his Mother placed;
And here below, now she's of heaven possest,
All generations are to call her blest.

And this is the last verse of Archdeacon Timms' hymn ('Sing we of the blessed Mother': *New English Hymnal*, hymn 185):

Sing the chiefest joy of Mary
When on earth her work was done,
And the Lord of all creation
Brought her to his heavenly home:
Virgin Mother, Mary blessèd,
Raised on high and crowned with grace,

---

[2] In 1997 the Common Worship Calendar restored 15 August as the Festival of the Blessed Virgin Mary in the Church of England. The Visit of the BVM to Elizabeth (31 May) is also a Festival, while the Conception and Birth of the BVM (8 December and 8 September) are Lesser Festivals.

[3] The Ven. George Timms (b. 1910) was Chairman of the Editors of the *New English Hymnal* (1986). He died on 15 November 1997.

May your Son, the world's redeemer,
Grant us all to see his face.

The controversy arises because both the Eastern Orthodox Church and the Roman Catholic Church teach that Mary has been assumed body and soul into heaven; this is not the object of a formal dogma in the Eastern Orthodox Church but it was solemnly defined for Roman Catholics by Pius XII in 1950. Anglican unease is due to two factors: a certain scepticism with regard to the non-scriptural apocryphal writings which tell of Mary's empty tomb and, more fundamentally, a belief that no teaching which is not biblical ought to be imposed on the faithful as a dogma – however attractive or reasonable that teaching may appear.

The first difficulty need not be a problem. The legends of Mary's Assumption are not historical and they are not treated as such in the definition of 1950, which is strictly agnostic as to whether anything happened at the observable, historical level. All that the definition says is that Mary was taken up body and soul into the glory of heaven: it merely affirms that what will be the destiny of all Christians – to be in body and soul in heaven, in the new spiritual body of the resurrection, is already the case as far as Mary is concerned: in the language of ARCIC 'her glory in heaven involves full participation in the fruits of salvation'.[4] She has passed beyond judgement and fully enjoys already what we hope to enjoy one day. Her Assumption does not separate Mary from the rest of us; it is one more pledge of the destiny promised to us all.

Anglicans can and, I believe, should accept all this quite happily. They still will have reservations about the dogmatic definition, which we would see as both unnecessary and going beyond that solid basis in Scripture which a dogmatic definition has normally been held to require. The Assumption is fully consonant with Scripture, but is that enough? Mind you, Anglicans are in the process of doing the same thing in another field.

---

4 Anglican–Roman Catholic International Commission, *The Final Report* (London, 1982), p. 96: Authority in the Church II, para. 30, footnote 6.

Theological support for women in the priesthood is at most consonant with Scripture; it cannot be proved from Scripture. But once you have women priests and bishops Anglicans are in fact saying that this is certainly true and must be accepted by all.

But let us not end on a painful note of controversy. In the Magnificat Mary rejoiced:

> He hath put down the mighty from their seat:
> and hath exalted the humble and meek.

Today the poor, the oppressed, the despised, 'the humble and meek' can take heart because a lowly maiden from Nazareth is now higher than the cherubim and more glorious than the seraphim, and in her exaltation there is hope and promise for all the humble and meek.

The homily ended with a passage from a sermon by Dom Gregory Dix which is quoted on p. 82 below.

✝

Taken up into Heaven

+ Soli Deo Gloria: The Assumption of the BVM (15.viii.93): Holy Trinity, Bath

> Heaven with transcendent joys her entrance graced,
> Next to his throne her Son his Mother placed;
> And here below, now she's of heaven possest,
> All generations are to call her blest.

I am happy to be with you this morning in Holy Trinity, Bath, and particularly because this is a church in which you honour one of the best and greatest of the Bishops of Bath and Wells, Thomas Ken, a man excluded from his see towards the end of the seventeenth century because he paid the Cost of Conscience and refused to accept the received wisdom of the day and the pressure to conform to the politic and the expedient.[5] The words I have just quoted come from a hymn of his and celebrate the mystery of this feast, Mary's full entry into the presence of her Son and the glory of heaven. We reject of course with contempt the alteration in this stanza perpetrated in at least one Anglican hymn book (not I imagine known, let alone used, in this church),[6] which replaces '*Next* to his throne' with '*Near* to this throne'. Bishop Ken was far too orthodox and catholic a divine to doubt for a moment that Mary's place was indeed *next* to the Son who had taken humanity from her womb!

Two of the feasts of this month of August speak of the glory of God which since the Incarnation has come to transform our humanity (body, soul and spirit) in a radically new way. On 6 August we celebrated the Feast of the Transfiguration of the Lord – the mystery in which the human form of Jesus was totally transformed by the eternal and uncreated glory of God. This anticipated the glory of the Resurrection and Ascension of Christ, and also pointed to the fact that in Christ, fully divine and fully human, our humanity is also destined to be transfigured. And not only our human nature, but the whole created order to which we belong also. For, as St Paul assures us in his Letter to the Romans, 'the creation itself will be set free from its bondage to decay and obtain the glorious liberty of the children of God'. The spiritual is not to be set over against the bodily. Our belief in the resurrection of the body – our own call to share in the Easter mystery – affirms the reality that the glory promised to us transforms both spirit and body.

And now today's solemnity of the Assumption of Our Blessed Lady witnesses in its own way to this destiny of redeemed humanity, this call to share in the Easter mystery. Christ alone

---

5 'Cost of Conscience' is the name of an organization that campaigned against the legislation for the ordination of women to the priesthood in the Church of England, to which the General Synod had given final approval on 11 November 1992.

6 *Hymns Ancient and Modern.*

is said to have *ascended* into heaven, for the word 'Ascension' means going up and ascribes an active role to the person who goes up. Christ ascends to the Father's throne by right, by right of his divinity and by right of his risen and glorified humanity. Mary is said to have been *assumed* into heaven – a word which means 'being taken up' and ascribes a passive role to the person so taken up. And in fact we are all destined to be taken up into heaven, to see the transfiguration and transformation of our total humanity, body, mind and spirit, and to receive a crown of glory – a share in the kingship of Christ. That is why today's second reading from St Paul's First Letter to the Corinthians[7] speaks of what is promised to us all and what we see – in anticipation – already achieved in Mary. For has not Christ promised us all:

> The glory which thou hast given me, I have given to them ... Father, I desire that they also, whom thou hast given to me, may be with me where I am, to behold my glory which thou hast given me in thy love for me before the foundation of the world.

If he has promised this to us all, how can we doubt that he has already granted it to his Mother?

In today's Gospel story Elizabeth proclaims three blessings:

1 Blessed are you among women.
2 Blessed is the fruit of your womb.
3 Blessed is she who believed.

Let us look at this last. It proclaims that Mary is the first of all Christians, 'a model of holiness, obedience and faith for all Christians', one who hears the word of God and keeps it, one who acknowledges humbly that God is her Saviour. And it is precisely because she is a type, figure and model of the Church, the Church which is both virgin bride and mother, that what is achieved in her is promised to us all, if we too, like her, believe and obey, open ourselves to be servants of the Lord, and rejoice

---

7 1 Corinthians 15.54–57.

in God our Saviour, and so, with all the lowly and meek, are exalted.

Mary's faith, obedience and humility are exemplary: they invite and challenge us to imitate her. Yet her holiness was not the result of goodness achieved in her own strength by her own deserving but the result of her choice by God for the unique role that was hers (*Theotokos*, the God-bearer) and her preparation by God for that role. It is because the Word of God is to take flesh from her, that she, God's Daughter, is to become God's Mother, that she must be fitted to become the perfect vessel and instrument for so awesome and so unique and unrepeatable a vocation. 'Blessed are you among women.' Yes indeed, but precisely *because* 'Blessed is the fruit of your womb.'

So the privileges of Mary are not there to call attention to herself but to call attention to the even greater mystery of her Son, Emmanuel, God among us, the Word made flesh. And she herself points away from herself in order to point us to her Son. As she said at the wedding feast of Cana, 'Do whatever he tells you.'

And so, in a formula which I discovered recently, by a poet or hymn writer whose name is not known, we can proclaim:

Mary the Dawn	Christ the perfect Day
Mary the Gate	Christ the heavenly Way
Mary the Root	Christ the mystic Vine
Mary the Grape	Christ the sacred Wine
Mary the Corn-Sheaf	Christ the living Bread
Mary the Rose tree	Christ the Rose blood red
Mary the Fount	Christ the cleansing Flood
Mary the Chalice	Christ the saving Blood
Mary the Temple	Christ the Temple's Lord
Mary the Shrine	Christ its God adored
Mary the Beacon	Christ the Heaven's Rest
Mary the Mirror	Christ the Vision blest.

☩

Crowned with Glory

+ Soli Deo Gloria: The Blessed Virgin Mary (15.viii.00): Chichester Cathedral at 18.00

From the first reading (Revelation 12):

> A great portent appeared in heaven, a woman clothed with the sun, with the moon under her feet and on her head a crown of twelve stars.

And from the Gospel (Luke 1), but in the more familiar words of the *Book of Common Prayer* Magnificat:

> He hath put down the mighty from their seat and hath exalted the humble and meek.

This contrast between the meekness and humility of the Poor Virgin of Nazareth and the splendid vision of the Woman of the Apocalypse crowned with twelve stars has perhaps nowhere been better portrayed than by the Anglican Benedictine monk and liturgical scholar Dom Gregory Dix in a sermon that he preached at Beaconsfield in 1941:

> Here she is, the Queen of all the Cinderellas in history: the humble peasant girl; the carpenter's wife, brought to bed in a stable; the refugee in Egypt; the mother of whom ill-natured neighbours said she was no better than she ought to be (she was not spared that taunt); the poor widow, who watched her Son die in agony because the great ones of the world feared this young man and put him out of the way; the silent humble old woman of the people, whose life was over for all that mattered, praying in obscurity for twelve or twenty years after the Ascension; and then – the Queen of heaven.[8]

---

8 Quoted by Dom Augustine Morris, 'Our Lady and the Reunion of Christendom', in E. L. Mascall and H. S. Box, *The Blessed Virgin Mary: Essays by Anglican Writers* (London: Darton, Longman & Todd, 1963), pp. 121–31, at p. 125. I am grateful to Robert Mercer CR for informing me of the source of this quotation.

And should you experience a moment's nervous hesitation at this title 'Queen of Heaven' and wonder whether it is not perhaps just a trifle un-Anglican, remember that one of the charges laid against William Laud, Charles I's Archbishop of Canterbury, at his trial by the Puritans, a trial that led to his condemnation and execution, was that he had erected over the porch of the University Church of St Mary the Virgin in Oxford a statue of the *Virgo Coronata* – the Crowned Virgin. The Puritans of course destroyed the image, but at the Restoration a replacement was installed – complete with crown.

In today's solemnity we celebrate the totality of the work of God's grace in the life of our Blessed Lady and its culmination in the welcome Christ gave to his Mother when she entered into the joys of heaven. There is a paradox here, as in almost all the great mysteries of the Christian faith. In one sense, Mary's honour and Mary's destiny are unique, for her vocation was unique; she alone was *Theotokos*, Mother of God incarnate, the one who carried the Son of God in her womb and brought him forth to the world at Bethlehem. So Thomas Ken, another great Anglican bishop of the seventeenth century (Bishop of Bath and Wells at the end of that century) could say, in the words of a hymn we shall sing at the Offertory: 'Next to his throne her Son his Mother placed'; not everyone can have that privileged place next to his throne, it is hers and hers alone.

And yet, and yet, Mary's true blessedness is that before she conceived the Word in her womb she conceived in her heart; she would not have been chosen to become Mother of God if she did not already treasure God's Word in her heart and thus could respond to the Angel's message with humble faith and prompt obedience. And in this Mary is a model for all Christians and her entrance into the glory of her Son is a model, a sign, a promise, an anticipation of the destiny of all Christian people, called to be taken up in body and soul into the glory of heaven, called to be crowned, each one of us, with the crown of God's gracious and transforming love, so that we too may reign with him in glory.

But Mary goes first and, as we contemplate her already crowned with that glory which we hope may one day be ours too, we may echo the very last recorded words of our own St Richard as he lay dying, words put to music by Fauré in an anthem we hear tonight:

> Maria, mater gratiae,
> mater misericordiae,
> tu nos ab hoste protege
> et in hora mortis suscipe.

> Mary, mother of grace,
> mother of mercy,
> protect us from the Enemy now
> and receive us at the hour of our death.

✠

Mary: Grace and Hope in Christ

✠ Soli Deo Gloria: The Assumption of the BVM (14.viii.05): Ufford

There is one constant feature which dominates the observance of this Feast of the Assumption of our Blessed Lady at all times and in all places: the celebration of Our Lady, Mary, *Theotokos*, as now 'fully present with God in Christ', predestined, called, justified and glorified, the poor humble lowly virgin of Nazareth now exalted or transformed, like the fairy-tale Cinderella, to become a queen, the Queen of Heaven.

But this year there is an additional feature which it would be wrong to ignore, especially in this church dedicated to the Assumption of the Blessed Virgin Mary. Earlier this year an Agreed Statement of the Anglican–Roman Catholic International Commission (ARCIC), *Mary: Grace and Hope in Christ*, was published. It marks a significant new degree of potential agreement and consensus which can only be a cause for profound thanksgiving, if it is received and ratified by our two churches. (Though we must balance that with the sad realization that in the curious game of Snakes and Ladders which characterizes ecumenical relations at the moment, closer agreement over the significance of Mary may be rendered ineffective by sharper disagreement about the ordination of women as bishops. I have personally been involved in Anglican–Roman Catholic relations at least since 1961 when I was sent as the Archbishop of Canterbury's priest student to the Université Catholique de Louvain, and have seen hopes grow and then wane again. But today, on this Feast and in this Church dedicated to the Assumption, let us concentrate not on snakes but on this particular ladder!)

At the Reformation Roman Catholics and Anglicans seemed to be moving in radically opposed directions with regard to Marian doctrine and Marian devotion. Late mediaeval Catholicism had tended to concentrate on Mary in a way that separated her both from Christ and from the Church, from her Son and her Son's disciples. For example, Mary was often held up to the faithful as a merciful, indulgent, easy-going Mediatrix of grace, a cosy Queen Mother figure who could be approached more easily than her Son, who as Judge had a sterner and more inflexible and unforgiving attitude to sinners. This attitude did violence both to Christ – our Judge, but also our only Saviour, Redeemer and Mediator – and to Mary, whose word to believers in all ages is the same as that addressed to the servants at the Wedding in Cana: 'Do whatever he tells you'; it drove a wedge between Mother and Son. It led many of the Reformers to deny the rightness of our asking Mary and the saints to pray for us, and it led to a terrible orgy of destruction – not least here in East Anglia – of statues, paintings and stained-glass windows depicting Our Lady and the saints.

Today the situation has been reversed. The Roman Catholic Church in the reforms of the Second Vatican Council has re-emphasized the need to subordinate all our thinking about Mary to the two poles of Christ and the Church and has made Marian devotion more scriptural, while the Church of England has begun – perhaps rather timidly in some places – to honour Mary again, to invoke her prayers and to introduce her image into our churches and her name into our hymns and carols. And once more in the Church of England, as in most churches of the Anglican Communion, 15 August has been restored as the principal feast of the Blessed Virgin Mary.

Mary is seen once more in both our traditions as – to use a technical term – the eschatological image of the Church – that is, the anticipation of what is the destiny of God's people and of every individual Christian – all of us called to share in Christ's Easter victory over death, to be 'fully present with God in Christ' (as the ARCIC text puts it),[9] all of us with Mary predestined, called, justified and glorified.

In the Creed we shall in a few moments profess our faith in 'the resurrection of the dead and the life of the world to come': resurrection of the dead – or, as the Apostles' Creed says, 'of the body' – not just the survival of the soul. Mary's presence in the fullness of her humanity, body and soul, in the glory of God, is a privilege, of course, given to one who was the Mother of God incarnate and the handmaid of the Lord in faith and obedience and commitment. But her Assumption is an anticipation, a sign of grace and hope, of our own destiny.

Christians affirm the essential good news of Creation and holiness of the body: the body is not a sordid tomb imprisoning a pure spirit: we were made to be creatures of flesh and blood. If it is the whole person (not the body only) which has been corrupted by sin (the root sin after all is the sin of pride), it is equally the whole person (not the soul only) which is to be redeemed and glorified. The doctrine of the resurrection of the body does not favour any particular explanation of *how* this will happen: it does safeguard the permanence of our personal identity as human persons and proclaim the redemption and transfiguration of that identity. So as we contemplate the glory of Mary in her Assumption into heaven, we celebrate the good-

---

[9] Anglican–Roman Catholic International Commission, *Mary: Grace and Hope in Christ. An Agreed Statement* (Harrisburg and London: Continuum, 2005), p. 34, para. 56.

ness of the whole created order, affirmed in Creation and in the Incarnation and in the Sacraments, and the call to holiness of body and soul as we look for the resurrection of the dead and the life of the world to come.

☩

The Prayers of the Saints

+ Soli Deo Gloria: Nativity of the Blessed Virgin Mary, transferred from 8 September (7.ix.03): St Michael's, Beaulieu-sur-Mer

A procession was winding its way one bank holiday Monday through the streets of the Norfolk village of Walsingham, a place of pilgrimage to the Blessed Virgin Mary since the eleventh century, whose shrine there was destroyed on the orders of Henry VIII and restored in the twentieth century, and is now frequented by Anglicans, Roman Catholics and Eastern Orthodox. A little group of demonstrators from a number of extreme protestant groups inspired by Ian Paisley were brandishing placards and screaming abuse. One of them with an extremely powerful voice and a strong Ulster accent was screaming out, 'She can't hear you; she's dead.' Now that in fact contradicts two central doctrines of the Christian faith, clearly affirmed in the Apostles' Creed – the communion of saints and the resurrection of the body.

The doctrine of the Communion of Saints teaches us that all Christian people, living and departed, are (to quote the *Book of Common Prayer*) 'knit together ... in one communion and fellowship, in the mystical body of ... Christ our Lord'.[10] That is to say that we are intimately related to one another, sharing the same life, dependent on the one Head, and that death cannot break this 'one communion and fellowship' that knits

---

10 Collect of All Saints' Day.

us all together. What binds us together is our common faith in Christ and our common baptism and our sharing in the Eucharist (with angels and archangels and with all the company of heaven), but its expression and its deepening depends on mutual love. Mutual love is itself expressed and deepened by mutual intercession, and it is one of the deep and unfathomable mysteries of divine providence that our own salvation, our own happiness, our own growth in holiness are dependent on mutual intercession.

Now there is no fundamental difference in my asking you or you asking me for the help of each other's prayers and our asking Our Blessed Lady or any of the other saints in heaven to pray for us. We do not pray *to* the saints any more than we pray *to* each other, for only God can answer prayer and bestow grace. Our opening hymn by Canon Stuckey Coles, a former Principal of Pusey House, makes this clear in verse 4:

> Let us weave our supplications,
> She with us and we with her.[11]

There was a tendency at the time of the Reformation for popular Catholic piety to treat Mary as practically a goddess, able to dispense favours as an independent source of grace and as much more lenient than her son. Luther quite rightly and properly reacted against this, but in his Commentary on the Magnificat, in which he exalted precisely her lowliness and her total dependence on God ('she does not want you to come to her, but through her to God'), he concluded, 'We pray God to give us a right understanding of this Magnificat ... through the intercession and for the sake of his dear Mother Mary.' Later Protestant Reformers and later generations of Protestants went beyond this position of Martin Luther, denying the legitimacy of asking for the prayers of saints, doubting whether the saints do pray for us, regarding any honour paid to the saints as dangerous infringement of worship due to Christ alone. And

---

[11] V. S. Stuckey Coles (1845–1929), 'Ye who own the faith of Jesus': *New English Hymnal*, hymn 188.

yet Scripture itself, in the Letter to the Hebrews, pictures the Communion of saints as a great sporting arena, with Christians on earth running a race 'surrounded by a great cloud of witnesses' – the Saints in the amphitheatre stands supporting us with their encouragement, their presence, their fellowship, their sympathy and, surely also, their prayers.

We believe in the Communion of Saints and the resurrection of the body or, in the Nicene Creed, 'the resurrection of the dead'. The dead in Christ are indeed alive in Christ, in one very important sense more alive than we are, because they are in the nearer presence of Christ with death behind them and no longer in front of them. As Jesus himself said, 'The Lord, the God of Abraham, the God of Isaac, the God of Jacob is not God of the dead, but of the living, for all live to him.'

Today we celebrate the Birthday of the Blessed Virgin Mary (we don't know of course the real date, but ...!) and the Fête Patronale of Beaulieu. The Gospel is the Magnificat – Mary's great hymn of praise in the presence of her cousin Elizabeth, the central hymn of Vespers or Evensong in the Roman Catholic, Anglican and Lutheran traditions. The Magnificat is a deeply spiritual combination of high exaltation ('All generations shall call me blessed', 'He that is mighty hath magnified me') and deep humility ('God my Saviour', 'He hath regarded the lowliness of his handmaiden', 'His mercy is on them that fear him').

So today we praise God for what he has done for us through her – through her acceptance of his word – we give thanks for her example of faith, trust, obedience and humility, and we remember Luther's words: 'She does not want you to come to her, but through her to God.'

Amen.

+

9

St Joseph

**Homily for the Feast of St Joseph,
given by Canon Roger Greenacre at the
Abbey of Notre-Dame du Bec,
at Mass on 19 March 2007**[1]

Father Abbot, I owe you first of all a word of most sincere gratitude. I didn't imagine that you had the intention of giving such attention to the fact that I am celebrating this year twenty-five years as an oblate of the Abbey of Bec. Gratitude, yes, but receiving at the eleventh hour your invitation to give the homily today, I couldn't help thinking – may God forgive me! – 'quel cadeau empoisonné'![2] But you spoke of a short meditation *en famille* rather than a grand panegyric and, because you are my Abbot and because St Joseph was a man of exemplary obedience, I could not say 'no'.

The person of St Joseph and the readings for today's liturgy offer us the possibility of exploring several themes; I shall only take one of them this morning.

The life of St Joseph is completely an *Amen* of submission, obedience and trust in God. But it is a *Yes*, an *Amen*, that is lived rather than spoken. The Gospels of Matthew and Luke report in their accounts of the nativity and childhood of Christ the words of the angels, of Mary, of Simeon, of King Herod, of

---

[1] The homily was written in French and published in *Les Amis du Bec-Hellouin*, 157 (March 2007), pp. 35–7. It has been translated for this publication.
[2] Literally, 'What a poisoned gift'.

Zechariah, of Elizabeth and of Jesus himself, but not one single word issues from the mouth of Joseph.

The whole of his life is an *Amen*, a prompt and faithful carrying out of the will of God. His life is marked by reticence, by self-effacement, in a word, by discretion. This is the word on which I invite you to meditate: discretion.

I shall tell you a little story – short, but true.

When I was a canon of Chichester Cathedral we once received the Queen of England and her consort, Prince Philip, Duke of Edinburgh, very solemnly. The Chapter awaited them at the great west door, but the bishop, accompanied by his chaplain, received them as they alighted from their car to escort them to us. The chaplain, a young priest, told me afterwards that the Duke of Edinburgh had said to him during that short walk, 'I see that we have the same duty: to walk three paces behind the boss!'

Three steps behind: that was also St Joseph's duty; never in front, never in the foreground but discreetly in the background, behind Mary and Jesus, a man who always acted, as the Gospel says, 'quietly'.

The same reticence, the same discretion, marks the liturgical tradition of the Church: the feast of St Joseph had to wait until the end of the fifteenth century to be included in the Roman Calendar. In the reign of Henry VIII it had still not found a place in the Latin liturgical books, which explains why it had no place in the *Book of Common Prayer* of the Church of England. Not until the end of the twentieth century did St Joseph take his place in the official calendar of the Church of England, on 19 March.

This reticence is explained by the fact that the Church hesitated to give too much importance to St Joseph, for fear of giving the impression that he was the true father of Jesus. But this reticence on the part of the Church coincided well with the discretion of St Joseph himself, a man who chose to stay in the background, and who, it seems, didn't say much. But as a great Irish writer said, 'It is always those who have nothing to say who say it at the greatest length.' It was perhaps because he was a 'quiet' man that he could hear the voice of the angel.

Make no mistake: St Joseph's discretion was not a sign of weakness; he was a man who had to take firm decisions, like that of which we heard in today's Gospel – to take the pregnant Mary as his wife, like that which led him to take Mary and Jesus off to Egypt: decisions that were crucial for the history of our salvation. He had the authority and he knew how to exercise it; St Luke tells us that Jesus submitted to the authority of his parents in Nazareth.

All of this story of salvation urges us to ask ourselves about the place of discretion in *our* lives. It's a question which poses itself first and foremost to those among us who exercise a ministry of authority in the Church, but it poses itself to all of us. Are we ready to walk three paces behind our boss, the Christ? Do we seek after the attention of others? Do we desire always to be under the spotlight? Are we more ready to speak than to listen?

On this feast of St Joseph, let us *all* commit ourselves to listening humbly and attentively to God and to our brethren. And let us ask St Joseph, who watched over Jesus with an attentive and fatherly love, to intercede today for the Body of Jesus, the Church, and for the healing of its wounds and its divisions. Amen!

Roger was further honoured by being invited to preside in a cope from the Abbot's Chair at Solemn Vespers that evening.

PART 3

The Blessed Virgin Mary in the Anglican Tradition

10

An Anglican Witness

Note

In 2002 Roger Greenacre wrote an article for the *Walsingham Review*, in which he described how he presented the place of Mary in the life and worship of Anglicans to members of other churches.[1] This chapter conflates translations of two such presentations. The first was published in the French Protestant weekly newspaper *Réforme* in 1987, as one of a number of articles inspired by the papal encyclical *Redemptoris Mater* published two months earlier.[2] The second, which formed the basis for the *Walsingham Review* article, was given at a colloquy held in Lourdes in 2001.[3] Roger's reflections from the *Walsingham Review* article on the enterprise in which he was engaged have been inserted at the appropriate points in italics.

Witnessing to the Place of Mary in the Life and Worship of Anglicanism

It has been my privilege to speak on this subject at a number of international gatherings, some of them at noted Marian shrines such as Czestochowa (in 1996) and, most recently, Lourdes (in 2001). I have tried to avoid two opposing temptations: the first,

---

1 'Trying to be Honest: Witnessing to the Place of Mary in the Life and Worship of Anglicanism', *Walsingham Review*, 130 (Assumptiontide 2002), pp. 6–8.
2 'La Mére cachée aux regards', *Réforme*, 16 May 1987, p. 6.
3 'Un Anglican témoigne', *Marie, signe pour les croyants: Les actes du colloque marial de Lourdes: Lourdes Magazine*, 109 (March–April 2002), pp. 15–17.

to concentrate negatively on the forces which menace Anglicanism today with increasing incoherence and disintegration; the second, simply to describe my own Marian theology and piety as if they represented the sole and the total Anglican picture.

Introduction

It would have been easy for me to give you a strictly personal and individual account of my own Marian spirituality. At the end of such a lecture you would have been able to say, 'But in the end there is practically no difference between our two communions in the area of devotion to Mary. What a joy and what a relief!' But I think that today I have the duty to be rigorously honest and to try to give you a comprehensive view of the place of Mary within Anglicanism. That is not an easy task.

If the history of Anglicanism has been from its inception one of the co-existence and interpenetration (often conflictual, but often productive) of several theological and spiritual traditions, catholic, protestant and liberal – the celebrated Anglican pluralism or 'comprehensiveness' – this last quarter of a century has presented us with the spectacle of novel and intensified tensions at the heart of the Anglican Communion which menace it with increasing incoherence and disintegration. But among these dark and stormy clouds (of which one is the liberal stream which relativizes the truth of the Incarnation), there are at the same time, thank God, also signs of hope.

Historical Survey

I always try to begin with an historical survey, describing how much was destroyed at the Reformation but also what survived.

One of the pioneers of the Oxford Movement in the nineteenth century, John Keble, priest and poet, gave one of his poems the title 'Mother out of Sight'. One could take this same title as a summary of the place of the Virgin Mary in Anglicanism at least until the nineteenth century. In the *Ecclesia Anglicana*, before the ruptures of the sixteenth century, the Virgin occupied a pre-eminent and very visible position. All of that was swept away and demolished during the tempests of the Reformation. The luxuriant tree of Marian devotion was pruned back to its roots, which continued to survive, in the Anglican liturgy. Mary wasn't completely out of sight; many stained-glass windows were kept, and even some statues escaped the general destruction.

Though the pruning of the sixteenth century was drastic and pitiless, it still permitted the emergence in the seventeenth century of a few promising green shoots of reflection and devotion, which were in turn to inspire the Fathers of the Oxford Movement. (In this context I like to quote from one of the most eloquent of the great seventeenth-century preachers, Mark Frank of Pembroke College, Cambridge.)

Thus, the Church of England underwent a radical spoliation of Marian devotion in the sixteenth century. But the elimination of popular devotions and the purification of texts and liturgical celebrations left some vestiges intact: the tree that had been pruned so severely wasn't dead, and the seventeenth century saw the appearance of some green shoots of reflection and Marian devotion among Anglican theologians, preachers and poets.

The Blessed Virgin was honoured by theologians and poets, often – in both cases – in a quite exuberant baroque style. It should be noted, however, that almost all of them – the most notable exception being William Forbes, Bishop of Edinburgh, in 1634 – denied that one could legitimately ask the Virgin and the saints directly for the assistance of their intercession. With the Revolution of 1688 and the schism of the Nonjurors (those who refused to take the oath of allegiance to William of Orange) this stream of devotion almost disappeared; the Church of England came to be dominated by a more purely protestant atmosphere and a cold, rationalist theology.[4] It was not until the twentieth century that the nonjuring Bishop Thomas Ken's hymn 'Her Virgin eyes saw God incarnate born', of which the last verse evokes the Assumption, was restored to honour and sung in churches.

The Oxford Movement, the catholic and catholicizing renewal which began in 1833, appealed explicitly to the same tradition. Initially their Mariology was marked by prudence and reserve – and by a quite robust opposition to the excesses (or what were considered to be such) of contemporary Roman Catholic Mariology. Among the leaders of the movement, John Keble was the only one who had been raised from childhood in the old high-church tradition. Perhaps for that reason, he was more open than his fellow leaders to Marian devotion, and it is in his poem 'Mother out of sight' that we perceive at once the depth and the discretion of that devotion.

John Keble's poem of 1846, 'Mother Out of Sight', perhaps more than any other text helped to break through the taboos of traditional Anglicanism:

> Therefore as kneeling day by day
> We to our Father duteous pray,
> So unforbidden may we speak
> An *Ave* to Christ's Mother meek:
> (As children with 'good morrow' come
> To elders in some happy home:)
> Inviting so the saintly host above
> With our unworthiness to pray in love.

One could almost say that with this text – which was written in 1844 but remained unpublished for a long time because Keble's friends judged that its publication would be imprudent – a door that had been shut in Anglicanism since the sixteenth

---

[4] This paragraph was written in 1987. Since then, scholarship has underlined the persistence of high churchmanship within the Hanoverian Established Church, despite the prominence of Latitudinarians in the later eighteenth century.

century was opened afresh. Eventually, the Oxford Movement went much further than the seventeenth-century writers. By the end of the nineteenth century, disciples of the Oxford Movement called 'ritualists' or 'Anglo-Catholics' adopted a style of devotion to the Blessed Virgin which it would be difficult to distinguish from the 'Roman' style. Today, Newman's Anglican disciples no longer share the degree of reticence with regard to invocation of the Blessed Virgin that he had before he was received into the Roman Catholic Church.

It is hardly necessary to add that the Marian theology and devotion of Anglo-Catholics is far from having gained the support of all Anglicans. In evangelical and liberal circles there is still a good deal of opposition to this Mariology, often for quite contradictory reasons. It should also be admitted that Anglo-Catholics themselves have often lacked both sensitivity and discernment.

Anglican–Roman Catholic Dialogue

After this historical introduction I then move on to look at Marian references in official texts of the dialogue between the Anglican Communion and the Roman Catholic Church. At the moment there are only two of any substance, though we are informed that ARCIC II is currently addressing the subject of Mariology.[5]

Today, the official dialogue between the Anglican Communion and the Roman Catholic Church has given us short Marian references in two of its texts. I feel that I must quote these, because they are official texts (and not merely my personal opinion). The first reference may be found in the second agreed statement on Authority in the Church, which appeared in the *Final Report* of the first Anglican–Roman Catholic International Commission (ARCIC I) and was signed by the members of that commission at Windsor in 1981:

---

5 *Mary: Grace and Hope in Christ* was duly published in 2005.

Anglicans and Roman Catholics can agree in much of the truth that these two dogmas are designed to affirm. We agree that there can be but one mediator between God and man, Jesus Christ, and reject any interpretation of the role of Mary which obscures this affirmation. We agree in recognizing that Christian understanding of Mary is inseparably linked with the doctrines of Christ and of the Church. We agree in recognizing the grace and unique vocation of Mary, Mother of God Incarnate (*Theotokos*), in observing her festivals, and in according her honour in the communion of saints. We agree that she was prepared by divine grace to be the mother of our Redeemer, by whom she herself was redeemed and received into glory. We further agree in recognizing in Mary a model of holiness, obedience and faith for all Christians. We accept that it is possible to regard her as a prophetic figure of the Church of God before as well as after the Incarnation.[6] Nevertheless the dogmas of the Immaculate Conception and the Assumption raise a special problem for those Anglicans who do not consider that the precise definitions given by these dogmas are sufficiently supported by Scripture. For many Anglicans the teaching authority of the bishop of Rome, independent of a council, is not recommended by the fact that through it these Marian doctrines were proclaimed as dogmas binding on all the faithful. Anglicans would also ask whether, in any future union between our two Churches, they would be required to subscribe to such dogmatic statements. One consequence of our separation has been a tendency for Anglicans and Roman Catholics alike to exaggerate the importance of the Marian dogmas

---

6 Footnote to the ARCIC statement: 'The affirmation of the Roman Catholic Church that Mary was conceived without original sin is based on recognition of her unique role within the mystery of the Incarnation. By being thus prepared to be the mother of our Redeemer, she also becomes a sign that the salvation won by Christ was operative among all mankind before his birth. The affirmation that her glory in heaven involves full participation in the fruits of salvation expresses and reinforces our faith that the life of the world to come has already broken into the life of our world. It is the conviction of Roman Catholics that the Marian dogmas formulate a faith consonant with Scripture.'

in themselves at the expense of other truths more closely related to the foundation of the Christian faith.[7]

In this text, the Commission gives attention to a major difficulty. But what strikes the reader above all is the very positive formulation of what Anglicans and Roman Catholics can affirm together about the role of the Virgin Mary in the salvation of mankind and in the life of the Church.

In his encyclical letter *Ut unum sint* of May 1995 Pope John Paul II proposed five themes that should be studied 'before a true consensus of faith can be achieved', of which the fifth was the Virgin Mary. The Pope explained more precisely the study that was needed. It was a case of reflecting on 'the Virgin Mary, as Mother of God and Icon of the Church, the spiritual Mother who intercedes for Christ's disciples and all humanity' (para. 79).

Ut unum sint has received a positive and even warm response on the part of Anglicans. I would now like to quote in full paragraph 32 of the official response of the bishops of the Church of England:

> There is one mediator between God and man, Jesus Christ. Mary's place in Christian faith and devotion is determined by God's choice of her to be the Mother of our Lord and Saviour Jesus Christ. Therefore, in continuity with the faith of the ancient Church, and with the support of the Third Ecumenical Council [the Council of Ephesus, 431], Anglicans acclaim Mary as Theotokos, and honour her place in the economy of salvation with special celebrations in the liturgical year. She was prepared by divine grace for her role as mother of our Redeemer, by whom she was herself redeemed and received in glory in the communion of saints. Her song Magnificat is part of the daily common prayer of the Church of England. In devotion she is the model for all faithful and obedient disciples and thus for the Church her-

---

[7] Anglican–Roman Catholic International Commission, *The Final Report* (London: CTS/SPCK, 1982), pp. 95–6: Authority in the Church (II), para. 30.

self. As in many parts of the Roman Catholic Church, for some Anglicans pilgrimages and other devotions are more important than for others. This variety is a strength within the Anglican tradition.[8]

The *Final Report* of ARCIC I had said that 'special difficulties are created by the recent Marian dogmas, because Anglicans doubt the appropriateness, or even the possibility, of defining them as essential to the faith of believers.'[9] In para. 33 of their response to *Ut unum sint*, the bishops take this point and comment,

> We recognize that the honour of Mary and the saints attests in a special way the unique mediation of Jesus Christ and the power of the gospel. We welcome the Pope's injunction 'not to impose any burden beyond that which is strictly necessary', and believe that his authority could be enhanced if this principle were seen to be application to this question [of the Marian dogmas].[10]

Positive factors which contribute to development

In conclusion, I would like to list some elements that have contributed to a real development in the Marian theology and piety among Anglicans:

- ❖ The Oxford Movement was able to restore to Anglicanism as a whole a theology centred on the mystery of the Incarnation, with the greatest importance attached to the Church, the sacraments and the communion of saints.
- ❖ The reform of the texts of the liturgy has given greater prominence to the Blessed Virgin Mary in almost all the

---

8 *May They All Be One: A Response of the House of Bishops of the Church of England to Ut Unum Sint* (GS Misc 495) (London: Church House Publishing, 1997), p. 12, para. 32.
9 ARCIC, *The Final Report*, p. 65: Authority in the Church (I), para. 24(c).
10 *May They All Be One*, para. 33.

churches of the Anglican Communion. A striking example is the restoration in the majority of those churches, including the Church of England, of 15 August as the principal feast of our Lady, even if it is not called 'the Assumption'.

- Before the reforms of the Second Vatican Council, Roman Catholic Mariology seriously disquieted other Christians and did not tend to foster a positive attitude on their part. Today, thanks to the Council, it is evident that catholic Mariology is firmly tied to the doctrines about Christ and about the Church and that one does not hesitate to affirm very clearly the subordination of Mary to her Son who is also her Saviour. Thus the first Anglican reactions to Pope John Paul II's encyclical letter *Redemptoris Mater* recognized with joy and with a certain relief that the Pope's thought is totally in line with that of the Council. That is not to say that all the problems have disappeared, but at least that the questions are not becoming more difficult to resolve.
- In 1967, thanks to the vision and the enthusiasm of a Roman Catholic layman, Martin Gillett, several friends belonging to different churches founded the Ecumenical Society of the Blessed Virgin Mary. They were conscious of the urgent need to transform that which was perceived as a major cause of division between Christians into a reason for thanksgiving and a source of prayer. They wanted to reflect together on Marian theology and to promote an ecumenical Marian piety. Today the honorary presidents are the Archbishop of Canterbury, Dr Runcie, and the Archbishop of Westminster, Cardinal Hume, and one of the three presidents is the Methodist theologian Gordon Wakefield. The Society is active at the local, national and international levels and the participation in it of Methodist, Lutheran and Reformed theologians is of great importance.
- An increased interest in, and appreciation of, sacred art, accompanied by the virtual disappearance of the former hostility to images, has done much to further the *visual* presence of Our Lady in our cathedrals and churches

today. I cannot think of any of our cathedrals which does not now contain a fairly prominent statue or icon of Our Lady, usually in what is called the 'Lady Chapel'.

❖ The Blessed Virgin has come back into our churches not only through the visual arts but also through music. There are now many fine congregational hymns and carols in honour of Our Lady: there has been also a rediscovery of the rich heritage of Marian music to be found in both the English and the wider European repertory, especially in plainchant and in Renaissance polyphony. In many of our cathedrals it is easier to introduce the *Hail Mary* as an anthem, sung in Latin and set to music by one of our great composers, than as a said prayer! There is today music of real quality by recent and contemporary composers, such as Benjamin Britten and John Tavener, inspired by Marian texts – Latin, Byzantine and English.

❖ An extraordinary phenomenon of the twentieth century was the restoration of the Shrine of Our Lady of Walsingham between the two World Wars. At the time it shocked most Anglicans who did not belong to the extreme Anglo-Catholic tendency. The popularity of Walsingham today as a centre of pilgrimage, healing and spiritual renewal that attracts Roman Catholics, Orthodox and Anglicans (and even some Methodists) has meant that people now come from Anglican parishes from all over England and Wales, not all of them marked by 'advanced' churchmanship.

❖ More recently, in Scotland, the Shrine of Our Lady of Haddington was restored in 1978 and began to attract pilgrims too. The ecumenical accent, which is very important at Walsingham, is even more striking at Haddington. Each year a large ecumenical pilgrimage (Catholic, Anglican and Reformed) takes place. It concludes with the joint recitation of what is called the 'protestant version' of the Angelus, composed by the Minister of Haddington.

❖ Finally, we cannot ignore the contribution – certainly ambiguous but important none the less – of the feminist movement. Though there is one current in it which is radically hostile to traditional Mariology and to Christian orthodoxy, there is also another which has stimulated many to examine with sympathy and attention what is for them a strange and novel theme – the role of Mary in Christian theology and spirituality.

11

I Sing of a Maiden: Devotion to the Blessed Virgin Mary in the Middle Ages[1]

It was a real homecoming, that summer evening in 1988. On that day, 6 June, after Evensong had been sung, a procession was formed to the Lady Chapel of Chichester Cathedral and the Bishop of Chichester, flanked by the Roman Catholic Bishop of Arundel and Brighton and the United Reformed Minister of Littlehampton, blessed the statue of Our Lady and Child, sculpted by John Skelton and presented to the Cathedral by the Ecumenical Society of the Blessed Virgin Mary to mark their seventh International Congress held here in 1986. The homecoming had indeed been prepared for just over a century earlier, when the Chapel, which had not been used for worship since the reign of Elizabeth I and had for some time been the Cathedral Library, was restored in memory of Bishop A. T. Gilbert (who died in 1870) and was subsequently adorned with a set of stained glass windows by Clayton and Bell depicting scenes from the life of the Blessed Virgin.

Too many people imagine that devotion to the Blessed Virgin – 'Our Lady Saint Mary' as our mediaeval ancestors loved to call her – was an invention of the Western Church in the Middle Ages and that it was totally eliminated as a 'Romish error' during the Reformation. In fact devotion to Mary and theological

---

[1] Southern Cathedrals Festival 1992 programme brochure, pp. 63–5; reprinted in the Newsletter of the Ecumenical Society of the Blessed Virgin Mary, 51 (October 1992).

reflection on her role in the history of salvation are rooted in the quantitatively meagre but theologically rich and suggestive scriptural material and in the writing of early theologians such as the second-century Bishop of Lyon,[2] St Irenaeus. They were enormously stimulated by the definition of Mary as *Theotokos* (Mother of God or, more literally, God-bearer) at the Third Ecumenical Council of Ephesus in 431. It is not too much of an exaggeration to say that this title was almost forced upon the Church by the controversy surrounding the mystery of the Incarnation of the Word of God. It was more the necessity of guarding and underlining the unity of the divine and the human in the one Person of Jesus Christ than the desire to honour his Mother which led both to the calling of the Council and to conciliar approval of the title *Theotokos*. Nevertheless, the Council of Ephesus encouraged a notable development in Mariology and this was at first far more marked in the East than in the West. The strong Marian emphases of the Byzantine liturgy and the iconographical and devotional tradition of Eastern Orthodoxy are reminders, if we need them, that there is nothing exclusively Latin about Marian devotion. The earliest known invocation addressed directly to Mary was written in Greek some time probably in the fourth century (or even earlier) and has inspired a formula found in the Latin, Greek, Coptic and Ethiopian traditions. As for the *Hail Mary*, the most popular of all Marian prayers, the text of this (combining Luke 1.28 and Luke 1.42) has been found inscribed on a Coptic potsherd dated about 600. A great leap forward in Mariology (to use a word which covers both theology and devotion) was made in Western Europe in the twelfth century, and most of the texts which feature in this programme of music come from this period or from the later Middle Ages. However, the hymn *Ave maris stella* (Hail, O Star that pointest ...)[3] is much older, from the ninth or, more probably, the eighth century: it has one of the most beautiful plainsong melodies of any of the old Breviary office hymns:

---

2 Roger invariably used the French spelling, rather than the English 'Lyons'.

3 The Latin literally means 'Hail, star of the sea'. 'Hail, O Star that pointest' is the English translation by Althelstan Riley (*New English Hymnal*, hymn 180).

MAIDEN, MOTHER AND QUEEN

Ave, maris stella,	Hail, star of the sea,
Dei Mater alma,	Nurturing Mother of God,
Atque semper Virgo,	And ever Virgin
Felix caeli porta.	Happy gate of Heaven.
Sumens illud Ave	Receiving that 'Ave'
Gabrielis ore,	From the mouth of Gabriel,
Funda nos in pace,	Establish us in peace,
Mutans Hevae nomen.	Transforming the name of 'Eva' (Eve).*
Solve vincla reis,	Loosen the chains of the guilty,
Profer lumen caecis,	Send forth light to the blind
Mala nostra pelle,	Our evil do thou dispel,
Bona cuncta posce.	Entreat (for us) all good things.
Monstra te esse matrem,	Show thyself to be a Mother:
Sumat per te precem,	Through thee may he receive prayer
Qui pro nobis natus	Who, being born for us,
Tulit esse tuus.	Undertook to be thine own.
Virgo singularis,	O unique Virgin,
Inter omnes mitis	Meek above all others
Nos, culpis solutos,	Make us, set free from (our) sins,
Mites fac et castos.	Meek and chaste.
Vitam praesta puram,	Bestow a pure life,
Iter para tutum,	Prepare a safe way:
Ut, videntes Jesum,	That seeing Jesus,
Semper collaetemur.	We may ever rejoice.
Sit laus Deo Patri,	Praise be to God the Father,
Summo Christo decus,	To the Most High Christ (be) glory,
Spiritui Sancto	To the Holy Spirit
Honor, tribus unus.	(Be) honour, to the Three equally.
Amen.	Amen.

* 'Ave' is 'Eva' spelt backwards.

To understand what happened in the twelfth century it is important to realize that the change was not primarily Mariological at all; it was a more general revolution affecting the whole temper of Christian devotion. A good introduction to it can be found in G. L. Prestige's 1940 Bampton Lectures *Fathers and Heretics*, in the chapter that is described as an epilogue: 'Eros: or, Devotion to the Sacred Humanity'.[4] He explains how in the pre-mediaeval period the Sacred Humanity of Our Lord was worshipped without being made the object of any specialized devotion: 'The devotion of the ancient Church was neither mainly subjective nor mainly individualistic. Its standard pattern of prayer was the liturgy, and the prayers of the liturgy are addressed not to God the Son, but through Christ to the Father.' Hymns and prayers addressed to Christ came into the liturgy from the fourth century onwards under Syrian influence, but they are biblical and liturgical in tone and concentrate more on Christ the Victor than on the Suffering Christ. The precursor of the new movement was St Anselm, successively Abbot of Bec and Archbishop of Canterbury, who died in 1109 and who, according to Sir Richard Southern, 'created a new kind of poetry – the poetry of intimate, personal devotion'. The two greatest figures in its development were St Bernard of Clairvaux (who died in 1153) and St Francis of Assisi (who died in 1226). The new spirituality was intensely personal, passionate and subjective and it fastened in a new way on the humanity of Jesus – both in the crib and on the cross. Its central focus was the human suffering of Jesus on the cross (and it is instructive in this context to study the history of the portrayal of the crucifixion in the visual arts); it found expression in devotion to the Name of Jesus, to his Heart and to his Five Wounds. The warmth and tenderness of this devotion is evident, for example, in the fourteenth-century Revelations of the Lady Julian of Norwich ('I saw the red blood trickling down from under the Garland hot and freshly and right plenteously').

---

4 G. L. Prestige, *Fathers and Heretics: Six Studies in Dogmatic Faith with Prologue and Epilogue, being the Bampton Lectures for 1940* (London: SPCK, 1940), pp. 373–426.

It is in this context that we must situate the similar development of a warm, tender and subjective devotion to Mary, no longer so much the majestic *Theotokos* as the very human Virgin Mother, to whom the monk came to render the same romantic allegiance that the knight or the troubadour of mediaeval chivalry gave to the lady of his devotion. Here again the precursor is St Anselm, who has left three remarkable prose-poems addressed to Our Lady. Here again too the study of the development of the image of Mary in Christian art is instructive. The justly celebrated Chichester Roundel on the south wall of the Bishop's Chapel, which was probably executed during the episcopate of St Richard, is a perfect example of this new tenderness.[5]

The growth of devotion to Our Lady had its consequences in the architecture of our churches and especially of our cathedrals. In Chichester, for example, the short apsidal Lady Chapel of the romanesque cathedral was first of all rebuilt as a two-bay chapel under Bishop Seffrid II (who died in 1204) and then had three further bays added to it under Bishop Gilbert of St Leofard (who died in 1305). It had other consequences too: the growth of pilgrimage to Marian shrines (such as Chartres in France and Walsingham in England); the growing popularity of the rosary; the addition to the daily round of the liturgy of cathedrals, collegiate churches and monasteries of a daily High Mass of Our Lady (in her chapel), supplementary offices and the singing of the Marian antiphons at the end of each of the choir offices. In Chichester Cathedral (and this was no exception) there was an additional Altar to Our Lady under the Arundel Screen to the south side of the entrance to the Choir and Bishop Arundel (who died in 1477) left detailed instructions for the daily singing of the anthem to Our Lady before her image there. Three of these final anthems (still sung in the Roman rite after Compline) feature in the concert programme: *Alma redemptoris Mater* (for use during Advent and the Christmas season), *Regina caeli laetare* (for use during the

---

[5] A digitally restored photograph of the Roundel by Dr Richard Foster appears on the cover of this book.

Great Fifty Days of Easter) and the *Salve Regina* (for use from after Pentecost until Advent).[6]

There was much in this mediaeval *cultus* of lasting beauty and value, but an overcharged theology and an overworked and unbalanced liturgical programme, where the original pattern came, as Louis Bouyer put it, 'to be immersed in a formless ocean of inorganic prayer', led inevitably to the vigorous protest of the Reformation. In one sense that protest was necessary, for what was at risk was the centrality of Christ and his unique role as Mediator and Redeemer. At the same time the protest led to a different kind of imbalance and to the ruthless destruction of much that was good and true and beautiful. For a while it seemed as if the Christian world would be for ever divided between those who gave exaggerated honour to Mary and those who ignored her. It needed the self-critical spirit of reform and renewal of Pope John XXIII ('The Madonna is not pleased when she is put above her Son') and of the Second Vatican Council ('The Church does not hesitate to profess this subordinate role of Mary')[7] to make possible a new ecumenical exploration and convergence. Anglican attitudes too had been (and still, to a certain extent, remain) reticent or even hostile, but at least a certain memory of the older tradition was kept alive by such things as the retention of some Marian feasts in the Prayer Book Calendar and the use of the Magnificat at Evensong, and that 'memory' sometimes surfaced – as in the *Preces Privatae* of Lancelot Andrewes, who died in 1626 and was Bishop successively of Chichester, Ely and Winchester. In one passage of these classic devotions we come across a phrase that is inspired by – or, rather, borrowed from – the Liturgy of St John Chrysostom as used even today in the Eastern Orthodox Churches:

---

6 All four Final Anthems are printed on pp. 112–14.

7 Dogmatic Constitution on the Church (*Lumen Gentium*), para. 62: W. M. Abbott (ed.), *The Documents of Vatican II* (London: Geoffrey Chapman, 1967), p. 92.

Commemorating the allholy, immaculate, more than blessed mother of God and evervirgin Mary, with all saints, let us commend ourselves and one another and all our life unto Christ God: unto Thee, o Lord, for unto Thee is due glory, honour and worship.[8]

Final Anthems of the Blessed Virgin Mary

From Advent to Candlemas

Alma Redemptoris Mater, quae pervia caeli
Porta manes, et stella maris, succurre cadenti,
Surgere qui curat, populo: tu quae genuisti,
Natura mirante, tuum sanctum Genitorem,
Virgo prius ac posterius, Gabrielis ab ore
Sumens illud Ave, peccatorum miserere.

Mother of Christ, hear thou thy people's cry,
Star of the deep, and Portal of the sky,
Mother of Him who thee from nothing made,
Sinking we strive, and call to thee for aid.
O, by that joy which Gabriel brought to thee
Thou Virgin first and last, let us thy mercy see.

Literal translation:

Loving Mother of the Redeemer, gate of heaven, star of the sea, assist your people who have fallen yet strive to rise again. To the wonderment of nature you bore your holy Creator, yet remained a virgin after as before. You who received Gabriel's joyful greeting, have pity on us poor sinners.

---

8 L. Andrewes, *The Preces Privatae of Lancelot Andrewes, Bishop of Winchester*, tr. F. E. Brightman (London: Methuen & Co. Ltd, 1903), p. 85.

From Candlemas to Wednesday in Holy Week

Ave, Regina Caelorum,	Hail, O Queen of Heaven enthroned;
Ave, Domina Angelorum:	Hail, by angels Mistress owned:
Salve, radix, salve, porta	Root of Jesse, Gate of Morn
Ex qua mundo lux est orta:	Whence the world's true Light was born!
Gaude, Virgo gloriosa,	Glorious Virgin, joy to thee,
Super omnes speciosa,	Loveliest whom in heaven they see;
Vale, o valde decora,	Fairest thou, where all are fair!
Et pro nobis Christum exora.	Plead with Christ our sins to spare.

During Eastertide

Regina caeli, laetare, alleluia:	Joy to thee, O Queen of Heaven, alleluia;
Quia quem meruisti portare, alleluia,	He whom Thou wast meet to bear, alleluia,
Resurrexit, sicut dixit, alleluia,	As He promised hath arisen, alleluia:
Ora pro nobis Deum, alleluia.	Pour for us to God thy prayer, alleluia!

From Trinity Sunday to Advent

Salve, Regina, Mater misericordiae;	Hail, holy Queen, Mother of Mercy;
vita, dulcedo et spes nostra, salve.	Hail, our life, our sweetness and our hope.
Ad te clamamus exsules filii Hevae.	To thee do we cry, poor banished children of Eve;
Ad te suspiramus, gementes et flentes	To thee do we send up our sighs, mourning and weeping
in hac lacrimarum valle.	in this vale of tears.
Eia, ergo, advocata nostra,	Turn then, most gracious advocate,
illos tuos misericordes oculos ad nos converte.	thine eyes of mercy towards us;
Et Iesum, benedictum fructum ventris tui,	and after this our exile
nobis post hoc exsilium ostende.	show unto us the blessed fruit of thy womb, Jesus.
O clemens, O pia, O dulcis Virgo Maria.	O clement, O loving, O sweet Virgin Mary.

12

Mother Out of Sight: Anglican Devotion to Mary[1]

John Keble

The symbolic date for the beginning of the Oxford Movement, the great movement of Catholic Revival in the Church of England, is generally accepted to be 14 July 1833, on which day John Keble preached his celebrated sermon on National Apostasy in the University Church of St Mary the Virgin. Of the acknowledged leaders of the Oxford Movement John Keble was certainly the most conservative, the most prudent and the most reserved, strongly convinced that he was in no sense an innovator but simply working for the reawakening and continuation of the old high-church tradition which he had learned as a child from his parents, the Anglicanism of the *Book of Common Prayer*, of the Caroline Divines and of the Nonjurors. Even he, however, was deeply upset when friends, even more cautious than himself, urged him to omit from *Lyra Innocentium*, a collection of his verse which he issued in 1846 (just after Newman's reception into the Church of Rome), a poem entitled 'Mother out of Sight' which contained these lines addressed to the Blessed Virgin Mary, 'for whom', his biographer Georgina Battiscombe tells us, he 'had always cherished a special personal devotion':[2]

---

[1] This paper was delivered to the East Sussex, West Sussex and Canterbury branches of the Ecumenical Society of the Blessed Virgin Mary during 1989. It was published by the Society as a pamphlet in 1990. The footnotes are by the author.

[2] G. Battiscombe, *John Keble: A Study in Limitations* (London: Constable, 1963), p. 284.

Therefore as kneeling day by day
We to our Father duteous pray,
So unforbidden may we speak
An Ave to Christ's Mother meek:
(As children with 'good morrow' come
To elders in some happy home:)
Inviting so the saintly host above
With our unworthiness to pray in love.[3]

Very moderate sentiments these, we would say now over 100 years later, and very carefully expressed, but enough to shock those whom his friend John Coleridge had described as 'persons of timorous, scrupulous, even captious natures, easily offended'.[4] The early Tractarians had become very cautious, partly because they genuinely believed in the principle of 'Reserve in Communicating Religious Knowledge' (the title of Tract 80 by Isaac Williams) and partly because they had absorbed the lesson of their imprudence in publishing Hurrell Froude's *Remains*, which contained such indiscretions as 'Really I hate the Reformation and the Reformers more and more' and provoked a storm of controversy.

I have been asked to speak specifically on Anglican Devotion to Mary and I have begun with Keble – though this could be confusing in any kind of strictly chronological historical account – because I think the title of his poem 'Mother out of Sight' is a fairly accurate description of that devotion up to and including John Keble.

Vestiges of Marian Devotion

We are in fact faced with a paradox. We are often reminded of the fact that vestiges and reminders of Marian devotion were at no time absent from the Church of England. Cathedrals,

---

[3] The full text can be found most accessibly in J. Keble, *The Christian Year and Other Poems* (London: Church Literature Association, 1976), pp. 216–18.
[4] cf. Battiscombe, *John Keble*, p. 285.

colleges and churches retained their dedication to St Mary the Virgin. A few statues – nearly all on the outside rather than the inside of these buildings – were retained, for example at Eton, at Winchester and at New College, Oxford; and one celebrated *Virgo Coronata* was even put up under the influence of Archbishop Laud in the new baroque porch at Oxford's University Church and was to figure in the charges against him at his trial. In many more churches stained-glass windows were suffered to remain and so allowed some kind of Marian icon to impress itself consciously or unconsciously upon the worshippers – and here we can only speculate as to the extent of the influence of the magnificent mediaeval glass in Fairford Church on the young John Keble.[5] And in the *Book of Common Prayer* the Magnificat forms the climax of Evening Prayer (even though since 1552 it can be replaced by the *Cantate Domino*), while the Calendar contains two red-letter days with propers (Purification and Annunciation) and three black-letter days (Visitation, Nativity and Conception), and the table of Lessons Proper for Holy Days even refers to the Annunciation of 'Our Lady'. The liturgy for Christmas Day moreover refers in its Collect to 'a pure Virgin' and in its Proper Preface to Christ being 'made very man of the substance of the Virgin Mary his mother, and that without spot of sin, to make us clean from all sin'.

Losses

But against this we have to set the losses. First of all, we must note the orgies of iconoclasm, anticipated by the destruction under Henry VIII of those shrines and images which had become an object of a particular *cultus* (as at Walsingham); these swept the country under Edward VI and again under

---

[5] Keble's childhood was spent in Fairford, and Georgina Battiscombe writes: 'Little John was greatly impressed by the famous series of mediaeval stained-glass windows in Fairford Church; in later years he spoke of the way in which their imagery had stamped the biblical scenes and characters upon his mind, and he planned a similar series of windows in his church at Hursley ...': Battiscombe, *John Keble*, p. 1.

Elizabeth I and once again during the seventeenth-century Civil War. Then, we must also remember the suppression of pilgrimages and the banning of rosaries; the removal of the *Hail Mary* from authorized primers and books of private devotion, and then the progressive elimination of Marian references from the Anglican liturgy. Let us remind ourselves that the first edition of the English Litany in 1544 contained the following phrases:

> Holy Virgin Mary, mother of God our saviour Jesu Christ, pray for us.
> All holy angels and archangels and all holy orders of blessed spirits pray for us.
> All holy Patriarchs, and Prophets, Apostles, and Martyrs, Confessors and virgins and all the blessed company of heaven, pray for us.

These three clauses disappeared in the 1549 Prayer Book. That same book also in its Calendar, which marked only red-letter dates, had suppressed all Marian feasts – including the greatest of them all, the Assumption, on 15 August – leaving only the Purification and the Annunciation which, as we now realize clearly, are really feasts of Our Lord. However, its Prayer for the whole state of Christ's Church did conclude with these words:

> And here we do geve unto thee moste high praise and heartie thankes, for the wonderfull grace and vertue, declared in all thy sainctes, from the begynning of the worlde: And chiefly in the glorious and moste blessed Virgin Mary, mother of thy sonne Jesu Christe our Lorde and God, and in the holy Patriarches, Prophetes, Apostles and Martyrs, whose examples (O Lorde) and stedfastnes in thy fayth, and kepyng thy holy commaundementes, graunt us to folowe. We commend unto thy mercye (O Lorde) all other thy servauntes, which are departed hence from us, with the signe of faith, and nowe do reste in the slepe of peace: Graunt unto them, we beseche thee, thy mercy and everlasting peace, and that, at the day

of the generall resureccion, we and all they which bee of the misticall body of thy sonne, may altogether be set on his right hand, and heare that his most ioyfull voyce: Come unto me, O ye that be blessed of my father, and possesse the kingdom, whiche is prepared for you from the begynning of the worlde.

This whole section, both the thanksgiving for Our Lady and the saints (though without mention of their prayers) and the petition for the faithful departed, was ruthlessly suppressed in the second Prayer Book of 1552, so that the prayer became exclusively one for the whole state of Christ's Church militant here on earth. And so it remained until 1662, when a new and much weaker section was added, which does not mention Mary by name but simply thanks God for all his servants departed this life in his faith and fear.

Reformation Theology

My subject is Anglican *Devotion* to Mary, but it is extremely perilous when devotion and theology are allowed to drift apart, and it seems to me that I must set these rather radical changes in devotional and liturgical practice in their context of Reformation theology. The Reformation was in its most positive sense a re-affirmation of evangelical priorities, and of evangelical priorities which stood in desperate need of clear and forceful re-affirmation: the centrality of Christ and of his work of redemption; the normative authority of the Scriptures; salvation by grace and justification by faith. But the Protestant Reformation was of course also – and less positively – a protest against everything that seemed to endanger or obscure these priorities. The protests often went too far and, instead of merely rejecting undoubted abuses in Catholic theology and devotion, rejected their very basis. With regard to the Western Catholic *cultus* of Our Lady and the saints, three ideas that were widely current did undoubtedly need to be energetically repudiated:

1. The idea that the saints had direct power to bestow favours and grant benefits.
2. The idea that Mary was more merciful and easygoing than her Son.
3. The idea that heaven was like the court of an earthly king; that the monarch himself was remote and inaccessible and that it was indispensable to have a 'friend at court', the ear of a courtier or – better still – of the Queen Mother.

We can therefore understand how in rejecting these false, unscriptural and dangerous ideas the Reformers insisted that Christ is our 'only Mediator and Advocate'. They were right, but, as in other spheres of Christian Doctrine, that little word *only* was taken too negatively. It is not my duty here to describe the Mariology of Luther, Zwingli and Calvin (though work done under the aegis of the Ecumenical Society of the Blessed Virgin Mary has brought many interesting – even surprising – and positive things to light). Luther was a conservative: he had a real love of Our Lady and was not ready to suppress all her feasts from the liturgy. Zwingli and Calvin were radicals and gave no place to saints' days of any kind. All three, however, were determined to eliminate the invocation of saints; Calvin even doubted whether the saints really intercede for us: 'They do not abandon their own repose so as to be drawn into earthly cares: and much less must we on this account be always calling upon them.'[6] In saying this, Calvin was in conflict with the clear teaching of the Lutheran *Saxon Confession* of 1551, which declares: 'There is no doubt that the blessed pray for the Church.'[7]

In England we can identify two currents. The first is one which we could perhaps call 'Henrician', the line taken officially in the reign of Henry VIII after his break with Rome. It was largely inspired by the work of Erasmus and the more

---

6 *The Institutes of the Christian Religion*, Book 3, Ch. XX. See Michael Perham, *The Communion of Saints* (London: Alcuin Club/SPCK, 1980), p. 47.
7 Quoted in D. Stone, *The Invocation of Saints* (London: Longman, 1903), p. 6.

moderate Catholic reformers, and it aimed both to suppress 'abuses' and 'superstition' and also to restore a more Christocentric attitude to devotion to the saints. A good example of this current is to be found in the Ten Articles of 1536, issued by the authority of King and Convocation:

> As touching the honouring of Saints, we will that all bishops and preachers shall instruct and teach our people ... that Saints now being in Christ in heaven be to be honoured of people in earth, but not with that confidence and honour which are only due to God, trusting to attain at their hands that which must be had only of God ... As touching praying to Saints, we will that all bishops and preachers shall instruct and teach our people ... that albeit grace, remission of sin, and salvation cannot be obtained but of God only by the mediation of our Saviour Christ ... yet it is very laudable to pray to Saints in heaven everlastingly living, whose charity is ever permanent, to be intercessors, and to pray for us and with us ... and in this manner we may pray to our blessed Lady, to St John Baptist, to all and every of the apostles or any other Saint particularly as our devotion doth serve us, so that it be done without any vain superstition, as to think that any Saint is more merciful, or will hear us sooner than Christ, or that any Saint doth serve for one thing more than other ...[8]

This is a careful and moderate statement, which ought to be acceptable to Roman Catholics and Anglicans alike today – and even to many in the Churches of the Reformation; I would draw your attention particularly to one phrase: 'whose charity is for ever permanent', for that is the real theological basis for believing in the continuing intercession of saints in heaven for their brothers and sisters on earth: a bond of mutual love finding expression in prayer.

There was some ambiguity in the sixteenth century about the precise meaning of the word 'invocation' in the phrase 'invo-

---

8 Cf. Stone, *The Invocation of Saints*, pp. 30–1.

cation of saints'. One document of Henry VIII's reign, *The Institution of a Christian Man* ('The Bishops' Book') contains the puzzling phrase: 'Nevertheless, to pray to Saints to be intercessors with us and for us to Our Lord ... so that we make no invocation of them, is lawful and allowed ...'[9] The word invocation in this sentence denotes requests to the saints to bestow directly of their own gift and power what can only be given by God; it is interesting to note that a revised text, published three years later and commonly known as 'The King's Book', changed that phrase 'so that we make no invocation of them' to read 'so that we esteem not or worship not them as givers of these gifts, but as intercessors for the same'.[10] The meaning to be attached to the phrase 'invocation of saints' is a point we will need to return to very shortly.

The second current found in sixteenth-century England was far more radical. It refused to allow any direct requests addressed to Our Lady and the saints for the help of their prayers; it even refused to allow the practice sometimes called comprecation; prayer addressed to God (as in the Roman Canon of the Mass) asking that we may benefit from the prayers of the saints; under the increasing influence of Calvin it came with time to doubt whether the saints do even pray for us at all.[11]

Much has been said and written by Anglicans hostile to devotion to Our Lady and the saints about the apparent condemnation of invocation of the saints in the Thirty-nine Articles of Religion. In its original form of 1553 – at the most advanced

---

9 Stone, *The Invocation of Saints*, pp. 32–3.
10 Stone, *The Invocation of Saints*, p. 33.
11 It should be noted, however, that one of the greatest of the seventeenth-century English Calvinists, the reluctant Nonconformist Richard Baxter, expresses in his hymn 'He wants not friends that hath thy love' his confidence of the continuing prayers of the departed:

Before thy throne we daily meet
As joint petitioners to thee;
In spirit each the other greet
And shall again each other see.
 (*New English Hymnal*, hymn 371)

point of Protestant dominance in the history of the Church of England – Article XXII condemned 'the doctrine of school authors (*'doctrina scholasticorum'*) concerning invocation of Saints', an attack on the great mediaeval scholastic theologians of the Latin Church; in its present form, as agreed in the reign of Elizabeth I, it condemns 'the Romish doctrine' ('doctrina Romanensium'). This is an unclear phrase, as is shown by the fact that the Irish Articles of 1615, drawn up under the influence of militant Calvinism, substituted the phrase 'the doctrine of the Church of Rome', a statement which excludes all ambiguity. 'Romish doctrine' cannot mean the teaching of the Council of Trent on this subject, which was given after the Articles were subscribed; in all probability it was aimed at the popular teaching current at the time in the Roman Church, which the Council of Trent perceived clearly to be in need of reform. We also need to take into consideration the point already made, the ambiguity surrounding the phrase the 'invocation of Saints'. This continued well into the seventeenth century and in Archbishop Ussher's Answer to a Jesuit Challenge of 1624 the phrase was used to denote addresses to the saints similar in wording to the adoration which we render to God.[12] It remained for one of the greatest of the seventeenth-century Anglican theologians, as we shall see, to bring definitive clarification to this ambiguity.

So in the sixteenth century we find even the most hardline Anglican Reformers anxious to pay honour to our Lady, to lay stress on her faith, her holiness, her sinlessness, on her perpetual virginity and so on. We find too that they have no problem about referring to her as 'Our Lady'. Nevertheless the judgement of Dr Ralph Townsend is surely incontrovertible:

> There is no doubt that the early Anglicans held Mary in high regard and great affection, but what is often missing in their writing is the poetry which is a necessary element of love. As Calvinist thinking penetrated Anglican liturgical practice and formulae in the course of the 16th and 17th centuries, so

---

12 Cf. Stone, *The Invocation of Saints*, p. 36.

the culture of devotion to the Virgin died. It is as if Anglicans say they esteem Mary, but do not show that they do.[13]

The Seventeenth Century

The seventeenth century, of course, saw a reaction against Calvinism, and what is characteristic of so much of the writing, even the prose, of some of the great Caroline Divines of the 'Arminian' or 'Laudian' high-church school is precisely 'the poetry which is a necessary element of love'. This change of mood is heralded by John Donne, who was born in the reign of Elizabeth I, ordained priest in the reign of James I, and died as Dean of St Paul's in 1631 in the reign of Charles I. A poem of his on the Virgin Mary shows a tender love for Our Lady and a very firm belief in the efficacy of her prayers:

For that faire blessed Mother-maid,
Whose flesh redeem'd us; that she-Cherubin,
Which unlock'd Paradise, and made
One claime for innocence, and disseiz'd sinne.
Whose wombe was a strange heav'n for there
God cloath'd himselfe, and grew,
Our zealous thankes wee poure. As her deeds were
Our helpes, so are her prayers; nor can she sue
In vaine, who hath such titles unto you.[14]

There is, as I say, a very firm belief here in the efficacy of Our Lady's prayers, but the poem is not addressed to Mary but to God.

The other great Anglican priest-poet of the age, George Herbert, who died in 1633, was the author of a poem which expresses great love of our Lady but draws back from requesting her prayers:

---

13 R. Townsend, *The Place of Mary in Early Anglican Thought* (Ecumenical Society of the Blessed Virgin Mary, May 1983), p. 7.
14 From 'A Litanie', lines 37–45.

Not out of envie or maliciousnesse
Do I forbear to crave your special aid: I would address
My vows to thee most gladly, blessed Maid,
and Mother of my God, in my distress.
Thou art the holy mine: whence came the gold,
The great restorative for all decay in young and old;
Thou art the cabinet where the jewell lay:
Chiefly to thee would I my soul unfold:
But now (alas!) I dare not; for our King,
Whom we do all joyntly adore and praise
Bids no such thing.[15]

Few of the other great seventeenth-century divines were formal poets – with the exception of Bishop Ken at the end of the century, whose poem 'Her virgin eyes' is to be found at least in the more reputable Anglican hymn books today and is frequently sung[16] – but they mostly had a powerful sense of imagery and a strong feeling for language.

If theology is to have at its centre the Bible and the liturgy, then, as Donald Allchin says, speaking of these men, 'the image will have a certain priority over the concept, for these texts are for the most part imagist rather than conceptual'.[17] In the great sermons and meditations of these men, Lancelot Andrewes, Jeremy Taylor, Mark Frank and their contemporaries, a tender devotion to Mary and a deep appreciation of her role in the mystery of redemption are expressed. So many of the classic themes of Catholic Mariology are also articulated here: Mary is Mother of God, Ever Virgin, the Second Eve, (even Star of the Sea!), Full of Grace, Free from Sin and the Model of all Christian virtues, especially of faith, humility and obedience. Yet it all remains somewhat rarified; the preacher and the poets can use language of a baroque exuberance, but it seems to find

---

[15] 'To All Angels and Saints' from *The Temple*.

[16] Another hymn book also prints it but alters Ken's phrase 'next to his throne' to 'near to his throne', thus forfeiting its claim to good repute.

[17] A. M. Allchin, *The Joy of All Creation* (London: Darton, Longman & Todd, 1984), p. 6.

hardly any echo in the consciousness or the devotion of ordinary churchgoers. There was little visual expression – even the great statue of the *Virgo Coronata* at St Mary's, Oxford, is outside the building rather than inside – as if to discourage prayer being focused upon it.[18] Surely this was due above all to the existence of a powerful brake – the strong sense that though you could celebrate Mary you could not directly address her, that it was wrong to say to her 'Pray for us' or 'Pray for me'. The inhibition expressed with such apparent regret by George Herbert in his poem was also expressed in the theology of the time. Of the theologians of the period only two, to my knowledge, break through this inhibition, and one of them only in part.[19]

The first is Herbert Thorndike, Prebendary of Westminster, who died in 1672. He writes as follows:

> There is the same ground to believe the communion of Saints, in the prayers which those that depart in the highest favour with God make for us; In the prayers which we make for those that depart in the lowest degree of favour with God, that there is for the common Christianity; Namely the Scriptures interpreted by the perpetual practice of God's Church.[20]

In another place he distinguishes three kinds of prayers:

---

18 However, as an undergraduate of Clare College, Cambridge, I worshipped for three years in a chapel which contained an eighteenth-century painted altarpiece of the Annunciation.

19 There is also the curious case of the controversial Richard Montague (or Mountague), successively Bishop of Chichester and of Norwich under Charles I. Though he would not allow that direct address to the saints (even *Ora pro nobis*) was legitimate, he was prepared to admit that they might exercise some sort of heavenly protection over those persons, bodies or countries which looked to them as patrons, cf. Perham, *The Communion of Saints*, pp. 66–7.

20 'Just Weights and Measures', in *The Theological Works of Herbert Thorndike* (Oxford: Library of Anglo-Catholic Theology (LACT), 1844), Vol. 5, p. 248.

1 those addressed to God, asking him to hear the prayers of saints on our behalf,
2 those addressed to the saints, requesting them to pray for us, and
3 those which seek directly from the saints what only God can give.

The first he approves and commends, the third he condemns strongly, the second he discusses at length but without coming to a very clear or forceful decision. 'I grant it no idolatry', he admits, but he is not happy about the practice and is worried that he can find no evidence for it before the fourth century. In the last resort he is agnostic, saying, 'I count it not fit for a private person to say what might be condescended to for the reunion of the Church.'[21]

The second theologian is William Forbes, a Scot from Aberdeen, who died in 1634 and was for a brief period under Charles I the first Bishop of Edinburgh. He was 'a man of exceptional sensitivity and perception' (to quote Donald Allchin again),[22] whose great book *Considerationes Modestae et Pacificae* (Modest and Eirenic Considerations) on controversial issues actually tried to bridge the gulf with Rome in a positive and friendly way – in a modest and pacific way. He discusses the whole issue at some length and in the course of his discussion resolves with total clarity the ambiguity attached to the concept of the invocation of saints. He distinguishes between what he calls 'religious invocation' or prayer in the strict meaning of the word, which cannot be addressed to anyone but God alone (and in making this affirmation he appeals among others to the correspondence of a sixteenth-century Patriarch of Constantinople, Jeremiah II, with German Lutherans) and what he

---

21 'Of the Laws of the Church', in *The Theological Works of Herbert Thorndike*, Vol. 4, Part II, pp. 768–84.
22 A. M. Allchin, *The Dynamic of Tradition* (London: Darton, Longman & Todd, 1981), p. 65. Bishop Forbes is also one of the Anglican theologians to whom reference is made in ARCIC II's statement *Salvation and the Church* (London: Church House Publishing, 1987), p. 10, note 1. His contribution to the debate on justification was typically irenic.

calls 'the bare addressing of Angels and Saints, whereby they are admonished and invited, that they should pray to God with us and for us ...' This latter 'we ..., who love to speak rather more cautiously and distinctly than do many others, term a calling unto (*advocationem*) rather than a calling upon (*invocationem*)', and he refuses to condemn it as unlawful or useless.[23] This is how he sums up his discussion:

> Let God alone be religiously adored: let him alone be prayed to, through Christ, who is the only and sole Mediator, truly and properly speaking, between God and men. Let not the very ancient custom received in the universal Church, as well Greek as Latin, of addressing the angels and saints after the manner we have mentioned, be condemned or rejected as impious, nor even as vain and foolish, by the more rigid Protestants. Let the foul abuses and superstitions which have crept in, be taken away. And so peace may thereafter easily be established and sanctioned between the dissentient parties, as regards this controversy. Which may the God of peace and of all pious concord vouchsafe to grant for the sake of his only begotten Son.[24]

But the good bishop's prayer was not destined to receive a speedy answer. He was to die after only two months in the episcopate, aged 49, but we can perhaps count him fortunate to have been spared the sight of the uprising in his own Cathedral Church of St Giles, only three years later, which was to spell the doom of episcopacy in Scotland, to lead on to the overthrow of Anglicanism in England, and to postpone for many centuries the calm, reasonable and irenic dialogue between Roman Catholics, Anglicans and the less rigid Protestants for which he had hoped and prayed and laboured.

---

23 *Considerationes Modestae et Pacificae*, cap. III: LACT (1850), Vol. 2, p. 211.
24 *Considerationes Modestae et Pacificae*, cap. V: LACT, Vol. 2, p. 313.

The Oxford Movement

The Oxford Movement in fact took up once more the task that Bishop William Forbes had set himself, and his own name and writings were to be rescued from near oblivion largely through the efforts of another Forbes – George, brother to the 'Scottish Pusey', Alexander Penrose Forbes, Bishop of Brechin.[25] On the delicate question of the Invocation of Saints the early Tractarians were characterized by caution, reserve and reticence; even in his retirement at Littlemore John Henry Newman insisted upon one change in the corporate recital of the offices of the Roman Breviary by his little community; whenever the phrase '*Ora pro nobis*' (pray for us) appeared, the phrase '*Oret pro nobis*' (may he or she pray for us) was substituted for it.[26]

John Keble's poem 'Mother out of Sight' therefore had an enormous psychological importance; it overcame an inhibition and released a brake which led to that great outpouring of devotion to Our Lady and the saints that has been a characteristic mark of Anglican Catholicism since the second wave of the Tractarian Movement. 'Mother out of Sight' can be seen now not only as the title of a poem but as an apt description of Marian devotion in the Church of England from the sixteenth to the nineteenth century. So, to end with our beginning, let us savour and ponder the central section of a poem we can now see as an historic breakthrough.

---

25 G. H. Forbes was responsible for the English translation of the *Considerationes* in the Library of Anglo-Catholic Theology (LACT), 1850–56.

26 Such, at any rate, is the claim made by D. Morse-Boycott in his popular account of the Catholic Revival in the Church of England, *They Shine Like Stars* (London: Skeffington & Son, 1947), p. 110, quoting the reminiscences of one John Oldcastle. Taken literally, this is difficult to substantiate, but William Lockhart, writing in the *Dublin Review* of October 1890, recalls: 'I remember, direct invocation *of* the saints was omitted, and instead we asked God that the Saint of the day might pray for us.' (I am most grateful to Dr Donald Withey for answering my query on this point.)

MAIDEN, MOTHER AND QUEEN

Mother of God! O, not in vain
We learn'd of old thy lowly strain.
Fain in thy shadow would we rest,
And kneel with thee, and call thee blest;
With thee would 'magnify the Lord',
And if thou art not here adored,
Yet seek we, day by day, the love and fear
Which bring thee, with all saints, near and more near.

What glory thou above hast won,
By special grace of thy dear Son,
We see not yet, nor dare espy
Thy crowned form with open eye.
Rather beside the manger meek
Thee bending with veiled brow we seek,
Or where the Angel in the thrice-great Name
Hail'd thee, and Jesus to thy bosom came.

Yearly since then with bitterer cry
Man hath assail'd the Throne on high
And sin and hate more fiercely striven
To mar the league 'twixt earth and heaven.
But the dread tie, that pardoning hour,
Made fast in Mary's awful bower,
Hath mightier proved to bind than we to break.
None may that work undo, that Flesh unmake.

Thenceforth, whom thousand worlds adore,
He calls thee Mother evermore;
Angel nor Saint His face may see
Apart from what he took of thee.
How may we choose but name thy name
Echoing below their high acclaim
In holy Creeds? Since earthly song and prayer
Must keep faint time to the dread anthem there.

How, but in love on thine own days,
Thou blissful one, upon thee gaze?
Nay, every day, each suppliant hour,
Whene'er we kneel in aisle or bower,
Thy glories we may greet unblamed,
Nor shun the lay by seraphs framed.
'Hail, Mary, full of grace!' O welcome sweet,
Which daily in all lands all saints repeat!

Fair greeting, with our matin vows
Paid duly to the enthroned Spouse,
His Church and Bride, here and on high,
Figured in her deep purity.
Who, born of Eve, high mercy won,
To bear and nurse the Eternal Son.
O, awful station, to no seraph given,
On this side touching sin, on the other heaven!

Therefore as kneeling day by day,
We to our Father duteous pray,
So unforbidden may we speak
An Ave to Christ's Mother meek;
(As children with 'good morrow' come:
To elders in some happy home:)
Inviting so the saintly host above
With our unworthiness to pray in love.

13

Mark Frank (1613–64): A Caroline Preacher[1]

Introduction

I first discovered the name of Mark Frank from an unlikely source, a French Marist father (of Czech or Polish descent) called Stanislas Cwiertniak. He was for a time on the staff of Notre-Dame de France in Leicester Square and was a fervent ally and supporter of his friend and fellow Marist, the pioneer ecumenist Maurice Villain. I had the privilege of meeting them both when Fr Cwiertniak was at the French church in London and when Roman Catholic priests with a knowledge and sympathetic understanding of Anglicanism were rarer than they now are. I forget now whether I first came across his book, *La Vierge Marie dans la Tradition Anglicane* (published in 1958) and then met him, or first met him and then came across his book. However, I acquired my own copy of the book in 1959. The book consists basically of extracts from Anglican authors (most, but not all, from the seventeenth century) arranged thematically and with an historical introduction. It was through this book that I first read and was impressed by Mark Frank (in French translation!) and it was my first introduction to his name. Cwiertniak made me curious, but in a way he did not help me much. In his book nothing is said about Frank except that he lived in the sixteenth century, which was not true (for he was born in 1613 and died in 1664), and the index simply indi-

---

[1] This talk was given at the Annual General Meeting of the Ecumenical Society of the Blessed Virgin Mary on 5 March 1994. It was published by the Society as a pamphlet in 1995. Except where stated, the footnotes are by the author.

cates *Sermons on Festivals* and nothing more. However, in 1960 I acquired a secondhand copy of *The Blessed Virgin and All the Company of Heaven* by Theodore Wirgman, Archdeacon of Port Elizabeth, published in 1905 and referred to in Cwiertniak's index. Wirgman's book, dedicated 'in piam memoriam J. H. Newman, S.T.P., Eccl. Romanae Cardinalis et E. B. Pusey, S.T.P., Eccl. Anglicanae Doctoris', correctly places Dr Frank in the seventeenth century. It was clear to me that Cwiertniak had drawn heavily on Wirgman, but where had Wirgman found Frank's sermons? This question was answered when I consulted a complete set of the *Library of Anglo-Catholic Theology* in the Library of Pusey House, Oxford, and found there the two volumes of *Sermons* by Mark Frank. I hardly need to remind you that in their programme of reawakening Anglicans to their true heritage, the Tractarians had embarked on two ambitious literary projects, *The Library of the Fathers* and *The Library of Anglo-Catholic Theology* (the works of some of the most notable seventeenth-century divines).[2]

Even a superficial reading of Frank's sermons was enough to captivate me; the combination of a vivid and eloquent style, deep learning, spiritual insight and theological profundity was quite remarkable. And yet none of the classic reference works to which I next turned – More and Cross, *Anglicanism*; *The Oxford Dictionary of the Christian Church*; *The Dictionary of English Church History* – even mentioned his name. Only later did I find two books that did mention him. The first was G. Lacey May, *Wings of an Eagle: An Anthology of Caroline Preachers* (1955), and the second a work May quotes, W. F. Mitchell's *English Pulpit Oratory from Andrewes to Tillotson* (1932); the latter hails Frank as 'the fairest star in the constellation of the "witty" preachers'. But here I risk digressing a little from the story of my detective-like enquiries[3] into this

---

2 The title of the series must surely be one of the earliest examples of the use of the term 'Anglo-Catholic'.

3 With apologies to *The Quest for Corvo* by A. J. A. Symons (London: Penguin Books, 1940), a biography (of the writer Frederick Rolfe) in the form of a detective enquiry.

unknown or forgotten divine. While perusing Frank in Pusey House Library in 1961 I shared my enthusiasm with Donald Allchin, then Librarian of Pusey House. And it is Donald Allchin who has done most to make Frank better known again, both in his contribution to *The Blessed Virgin Mary: Essays by Anglicans*, published in 1963,[4] and in *The Joy of All Creation*, first published in 1984 and very recently brought out in a new edition. But I must also mention a communication read by Professor Howard Root, then Director of the Anglican Centre in Rome, at the 1987 International Mariological Congress in Malta on Frank's Sermon on the Annunciation.[5]

Who was Mark Frank?

But who was Mark Frank? He was born in 1613 at Brickhill in Buckinghamshire and admitted to Pembroke College, Cambridge, in 1627, becoming a Fellow in 1634. In 1641 he preached a courageous sermon at Paul's Cross on obedience to the King and to the liturgy and customs of the Church of England before the Lord Mayor and Corporation of the City of London at a time when they were strongly backing Parliament in its opposition to Charles I. This sermon attracted the notice and approval of the King but this was of little help to the preacher, for two years later the Earl of Manchester was busy weeding out 'malignants' from the University of Cambridge on behalf of Parliament. Mark Frank was one of those who refused to sign the Solemn League and Covenant and he was deprived of his fellowship to endure exile and poverty until the

---

4 *Editor's note*: in a footnote to this essay, Allchin wrote, 'I am grateful to the Revd Roger Greenacre for first drawing my attention to the sermons of Mark Frank': A. M. Allchin, 'Our Lady in Seventeenth-Century Anglican Devotion and Theology', in E. L. Mascall and H. S. Box (eds), *The Blessed Virgin Mary. Essays by Anglican Writers* (London: Darton, Longman & Todd, 1963), pp. 53–76 at p. 65.

5 Since this paper was delivered in March 1994 there has been published *Covenant of Grace Renewed: A Vision of the Eucharist in the Seventeenth Century* by Kenneth Stevenson, which refers to Frank and quotes one of his Candlemas sermons (London: Darton, Longman & Todd, 1994), pp. 189–90.

Restoration of the Monarchy and of the Church of England in 1660. He was reinstated in his fellowship in that year and further honours followed thick and fast; he became Archdeacon of St Albans, Treasurer and prebendary of St Paul's Cathedral, Chaplain to the Archbishop of Canterbury, Rector of Barley, near Cambridge (where he succeeded the distinguished theologian Herbert Thorndike), and in 1662 Master of Pembroke. But two years later in 1664 at the age of fifty-one he died, and was buried in St Paul's Cathedral.

This bare *curriculum vitae* tells us very little about the man and his personality; nearly everything we know about him comes to us through his only published work, his *Sermons*, first published posthumously in 1672 and re-issued in 1849 in the *Library of Anglo-Catholic Theology*. Of Frank we could repeat what St Gregory the Great wrote of St Benedict, when he claimed that his greatness came entirely from his Rule, the 'key to the teacher's life, for he could not have lived otherwise than he taught'. First of all, however, we need to set him in context, the context of mid-seventeenth-century Cambridge.

If the Tractarian revival of the Catholic tradition in the Church of England is called the Oxford Movement because most (but not all) of its leading figures were members of the University of Oxford, its seventeenth-century precursor could perhaps be called the Cambridge Movement.[6] It was above all a reaction against the then dominant Calvinist doctrine of grace and so is often called 'Arminian' after the Dutch theologian Arminius. It was also strongly sacramental, liturgical and patristic in tone and is often called 'Laudian' after Charles I's Archbishop of Canterbury, himself an Oxford man. Many of the leading protagonists of this school, however, came from Cambridge and included such pioneers as Bishops Overall, Andrewes (a former fellow and Master of Pembroke) and Neile and many who could have been known to Frank such as Rich-

---

6 It is usual, however, to reserve the use of this title for the efforts of John Mason Neale and others to apply the theological insights of the Oxford Movement to the fields of church architecture and liturgical practice in the mid-nineteenth century.

ard Montague, Matthew Wren (fellow of Pembroke and then Master of Peterhouse) and John Cosin (Wren's successor at Peterhouse), all of whom became bishops.[7]

It would be particularly interesting to pursue the connection between Cosin and Frank; Frank was at Pembroke at the time when, just across the road, Cosin as Master of Peterhouse was acquiring a good deal of notoriety for his liturgical practice both at Peterhouse and at Durham Cathedral where, during his time as prebendary, his lighting of candles on Candlemas Day had provoked a violent protest from another of the prebendaries. Frank's own two surviving Candlemas sermons indicate a man who shared many of Cosin's enthusiasms.

The Sermons

It is time now to turn to the sermons themselves and to begin with some comments on the preacher's style. If Mark Frank was one of the finest of the 'witty' preachers, the wit in question is not a matter of humour; it is rather the combination of all the skills of oratory, imagination, learning and language in the service of what was seen as one of the highest and most serious art forms, the art of the pulpit. Of the preaching of Lancelot Andrewes, King James could comment – admiringly not disapprovingly – 'he playeth with his text, patting it to and fro, as a cat doth with a mouse', while George Herbert called this technique of squeezing the last drop of meaning out of a verse of Scripture 'crumbling the text'. Frank does this, but, as May remarks, he is half way between Donne and Taylor and the exponents of a plainer style that came in during the reign of Charles II; he eschewed over-lengthy sentences and quotations and made intelligibility his principal aim.

---

7 Cf. Nicholas Tyacke, *Anti-Calvinists: The Rise of English Arminianism c 1590–1640* (paperback edn: Oxford: Oxford University Press, 1990), esp. Ch. 2: 'Cambridge University and Arminianism'. For a poignant evocation of this Cambridge scene in fiction, see Rose Macaulay, *They Were Defeated* (London: Collins, 1960).

The sermons are intensely biblical; the margins of the *Library of Anglo-Catholic Theology* edition are filled with the texts which are quoted in English, Latin and Greek or (more rarely) Hebrew either directly or by allusion, but the whole of his thinking and his language is steeped in the Bible. They are also intensely patristic; among the Western Fathers he cites are Leo, Ambrose, Augustine, Peter Chrysologus, Pope Gregory, Bede, Bernard (a particular favourite) and Peter Damian and among the Eastern Fathers John Chrysostom, Gregory of Nyssa and Epiphanius. He can at times – as we shall see – be quite strongly critical of Rome, but he reserves his strongest and most deeply felt criticism for the Puritans. He is, I believe, the Mariological preacher *par excellence* of the seventeenth century in the Church of England, but before we take a closer look at some of the sermons which directly address this theme, let us first of all, in order to set his Mariological preaching in its context, give some examples of his general theological position.

He does not spend much time in his sermons debating the vexed topic of predestination. When he does broach the subject he is clearly anti-Calvinist, as in this passage in the Fourth Sermon on Christmas Day, in which he attacks those who will allow Christ 'neither to save, nor come to save, anybody but "the elect"', who limit his coming 'only to a few, and all the rest excluded by some inevitable decree':

> It is neither a true nor faithful saying, nor much worth the accepting, as many receivers as it has, that says otherwise, that binds up his coming only to the elect. For if not for all, they may be out, for all their brags; may be too righteous to be in, among the sinners; among the righteous, that he says himself he came not for. This saying that we are for, 'that Christ Jesus came into the world to save sinners, is a faithful saying, worthy of all acceptation,' even the chiefest the world affords, – to be received by all, whilst itself rejects none.[8]

---

8 M. Frank, *Sermons by Mark Frank, D.D.* (Oxford: John Henry Parker, 1849), Vol. 1: The Fourth Sermon on Christmas-Day, p. 113.

His sense of the Church and of the Church's liturgy is extremely strong; here, for example, is how he expounds his text 'Blessed is he that cometh in the Name of the Lord' on the First Sunday in Advent:

> The multitudes before is the Jewish synagogue; the multitudes behind, the Christian Church; a multitude, indeed, that cannot be numbered, of emperors, and kings, and princes; bishops and priests; doctors, martyrs, confessors, and virgins, all in their several orders and generations, crying, 'Hosanna to the Son of David,' ... All these multitudes – the Jew, with his multitude of patriarchs, priests, and Levites, and singers, and prophets, with his sacrifices of bulls, and rams, and goats, and sheep, of types and figures, all crying out Messiah is coming – the Christians, apostles, martyrs, confessors, doctors, virgins, bishops, priests, and deacons, and all several orders in their choirs and churches throughout the world, crying out, He is come; all the corners of the earth resounding out Hosannas and Allelujahs to him. *Una est fides praecedentium atque sequentium populorum*, says St Gregory; all believing and professing the same He that cometh here; they, the Jews, before, crying 'He that cometh;' we, the Christians, crying, 'He that is come,' or rather, He that cometh still, that every day comes to us by his grace, and through his word, and in his sacraments: 'Blessed is he that cometh' still, not a tense or tittle changed ...
>
> So now the congregation is full, what should we do but begin our service? when we have Law, and Prophets, and Gospel to countenance and bear us company in our Te Deum and Benedictus, at our prayers and praises, in our joys and festivals; all of them crying nothing but Christ, nothing but Christ, blessed be he, blessed be he, and blessed be his coming, and blessed be his day, and blessed be his deeds; the whole practice of all Christian churches and congregations that ever were gathered together *in nomine Domini*, 'in the name of the Lord,' till these mere nominal verbal Christians, that are afraid of the name of Him that cometh, of the Name

of Jesus, of blessing it or bowing at it; all Christians, all that came before in the name of Christ, till these pretenders that follow nobody but their own fancies; all agreeing in the same welcome to their Redeemer, joining in the same prayers and praises: what should we do but add our voices and sing with them?[9]

This excerpt gives us a glimpse both of his eloquence and also of his bitterness towards the Puritans; it gives too a glimpse of his sense of hierarchy and of the plurality of vocations within the Church – a plurality which ought to embrace the vocation to the religious life, since there is a reference to the order of virgins and an earlier reference to 'orders of religious men'. In one of his Candlemas sermons he refers to 'Anna the religious' and Canon Allchin points out that he was known as a young man to have had a close association with the Little Gidding community and a deep friendship with the nephew of Nicholas Ferrar, the community's founder, who was also called Nicholas Ferrar. But his Advent Sunday sermon at least seems to have been preached during the period of Puritan dominance after the dissolution of the Little Gidding community,[10] for he continues:

Indeed true it is, God has turned our songs of joy into the voice of weeping (as the prophet complains); taken away our feasts and gaudy days; and we may well cry, and cry aloud in that sadder sense of the word 'crying:' yet for all that, must we not lay down the other, or forget the song of prayer and praise, especially upon the point of Christ's coming to us.[11]

---

9 Frank, *Sermons*, Vol. 1; A Sermon on the First Sunday in Advent, pp. 7–8.
10 None of the sermons is dated, except for that delivered in 1641 at St Paul's Cross. But if some, such as the Sermon on the First Sunday in Advent, were almost certainly preached during the period of his deprivation, others were clearly delivered after the Restoration of Charles II. There are clear references to this event in the Sixth Sermon on Christmas Day and in the two sermons preached in St Paul's Cathedral.
11 Frank, *Sermons*, Vol. 1: A Sermon on the First Sunday in Advent, pp. 8–9.

This strong sense of, and delight in, the Church's liturgy includes a delight in music that finds expression in many of his sermons and particularly in this Advent sermon:

> Three parts there are in it as in other songs, *bassus*, *tenor*, and *altus* – the bass, the tenor and the treble. 'Hosanna to the Son of David;' there is the bass, the deepest and lowest note, the humanity of Christ *in filio David*, being 'the Son of David:' the bass sings that, that is low indeed for him, we can go no lower. 'Blessed is he that cometh in the name of the Lord;' there is the tenor or middle part, he and the name of the Lord joined together, God and man united – that is a note higher than the first, the Mediator between God and man; God in the highest, Son of David in the lowest; the middle note then follows. And *Hosanna in altissimis*, the *altus* or treble, the highest note of all: we can reach no higher, strain we never so high.[12]

His sense of the Church appropriately includes a strong sense of authority, of an authority in which tradition forms an important constitutive element. In his hard-hitting sermon of 1641, preached at Paul's Cross, he can say:

> Authority used to be a logical argument to guide our reason: and have we lost our logic too, as well as our obedience? The consent of wise, grave, learned fathers, (till you know where to find better,) with any man not too high in his own conceit, is certainly of a value somewhat above his private imagination. For, who tells you they are deceived? Your private minister? And are you sure he is not? And are they deceived? And is it not as likely that you and he should be? Were they not as wise as you – as just as you – as devout as you? Have you reason, and had not they? Do you use Scripture, and did not they? Had they interests, and have not you? That all should be deceived, till you, and your new ministers came into the world, is morally impossible.[13]

---

12 Frank, *Sermons*, Vol. 1: A Sermon on the First Sunday in Advent, p. 10.
13 Frank, *Sermons*, Vol. 2: A Sermon Preached at S. Paul's Cross, p. 421.

He goes on to make a strong defence of episcopacy in words which would hardly have been music to the ears of the Lord Mayor and Corporation:

> Bishops are fathers by their title, the fathers of the Church; so the first Christians, so all since, till this new unchristian Christianity started up. Fathers in God, it is their style; however some of late, sons of Belial, would make them fathers in the devil, antichrists; perhaps, that they might make them like themselves. Strange antichrists to whom Christ hath left the governing of his Church these 1500 years![14]

Having made himself on this occasion so thoroughly unpopular with his audience, he continues with a defence of outward ceremonies:

> May not I as lawfully serve my God in a reverent posture, as thou in a saucy and irreverent garb? Is it superstition in me to stand, because thou sittest or leanest on thy elbow? Is it idolatry in me to kneel, because thou wilt not foul thy clothes, or vex thy knees? Strange must it needs be, that sitting, leaning, lolling, must be law and canon, where no set behaviour is expressed, and my reverence only be against it; made innovation which law never forbad, custom has retained. When you can bring me law against my standing, bowing, kneeling, which yourselves know custom hath observed, where uniform order has been kept, I shall either submit or answer.[15]

He uses his Whitsunday sermons also to speak about the authority of Councils and of the episcopate. Thus in his Third Sermon he can say:

> In matters of doubt and controversy, send to the Church, to Jerusalem, to the Apostles and Elders there convened in

---

14 Frank, *Sermons*, Vol. 2: A Sermon Preached at S. Paul's Cross, p. 433.
15 Frank, *Sermons*, Vol. 2: A Sermon Preached at S. Paul's Cross, p. 431.

council, and let them determine it, so we find it done. In a lawful and full assembly of the learned Fathers of the Church such shall be determined; – that is the way to settle truth.[16]

And speaking of the bishops as successors of the Apostles, he can say in the Fourth Sermon:

> That soul which breaks the bond of unity, and divides itself from the Church of Christ, from the company of the Apostles and their successors, the still fathers of it, cannot hold this holy wind, cannot enclose this holy fire; they are broken and cracked, crack only of the Spirit, but are really broken from that body in which only the Spirit moves.[17]

Mark Frank has also a very high doctrine of the ministerial priesthood, of the link between priesthood and the sacraments and of the sacrificial role of the Christian priesthood. In his First Sermon on the Circumcision he can say:

> The new Church has its new sacraments ... new sacrifices ... a new priesthood to offer them; 'an unchangeable priesthood' now. Christ our high-priest, and the 'ministers of the new testament' as so many under-priests, to offer them up to God. Christ offered himself as sacrifice; offers up also our prayers and praises to his Father; has left his ministers, in his name and merits, to do it too. And this, a lasting priesthood, to last for ever.
>
> We have a new altar, too – so S. Paul – 'an altar that they which served the tabernacle have no power to eat of.' Take it for the cross, on which Christ offered up himself; or take it for the holy table, where that great sacrifice of his is daily commemorated in Christian churches: *habemus*, says the Apostle; such an one we have, and I am sure it is 'new.'[18]

---

16 Frank, *Sermons*, Vol. 2: The Third Sermon on Whitsunday, p. 234.
17 Frank, *Sermons*, Vol. 2: The Fourth Sermon on Whitsunday, p. 244.
18 Frank, *Sermons*, Vol. 1: The First Sermon on the Circumcision, pp. 252–3.

The idea he pursues in his Second Sermon on the Purification, when he invites his hearers to contemplate Simeon (whom he holds to be a priest) taking the child Jesus into his arms, and makes a comparison that we might not expect to find in any pre-Tractarian Anglican:

> But the Christian priest does more, blesses the child too. No priest of the law could do that: it is the minister of the Gospel only that can do that; that has that authority, to consecrate, and bless, and take, and all. He it is that blesses the dead elements, and quickens them into holy things by the ministration of his office, by the virtue of his function. Till he blesses, they are but common bread and wine; when he has taken and offered them, then they are holy; then they are the means, and pledges, and seals of grace; then they convey Christ unto the faithful receiver's soul. This is the mystery of the Gospel and so I speak it; not literally of Christ's person, but mystically of his body and blood, as offered and taken in the sacrament.[19]

The Blessed Virgin Mary

It is time now – at last – to turn to the sermons which have a directly Mariological bearing. I begin with the Second Sermon on Christmas Day with its brilliant and beautiful opening:[20]

> *And she brought forth her first-born son, and wrapped him in swaddling clothes, and laid him in a manger, because there was no room for them in the inn.*

---

19 Frank, *Sermons*, Vol. 1: The Second Sermon on the Purification, p. 362. He goes on to say of the Eucharist that it 'cannot be offered but by the hands to which Christ committed that power and authority'.

20 Frank rather specializes in dramatic openings. This is how he begins his Sermon on St Stephen's Day: 'Yesterday's Child is today, you see, become a man. He that yesterday could neither stand nor go, knew not the right hand from the left, lay helpless as it were in the bosom of his mother, is today presented to us standing at the right hand of God in the glory of the Father ...': Frank, *Sermons*, Vol. 1: A Sermon on S. Stephen's Day, p. 213.

I shall not need to tell you who this 'she,' or who this 'him.' The day rises with it in its wings. This day wrote it with the first ray of the morning sun upon the posts of the world. The angels sung it in their choirs, the morning stars together in their courses. The Virgin Mother, the Eternal Son. The most blessed among women, the fairest of the sons of men. The woman clothed with the sun: the son compassed with a woman. She the gate of heaven: he the King of Glory that came forth. She the mother of the everlasting God: he God without a mother; God blessed for evermore. Great persons as ever met upon a day.

Yet as great as the persons, and as great as the day, the great lesson of them both is to be little, to think and make little of ourselves; seeing the infinite greatness in this day become so little, Eternity a child, the rays of glory wrapt in rags, Heaven crowded into the corner of a stable, and He that is everywhere want a room.

I may at other times have spoken great and glorious things, both of the persons and the day: but I am determined to-day to know nothing but Jesus Christ in rags, but Jesus Christ in a manger. And I hope I shall have your company along ...[21]

A little later in the same sermon he ponders on the lowliness of Mary:

But, if he would be born of a woman, could he not have chosen an othergates than 'she,' than a poor carpenter's wife? Some great queen or lady had been fitter far to have made as it were the Queen of Heaven, and mother to the heir of all the world. But *respexit humilitatem ancillae*, it was the lowliness of this his holy handmaid that he looked to; it was for her humility he chose to be born of her before any other: that we may know, 1, whom it is that the Eternal Wisdom will vouchsafe to dwell with, even the humble and lowly; that, 2, we may see he even studies to descend as low as pos-

---

[21] Frank, *Sermons*, Vol. 1: The Second Sermon on Christmas-Day, p. 77.

sible, that so even the meanest might come to him without fear; that, 3, we should henceforth despise no man for his parentage, nor bear ourselves high upon our birth and stock.

Our descent and kindred are no such business to make us proud. Christ comes as soon to the low cottage as to the loftiest palace, to the handmaid as to the mistress, to the poor as to the rich; nay, prefers them here, honours a poor humble maid above all the gallant ladies of the world.[22]

He continues with a reflexion on the way in which every Christian like Mary has to 'bring forth' Christ:

I hope we have showed you mystery enow, and you have seen humility enough. But it is not enough to see the one or the other, unless now we take up the Virgin Mary's part, which is behind, bring forth this First-born to ourselves; suffer him to be born in us, who was born for us; and bring forth Christ in our lives, wrap him and lay him up with all the tenderness of a mother. The pure virgin pious soul is this 'she' that brings forth Christ, the nourishing and cherishing of him and all his gifts and graces, is this wrapping him in swaddling clothes; the laying up his word, his promises and precepts in our hearts, is the laying him in the manger.[23]

Whenever Mark Frank is preaching at a Eucharist, as on this occasion, he always works up to a sacramental conclusion; this is how he does it on Christmas Day:

What though there be no room for them in the inn? I hope there is in our houses for him. It is Christmas time, and let us keep open house for him; let his rags be our Christmas raiment, his manger our Christmas cheer, his stable our Christmas great chamber, hall, dining-room. We must clothe with him, and feed with him, and lodge with him at this

---

22 Frank, *Sermons*, Vol. 1: The Second Sermon on Christmas-Day, pp. 79–80.
23 Frank, *Sermons*, Vol. 1: The Second Sermon on Christmas-Day, pp. 89–90.

feast. He is now ready by and by to give Himself to eat; you may see him wrapped ready in the swaddling clothes of his blessed sacrament; you may behold him laid upon the altar as in his manger. Do but make room for him, and we will bring him forth, and you shall look upon him, and handle him, and feed upon him: bring we only the rags of a rent and torn and broken and contrite heart, the white linen cloths of pure intentions and honest affections to swathe him in, wrap him up fast, and lay him close to our souls and bosoms. It is a day of mysteries: it is a mysterious business we are about; Christ wrapped up, Christ in the sacrament, Christ in a mystery; let us be content to let it go so, believe, admire and adore it.[24]

Let us turn now to the First Sermon on the Epiphany. It is interesting to note that Frank is well aware of the full range of meaning to be given to the Feast. He speaks of the 'three Epiphanies the Church reckons upon this day', that to the Wise Men, that at his Baptism and that at Cana, 'all three commemorated upon this day; the first in the Gospel, the other two in the two Second Lessons for the day'. He is eloquent about the Wise Men's journey:

Many a weary step had they trod, many a fruitless question had they asked, many an unprofitable search had they made to find him; and, behold, yet they will not give over. Twelve days it had cost them to come to Jerusalem, through the Arabian deserts, over the Arabian mountains, both Arabia Deserta and Petraea: the difficulty of the way, through sands and rocks – the danger of the passages, being infamous for robbers – the cold and hardness of a deep winter season – the hazard and inconvenience of so long, so hard, so unseasonable, so dangerous, and I may say so uncertain a journey, could no whit deter them from their purpose: to Jerusalem they will, through all these difficulties.[25]

---

[24] Frank, *Sermons*, Vol. 1: The Second Sermon on Christmas-Day, p. 90.
[25] Frank, *Sermons*, Vol. 1: The First Sermon on the Epiphany, p. 277.

He is, however, even more eloquent when he describes their arrival at the house at Bethlehem:

> I do not wonder interpreters make this house the church of God. It is the gate and court of heaven, now Christ is here; angels sing round about it, all holiness is in it, now Christ is in it: here all the creatures, reasonable and unreasonable, come to pay their homage to their Creator; hither they come, even from the ends of the earth, to their devotions; 'a house of prayer' it is 'for all people,' Gentiles and all; hither they come to worship, hither they come to pay their offerings and their vows; here is the shrine and altar, the glorious Virgin's lap, where the Saviour of the world is laid to be adored and worshipped; here stands the star for tapers to give it light; and here the wise men this day become priests – worship and offer, present prayers and praises, for themselves and the whole world besides; all people of the world, high and low, learned and ignorant, represented by them.[26]

We pass now to the two sermons preached on Candlemas Day, the first in the morning preached at the Eucharist, the second preached on the same day at Evensong.

Near the beginning of the first sermon he alludes to the traditional ceremonies associated with the day:

> For this day also of his presentation, as well as those other days of his birth, circumcision and manifestation – Candlemas-day as well as Christmas-day, New-year's-day or Epiphany, is a day of blessing; a day of God's blessing us, and our blessing of him again; of Christ's being presented for us, and our presenting to him again; of his presenting in the temple, and our presenting ourselves in the church, to bless God and him for his presentation, his presentation-day, and our Candlemas, our little candles, our petty lights; our souls reflecting back to this great Light, that was this day presented in the temple and then darted down upon us.[27]

---
26 Frank, *Sermons*, Vol. 1: The First Sermon on the Epiphany, p. 280.
27 Frank, *Sermons*, Vol. 1: The First Sermon on the Purification, p. 340.

He goes on to enumerate those who were present that day and 'none so good but stands in need of him ... that will want a Saviour ... if not among sinners, yet among the righteous':

> Mary the blessed, Joseph the just, Simeon the devout, Anna the religious, all in to-day, secular and religious, of all sexes and orders; all come in today, as at the end of Christmas; like the chorus to the angels' choir, to bear a part in the angels' anthem, to make up a full choir of voices to glorify God for this great present, which brings peace to the earth, and goodwill among men.[28]

If he affirms, as of course does the Tradition of Catholic Christendom, that Mary too has need of a Saviour, he can still in the course of this sermon refer to her as 'that most pure and immaculate Virgin'. He permits himself an ironic comment on his contemporaries too:

> From Bethlehem to Jerusalem is a pretty walk to go with a young child to offer; but where God commands, there is no gainsaying. There is no burden neither to such souls as just Josephs and blessed Marys, and the child will get no cold by the way it goes to God: our niceness makes the trouble, and betrays us to the fear. The child gets no hurt by being carried to the font; nor did it in devouter times, when it was wholly dipped, no more than so great a pain as circumcision hurt the infant's health. Our tenderness and fooleries, who have not faith enough to trust God with them, or to submit mildly to God's ordinances, are the only causes of all miscarriages in holy business.[29]

The morning sermon works up to a magnificent peroration which is, as we would expect, thoroughly and explicitly eucharistic. We can detect a note of regret for the passing of the former Candlemas ceremonies and an allusion surely to the

---

28 Frank, *Sermons*, Vol. 1: The First Sermon on the Purification, p. 341.
29 Frank, *Sermons*, Vol. 1: The First Sermon on the Purification, p. 351.

two candles on the altar in the reference to the 'two candles of faith and good works':

> It is Candlemas to-day, – so-called from the lighting up of candles, offering them, consecrating them, and bearing them in procession; a custom from the time of Justinian the Emperor, at the latest about 1100 years ago; or as others say Pope Gelasius, anno 496, or thereabouts; – to show that long expected Light of the Gentiles was now come, was now sprung up and shined brighter than the sun at noon, and might be taken in our hands. Let the ceremony pass, reserve the substance; light up the two candles of faith and good works, light them with the fire of charity; bear we them burning in our hands, as Christ commands us; meet we him 'with our lamps burning,' consecrate we also them, all our works and actions, with our prayers; offer we them then upon the altars of the Lord of Hosts, to his honour and glory; and go we to the altars of the God of our salvation, *bini et bini*, as St Bernard speaks, as in procession, 'two and two', in peace and unity together; and with this solemnity and preparation, we poor oxen and asses may come and approach to our Master's crib. The crib is the outward elements, wherein he lies wrapped up; they are the swaddling clothes and mantles, with which his body is covered when he is now offered up to God, and taken up by us. Take them, and take him; the candle of faith will there show you him, and the candle of charity will light him down into your arms, that you may embrace him. We embrace where we love, we take into our arms whom we love; so that love Jesus and embrace Jesus – love Jesus and take Jesus – love Jesus and take him into our hands, and into our arms, and into our mouths, and into our hearts.[30]

The same candlelight theme reappears in the evening sermon; here is a part of his conclusion which leads into a moving and passionate doxology:

---

30 Frank, *Sermons*, Vol. 1: The First Sermon on the Purification, p. 358.

Light up now your candles at this evening service, for the glory of your morning sacrifice: it is Candlemas. Become we all burning and shining lights, to do honour to this day, and the blessed armful of it. Let your souls shine bright with grace, your hands with good works; ... Walk we 'as children of the light,' as so many walking lights; and offer we ourselves up like so many holy candles to the Father of Light.[31]

We come finally to the Sermon on the Annunciation in which he expounds most fully his Marian theology. Let us begin at the beginning:

And the Angel came in unto her, and said, Hail, thou that art highly favoured, the Lord is with thee: blessed art thou among women.

The day will tell you who this 'blessed among women' is: we call it our Lady-day; and the text will tell you why she comes into the day, because the Angel to-day came in to her. And the Angel will tell you why he today came in to her; she was 'highly favoured,' and 'the Lord was with her,' was to come himself this day into her, to make her the most 'blessed among women,' – sent him only before to tell her so, – to tell her, he would be with her by and by himself.

This makes it Annunciation-day, the Annunciation of the Virgin Mary, as the Church calls it, and the annunciation to her, as we may call it too.[32]

He explains very clearly the double sense of the word 'annunciation' in a way that anticipates the twentieth-century liturgical change which now calls the feast the Annunciation of the Lord, the Annunciation of our Lord to the Blessed Virgin Mary:

So the Incarnation of Christ, and the Annunciation of the blessed Virgin, – his being incarnate of her, and her blessed-

---

31 Frank, *Sermons*, Vol. 1: The Second Sermon on the Purification, p. 376.
32 Frank, *Sermons*, Vol. 2: A Sermon on the Annunciation, p. 33.

ness by him, and all our blessednesses in him with her, make it as well our Lord's as our Lady's day. More his, because his being Lord made her a Lady, else a poor carpenter's wife, God knows; all her worthiness and honour, as all ours, is from him; and we to take heed to-day, or any day, of parting them; or so remembering her, as to forget him; or so blessing her, as to take away any of our blessing him; any of his worship, to give to her. Let her blessedness, the respect we give her, be *inter mulieres*, 'among women' still; such as is fit and proportionate to weak creatures, not due and proper only to the Creator, that *Dominus tecum*, Christ in her be the business: that we take pattern by the Angel, to give her no more than is her due, yet to be sure to give her that though, and that particularly upon the day.[33]

In his anxiety to present a balanced theology he then indulges in one of his very rare attacks on the Roman Catholic Church, only to follow it with an even stronger attack on the Puritans, whom in a striking and poignant phrase he accuses of wounding our Lord 'through our Lady's sides':

> The only wonder indeed to us, will be to hear of an *Ave Mary*. Indeed, I cannot myself but wonder at it, as they use it now, to see it turned into a prayer. It was never made for prayer or praise – a mere salutation. The Angel's here to the blessed Virgin never intended it, I dare say, for other, either to praise her with, or to pray unto her. And I shall not consider it as such. I am only for the Angel's *Ave*, not the popish *Ave Maria*; I can see no such in the text.
>
> Nor should I scarce, I confess, have chosen such a theme today, though the Gospel reach it to me, but that I see it is time to do it, when our Lord is wounded through our Lady's sides; both our Lord and the mother of our Lord, most vilely spoken of by a new generation of wicked men, who, because the Romanists make little less of her than a goddess, they

---

[33] Frank, *Sermons*, Vol. 2: A Sermon on the Annunciation, p. 34.

make not so much of her as a good woman: because they bless her too much, these unbless her quite, at least they will not suffer her to be blessed as she should.[34]

He tries carefully to steer a middle path between two extremes and he insists, as do indeed all the recent conciliar and papal texts from the Roman Catholic Church, that all Mary's glory comes from the Lord:

> She hath a Lord, – is a subject as well as we. And lastly, all her blessedness is but *inter mulieres*, 'among women'; how much soever she excels all women, she is but *inter mulieres*, among such creatures, in the rank of creatures; no goddess, nor partner with the Godhead, either in title or worship.
>
> By considering and laying all these points together, we shall both vindicate the blessed Virgin's honour, as well as from all superstitious as profane abuses, and ourselves from all neglect of any duty to the mother of our Lord, – one so highly favoured and blessed by him, whilst we give her all that either Lord or Angel gave her; but yet dare not give her more.[35]

Though he claims not to give our Lady 'other titles than the Scripture gives her', he does in fact go further:

> ... But to such a virgin, one so highly favoured as to be made the mother of God, (for the mother of Christ is no less, he being God,) what messenger could come less than an angel? Prophets and patriarchs were too little for so great an embassage, and angels never came upon a greater.[36]

And again:

---

34 Frank, *Sermons*, Vol. 2: A Sermon on the Annunciation, pp. 35–6.
35 Frank, *Sermons*, Vol. 2: A Sermon on the Annunciation, p. 37.
36 Frank, *Sermons*, Vol. 2: A Sermon on the Annunciation, p. 38. Again, a little later, on the title *Deipara* – 'as the Church, against all heretics, has ever styled her the Mother of God' (p. 40).

Of a high and illustrious name besides; *Maria* is *maris stella*, says St Bede: 'the star of the sea,' a fit name for the mother of the bright Morning Star that rises out of the vast sea of God's infinite and endless love. Maria the Syriac interprets *domina*, 'a lady,' a name yet retained, and given to her by all Christians; our Lady, or the Lady Mother of our Lord.[37]

He goes on, in a profound meditation on the greeting *Dominus tecum*, 'The Lord is with thee', to make his highest claim for the Blessed Virgin, 'that God is with her', so Professor Root sums it up, 'as he is and has been with no other creature'.[38]

He is not with her, as he is with any else. *Tecum in mente, tecum in ventre*, as the Fathers gloss it; *Tecum in spiritu, tecum in carne*, with her he was, or would be presently, as well in her body as in her soul, personally, essentially, nay bodily with her, and take a body from her, – a way of being with any never heard before or since, – a being with her beyond any expression or conception whatsoever.[39]

It will seem strange to us today that, in spite of his almost lyrical exaltation of Our Lady, Mark Frank will not allow the legitimacy of the *Ave Maria* or of any direct invocation addressed to her or to any of the saints. Both in this sermon and in the two sermons delivered on All Saints' Day he goes out of his way to defend the honour due to the saints. This embraces their burial places, for 'even the lodgings of their very ashes seem to exult with a kind of joy to be made the receptacles and cabinets of those jewels of the Almighty, and their sepulchres and memorials are blessed for ever more'. He commends the custom of the primitive Church of naming the saints in thanksgiving 'even at the altar itself'; the saints are to be

---

37 Frank, *Sermons*, Vol. 2: A Sermon on the Annunciation, pp. 39–40.
38 H. Root, 'An Anglican Divine on Mary: Mark Frank', in *Acta Congressus Mariologici-Mariani Internationalis in Republica Melitensi Anno 1983 Celebrati* (Rome: Pontificia Academia Mariana Internationalis, 1987), p. 321.
39 Frank, *Sermons*, Vol. 2: A Sermon on the Annunciation, pp. 43–4.

honoured, but honoured 'with our praises, I say, but not our prayers'. It is not that he denies that they now 'guard us round with ... their earnest prayers for their afflicted brethren', but he prefers to lay emphasis on the fact that they also require our prayers 'for their perfection and consummation, and our own – for "they without us shall not be made perfect"'. More than that he affirms Scripture will not allow.[40]

But let us return to – and conclude with – the Sermon on the Annunciation. He sums up his message in these words:

> Give we her in God's name the honour due to her. God hath styled her 'blessed' by the Angel, by Elizabeth; commanded all generations to call her so, and they hitherto have done it, and let us do it too.[41]

And, since the Eucharist is being celebrated, he has to draw together, as is his wont, the theme of the day and the theme of the Sacrament:

> Yet not to such at any time more fully than in the blessed Sacrament to which we are now a-going. There he is strangely with us, highly favours us, exceedingly blesses us; there we are all made blessed Marys, and become mothers, sisters, and brothers of our Lord, whilst we hear his word, and conceive it in us; whilst we believe him who is the Word, and receive him too into us. There angels come to us on heavenly errands, and there our Lord indeed is with us; and we are blessed, and the angels hovering all about to peep into those holy mysteries, think us so, and call us so.[42]

---

40 Frank, *Sermons*, Vol. 2: The First and Second Sermons on All Saints, pp. 336–75, *passim*.
41 Frank, *Sermons*, Vol. 2: A Sermon on the Annunciation, p. 50.
42 Frank, *Sermons*, Vol. 2: A Sermon on the Annunciation, pp. 50–1.

Conclusion

At this critical juncture in the history of the Church of England I find the life and writings of Mark Frank particularly moving. It is a time when many Catholic Anglicans are abandoning the Church of England, moving from a conviction that their Church has betrayed its Catholic heritage to a profound doubt as to whether that heritage was ever anything more than an illusion, a beautiful dream but only a dream.

The study of the Arminian movement in the seventeenth century forces one to confront fundamental questions about the catholicity of the Church of England, to try to explain how after the long, harsh winter of Calvinist domination a profound, tender and passionate Catholic instinct in doctrine and spirituality could spring up and produce such natural, healthy and luxuriant foliage so soon after the tree of catholic doctrine and devotion seemed to have been cut down to the very roots in the 'stripping of the altars' in the Elizabethan period. What, if anything, does that say about the hidden roots that remained? What, if anything, does that give us as a message of hope in another bleak period today?

Bibliography

M. Frank, *Sermons by Mark Frank, D.D.*, 2 volumes (Oxford: Library of Anglo-Catholic Theology: John Henry Parker, 1849).

The Dictionary of National Biography, Vol. 20 (London: Smith, Elder, 1889).[43]

A. T. Wirgman, *The Blessed Virgin and all the Company of Heaven* (London: Cope & Fenwick, 1908).

W. F. Mitchell, *English Pulpit Oratory from Andrewes to Tillotson* (London: SPCK, 1932).

G. Lacey May, *Wings of an Eagle: An Anthology of Caroline Preachers* (London: SPCK, 1955).

---

43 *Editor's note*: see also now K. W. Stevenson, 'Mark Frank', in *Oxford Dictionary of National Biography* (Oxford: Oxford University Press, 2004), which cites Allchin's *The Joy of All Creation* and this paper.

S. Cwiertniak, S.M., *La Vierge Marie dans la Tradition Anglicane* (Paris: Fleurus, 1958).

A. M. Allchin, 'Our Lady in Seventeenth-Century Anglican Devotion and Theology', in E. L. Mascall and H. S. Box (eds), *The Blessed Virgin Mary. Essays by Anglican Writers* (London: Darton, Longman & Todd, 1963).

A. M. Allchin, *The Joy of All Creation* (1st edn, London: Darton, Longman & Todd, 1984; 2nd edn, substantially revised and with new material: London: New City, 1993).

H. Root, 'An Anglican Divine on Mary: Mark Frank', in *Acta Congressus Mariologici-Maraani Internationalis in Republica Melitensi Anno 1983 Celebrati* (Rome: Pontificia Academia Mariana Internationalis, 1987).

K. Stevenson, *Covenant of Grace Renewed: A Vision of the Eucharist in the Seventeenth Century* (London: Darton, Longman & Todd, 1994).

14

The Virgin Mary in the Liturgical Texts of the Anglican Communion[1]

Henry VIII

At the risk of oversimplification, it can be said that the first phase of the English Reformation under King Henry VIII (1509–47) did not involve liturgical change. His quarrel with Rome was to sever communion between the English Church and the See of Rome, when he had himself declared Supreme Head of the Church of England, which was for him no mere honorific title but a grim and tyrannical reality. He combined strong antipapalism (though his earlier fidelity to Rome and his fierce repudiation of Luther's sacramental teaching had earned him the title *Fidei Defensor* – Defender of the Faith – from a grateful Pope) with very conservative religious views and strong opposition to Protestantism. It was above all his need for money that led him to suppress the Religious Orders and to despoil shrines and sanctuaries – among them the Shrine of Our Lady of Walsingham – but there were among his bishops many who, under the influence of Erasmus, were in favour of some reforms, notably in the *cultus* of the saints. Others of his bishops – and above all Thomas Cranmer, Archbishop of Canterbury – had been won over to Protestant doctrines but were obliged to keep these largely to themselves to avoid incurring the dangerous hostility of the King.

---

[1] This article was first published in *De Cultu Mariano Saeculo XX: Acta of the International Mariological-Marian Congress, Częstochowa, 1996* (Vatican City: Pontificia Academia Mariana Internationalis, 1999), pp. 213–30. Except where stated, the footnotes are by the author.

Towards the end of his reign the King allowed some cautious changes in the liturgy, among them an English Litany to be sung in procession before the Sunday Latin High Mass. This Litany was the work of Archbishop Thomas Cranmer and is substantially the same Litany that appeared later in the English Prayer Book, but in its 1544 version it contained the following three clauses:

> Holy Virgin Mary, Mother of God our Saviour Jesu Christ, pray for us.
> All holy angels and archangels and all holy orders of blessed spirits, pray for us.
> All holy Patriarchs, and Prophets, Apostles, and Martyrs, Confessors and Virgins and all the blessed company of heaven, pray for us.

The First Prayer Book (1549)

Henry VIII was succeeded by his son Edward VI (1547–53), who at the time of his accession was only nine years old. During his reign the Protestant party took over power both in Church and State. Liturgical changes were soon introduced and their chief architect, a liturgist of no mean skill and a translator from Latin into English of real genius, was Archbishop Cranmer. The First English *Book of Common Prayer* (a single book combining Missal, Breviary, Ritual and Pontifical) was issued in 1549 and was – at least at first sight – comparatively conservative. For our present purposes we must restrict our inspection of the new liturgy to the place of the Blessed Virgin and note the following features:

1 *The Calendar* notes only major feasts. Although both the 'Purification of St Mary the Virgin' (as it is styled) and the 'Annunciation of the Virgin Mary' (as it is styled) are retained, the Assumption and all other Marian feasts have disappeared. The Virgin Mary is, however, mentioned in the Collect and in the Proper Preface of Christmas.

2 *Evening Prayer:* the Magnificat is ordered to be said or sung daily at the Office of Evensong.
3 *The Litany* is practically identical with that issued in 1544 in the previous reign, but the three invocations and their response – 'Pray for us' – have been removed. From this point no direct invocation of the saints is found in any official and mandatory liturgical text of the Church of England. It is also clear that from this time the *Hail Mary* was removed even from authorized books of private devotion.
4 *At the Eucharist* the Intercession includes not only the living but also the departed and the saints in glory in these words:

> And here we do give unto thee most high praise and hearty thanks for the wonderful grace and virtue declared in all thy saints from the beginning of the world: And chiefly in the glorious and most blessed Virgin Mary, mother of thy Son Jesu Christ our Lord and God, and in the holy Patriarchs, Prophets, Apostles and Martyrs, whose examples, O Lord, and steadfastness in thy faith and keeping thy holy commandments, grant us to follow.
>
> We commend unto thy mercy, O Lord, all other thy servants, which are departed hence from us with the sign of faith and now do rest in the sleep of peace. Grant unto them, we beseech thee, thy mercy and everlasting peace, and that, at the day of the general resurrection, we and all they which be of the mystical body of thy Son may altogether be set on his right hand and hear that his most joyful voice: 'Come unto me ...'

The Second Prayer Book (1552)

In 1552 the First Prayer Book was replaced by the Second, one of stark and uncompromising Protestantism. It had perhaps been Cranmer's intention all along to proceed by stages, but the short life of the 1549 Prayer Book was ensured not only by the vigorous criticism of certain foreign Protestant theologians who had taken refuge in England at this time – among whom was a Polish nobleman John Laski (or à Lasco) – but by the fact that some of the more catholic-minded bishops tried to quote this liturgy in defence of traditional doctrine. If we compare the Second Prayer Book with the First, we find

1. in the *Calendar* there is no change with regard to Marian feasts,
2. that at *Evening Prayer*, although the Magnificat is retained, an alternative Canticle (Psalm 98) is allowed in its place,
3. that the Intercession in the *Eucharistic Liturgy* is now a prayer 'for the whole state of Christ's Church militant here in earth' and contains neither thanksgiving for the saints nor prayer for the departed.

Edward VI died in 1553 at the age of 15 and was succeeded by his half sister Mary (1553–58), who not only abolished all the English service books but, in just over a year, was able to see the Church and Nation of England reconciled with Rome. But this was not to last very long, for Mary herself died, without issue, four years later.

Elizabeth I

The new sovereign was Elizabeth I (1558–1603), half sister to Edward VI and to Mary I. An astute, hard-headed and intelligent woman, she would personally have favoured a return to something very like the state of religion at her father's death or in the early years of her brother's reign but was obliged to accept a more Protestant settlement than her own preferences indicated. It was in fact the second, rather than the first, Prayer Book of Edward VI which was restored, though with a number of significant changes to make it less offensive to her catholic-minded subjects.

In 1561 a new Calendar was promulgated, which distinguished between red-letter days (printed in red), which had a full liturgical observance, and black-letter days (printed in black) for which no liturgical provision at all was made. Nevertheless the list of black-letter days included three Marian feasts; her Visitation on 2 July, her Nativity on 8 September and her Conception (not described as Immaculate either here or in the mediaeval Calendar of the English Church) on 8 December. Their presence had little significance at the time, but was much later to furnish an occasion for their observance and to stimulate Marian devotion. This new Calendar remained substantially the same until the twentieth century. The Assumption, however, remained excluded from all these Calendars, only retaining a shadowy hold on the Anglican tradition by being retained in the Calendar of the University of Oxford.

Gains and Losses

Before going on to further changes in liturgical texts in the seventeenth century, it is probably time to pause for a moment to draw up a balance sheet of gains and losses.

On the negative side, we must note the orgies of iconoclasm – anticipated by the destruction under Henry VIII of shrines and images which were judged to have attracted superstitious veneration; these swept the country under Edward VI and again under Elizabeth I and were to be repeated and completed in the seventeenth century during the Civil War between Charles I and Parliament. We must also note the suppression of pilgrimages and the banning of rosaries; the removal of the *Hail Mary* from even books of authorized private devotion and the progressive elimination of Marian references from the Anglican liturgy.

On the positive side, some vestiges and reminders of Marian devotion were at no time absent from the Church of England. Cathedrals, colleges and chapels retained their dedication to St Mary the Virgin; a few statues – though nearly all on the outside rather than the inside of these buildings – were retained, for example at Eton, at Winchester and at New

College, Oxford; and in many more churches stained-glass windows were suffered to remain and so allowed some kind of Marian icon to impress itself consciously or unconsciously upon the worshippers. One of the leaders of the nineteenth-century Oxford Movement, John Keble, was to acknowledge the strong influence of the mediaeval glass in Fairford Church, where he worshipped as a boy, upon his mind and his imagination. To these must be added the use of the Magnificat at the Office of Evening Prayer and the remaining Marian references in the Liturgy – especially on Christmas Day and the Feasts of the Purification and Annunciation. Even in the *Book of Homilies* (authorized texts to be read in place of the sermon in those churches where ministers 'have not the gift of preaching sufficiently to instruct the people'), which were written under extreme Protestant and anti-Roman influence in the sixteenth century, we can find references to Mary as, for example, 'this most noble and most virtuous Lady'.

It is important to give an *honest* picture. I am not trying to delude you into thinking that the Blessed Virgin was given due and proper honour in the Church of England at this time: I *am* trying to help you to understand how later on a certain richness of Marian devotion could be reintroduced into the Church of England, since, although the tree of catholic doctrine and devotion appeared to have been cut down to the roots in the sixteenth century, there was enough life in those roots to allow a genuine Marian piety to emerge from the bare and wintry ground and to produce fruit when a less inclement climate would prevail.

The Caroline Divines

And, in fact, the seventeenth century was to see a striking movement which was at one and the same time a reaction against Calvinism and a return to more catholic ideas. The high-church revival of the so-called Caroline Divines (theologians who flourished in the reigns of Charles I, 1625–49, and

Charles II, 1660–85) had been made possible not only through the pioneering work of a theologian of real genius, whom it is indeed possible to call 'the Father of Anglicanism', Richard Hooker (c. 1554–1600), but from the fact that from the beginning the authoritative foundation documents of Anglicanism made appeal not to *Scriptura sola* but to the sovereign authority of Scripture as interpreted by the Creeds, the definitions of the early Councils and the consensus of the Fathers. It would be dangerously misleading to assert that the Caroline Divines formed a homogeneous group with an identical theological platform; it can, however, safely be affirmed that they were all deeply under patristic influence, that they looked to the Greek Fathers as much (if not more) than to the Latin Fathers, and that their centre of interest was no longer an exclusive concentration on the Doctrine of Salvation and the controversies concerning grace, justification and predestination but had moved to the doctrine of the Incarnation. It can also be said of them that their approach was less schematic than that of their sixteenth-century predecessors; it was devout, imaginative and sacramental and gave priority to the image over the concept. There were notable poets among them (such as John Donne and George Herbert) as well as great preachers and theologians. It saw also a revival of liturgical splendour – and it was this which notably aroused the fury of the Puritans; one of the charges against William Laud, Archbishop of Canterbury, who was executed in 1645 during the Civil War, was the new baroque porch erected under his influence outside the University Church of St Mary the Virgin, Oxford, with its statue of the Crowned Virgin.

The Blessed Virgin began in the seventeenth century to be honoured more publicly in the Church of England, notably in some of the sermons preached on Christmas Day, on the Purification and on the Annunciation by some of the great preachers of this period. But although many of them did not hesitate to speak of her as Our Lady, as Mother of God, as Ever-Virgin, as the Second Eve, even as Star of the Sea; to extol her faith and her obedience as models for all Christians to imitate, and to deplore what they saw as Puritan irreverence ('when our Lord is wounded through our Lady's sides', as one of them, Mark Frank, said in a sermon on the Annunciation),[2] yet they still considered any direct invocation of Our Lady, as in the *Hail Mary*, to be contrary to scriptural and primitive teaching. Only two of them, to my knowledge, were able to break through this powerful inhibition, which was to act as such a strong brake on Marian devotion: Herbert Thorndike (prebendary of Westminster) and William Forbes, Bishop of Edinburgh. Thorndike made an important distinction between three kinds of prayer used in honouring the saints. First, there are those addressed to God, asking him to hear the prayers of saints on our behalf, secondly, those addressed to the saints requesting them to pray for us; thirdly, those which seek directly from the saints what only God can give. The first he approves and commends (though even this practice, sometimes called *comprecation*, was not at that time to be found in any Anglican liturgical text); the third he condemns strongly; the second he discusses at some length without being able either to commend or condemn. Bishop Forbes, on the other hand, feels able to accept the second kind of prayer (a request addressed to the saints asking them to pray for us), describing it as a 'very ancient custom received in the universal Church, as well Greek as Latin'. It is also worth noting that a book of private prayers, *Preces Privatae*, composed by the saintly and influential Lancelot Andrewes (Bishop successively of Chichester, Ely and Winchester), contains a phrase that is taken directly from the Byzantine liturgy:

Commemorating the all-holy, immaculate, more than blessed Mother of God and ever-virgin Mary, with all saints, let us commend ourselves and one another and all our life unto Christ God ...

---

[2] M. Frank, *Sermons by Mark Frank, D.D.* (Oxford: John Henry Parker, 1849), Vol. 2: A Sermon on the Annunciation, p. 35.

The Scottish Liturgy of 1637

Remaining for the moment in the seventeenth century, we need to record two revisions of the Prayer Book in that century. The first of these was the Scottish Liturgy of 1637. King James VI of Scotland, who became James I of England in 1603, had already restored episcopacy to what had then been the Presbyterian Church of Scotland; his son Charles I followed this up by attempting to impose upon Scotland a Prayer Book. This was not the current English Prayer Book, but one which, in many respects, marked a return to the more catholic temper of Edward VI's first Prayer Book of 1549. I have three comments to make about it:

- ❖ Firstly, its publication caused riots which led to a rising in Scotland. This in turn led to the abolition not only of this Liturgy but also of episcopacy, which in turn precipitated the outbreak of Civil War in England in 1642 and the consequent downfall and suppression of Anglicanism in England until the Restoration of the Monarchy under Charles II in 1660.
- ❖ Secondly, the publication of a Scottish Liturgy marks the beginning of the principle that the English Liturgy is not necessarily authoritative in other countries, but that, as it would be expressed today, each self-governing church of the Anglican Communion is free to authorize its own liturgy. In the 1630s it was the Scottish bishops who insisted that Scotland should have its own Book and not simply adopt the English Book.
- ❖ Thirdly, this Scottish Liturgy, although doomed to extinction almost from the moment of its birth, was to have considerable influence on the reform of the English Prayer Book in 1662 and on subsequent Scottish and American liturgies. For our present purpose it is important to note that in the Intercessions in the eucharistic rite a commemoration of the saints, omitted in 1552, was restored although without naming the Blessed Virgin Mary.

The English Prayer Book of 1662

Turning now to the English revision of 1662, still the official Liturgy of the Church of England (for all the newer rites are, strictly speaking, 'alternative' services), we have, again for our present purpose, to note both a somewhat abbreviated version of the commemoration of the saints found in the Scottish Liturgy and also the fact that in a new Table of Proper Lessons the Feast of the Annunciation is described as the 'Annunciation of our Lady', the first officially authorized use of that title in an Anglican Prayer Book.

The second half of the seventeenth century and the eighteenth century saw an onslaught from Socinian or Unitarian ideas upon the churches which issued from, or were strongly influenced by, the Reformation. The English Presbyterians, who, at one point early in the Civil War, after the abolition of the Prayer Book and the episcopate, looked as if they were going to take the place of Anglicanism and who, though now weaker, still dominated the resistance to Anglicanism at the Restoration of the Monarchy and of Anglicanism in the years following 1660, gradually found themselves even more gravely weakened by the inroads made in their ranks by the Unitarians. Some of the more rationalist or 'latitudinarian' among the Anglican clergy were also attracted by Unitarian ideas. It was, however, the strong emphasis upon the Mystery of the Holy Trinity and upon the Doctrine of the Incarnation in the *Book of Common Prayer* (of which some examples, to name but a few, were the constant repetition of the *Gloria Patri*, the use of the Apostles' Creed and even on some feasts of the *Quicunque vult* at the Daily Office and of the Nicene Creed at the Eucharist, the retention of the *Te Deum* and the *Gloria in excelsis* and the prominent place of Trinity Sunday and the Sundays after Trinity in the Calendar) which made it difficult for Unitarian ideas to take root in Anglicanism and which made it also impossible to ignore completely the place of the Blessed Virgin Mary in the economy of salvation.

The Eighteenth Century

In the eighteenth century the catholic tradition in the Church of England, which had seemed to flourish in the preceding century, was seriously weakened by the schism of the Nonjurors – those bishops and priests (and their followers) whose exalted doctrine of kingship and whose inability to swear allegiance to William and Mary in 1689 after the deposition and flight of the Roman Catholic King James II (to whom they considered they were still bound by the oaths of allegiance they had taken to him) caused them to be deposed from office. Some of these Nonjurors produced liturgies which looked to the 1549 Prayer Book and even to the Eastern rites, but in the official Church of England there was not only no change in the liturgy but a period of liturgical stagnation and decadence. Only one phenomenon deserves to be recorded here and even that only for the promise which its later development was to bring, namely the growing popularity of hymns and of hymn singing, though these at first were confined to those in the Evangelical tradition in Anglicanism, to the Methodists and to the other Protestant Nonconformist bodies.

The Oxford Movement

When we turn to the Oxford Movement – also known as the Tractarian Movement or the Catholic Revival – which began in Oxford in the 1830s, we are confronted with a paradox. The Movement at first strenuously claimed that it was *not* innovating, that it was simply giving new life to a tradition that had been gloriously promoted by the Caroline Divines and the Nonjurors but had more recently been forgotten. This explains the strong anti-Roman emphasis of that initial period, partly genuine and partly a matter of self-defence in the face of accusations of 'popery': it also explains their determination to practise strict compliance with the text and rubrics of the 1662 *Book of Common Prayer* (for example in reviving the public recitation of the Daily Office) and to give as catholic an interpretation as possible to that book.

Increasingly, however, they became conscious of its limitation and defects, no longer able to call it, as some of the more old-fashioned high churchmen did, 'the most perfect upon earth', but referring to it rather as merely 'crumbs from the Apostles' table'. They came too to appreciate the riches of the Breviary and to supplement the Prayer Book offices by reciting the Breviary offices. Most did this privately, but it was done publicly by John Henry Newman and his little group of disciples at Littlemore. But at this stage one significant change was made. All the time that he remained in the Church of England Newman felt it his duty either to omit any prayers or antiphons directly addressed to Our Lady and the saints or at least to change '*Ora pro nobis*' into '*Oret pro nobis*'.

Interestingly, it was one of the most cautious and moderate of the early Tractarians, John Keble, who first defended the use of the *Hail Mary* in a poem of 1846 entitled (significantly) 'Mother Out of Sight':

Therefore as kneeling day by day
We to our Father duteous pray,
So unforbidden may we speak
An *Ave* to Christ's Mother meek:
(As children with 'good morrow' come
To elders in some happy home:
Inviting so the saintly host above
With our unworthiness to pray in love.[3]

From these cautions beginnings we can trace a gradual increase of Marian sensitivity, theological reflection and devotion. Contributory factors in this development are the following:

1 Like the Caroline Divines, the Tractarians and their disciples had an unschematic, poetic and sacramental approach

---

[3] The full text can be found most accessibly in J. Keble, *The Christian Year and Other Poems* (London: Church Literature Association, 1976), pp. 216–18.

to the Faith. In the case of the Tractarian Movement this was enhanced by its connection with the nineteenth-century romantic and gothic revival and its idealization of the Middle Ages. It was impossible to ignore the place of Our Lady in mediaeval art and so in the church art of the later nineteenth century she began increasingly to be depicted in stained glass, in mosaic and in sculpture.

2 The earlier high-church appeal to the consensus of the Early Church often seemed to stop at the Fourth Ecumenical Council of Chalcedon in 451. This seemed to the Tractarians and to their successors to be unnaturally restrictive and their criterion moved to the consensus of the Undivided Church, which, as they understood it, meant the common tradition of the Greek East and the Latin West until their tragic separation. So Lord Halifax, a disciple of Dr Pusey and Dr Liddon, who had a firm if unsophisticated grasp of the essentials of the faith, could write to a fellow layman:

> As I grew older and was brought face to face with the fact that Christians were divided on matters of faith, I do not think I asked myself whether this or that commended itself to my judgment, or what might seem to be the more probable view, but I endeavoured to make sure what it was the whole Church had taught on the subject, what were matters of faith, what, however good and true in themselves, were only matters of opinion, what, in regard to such latter matters, had been the generally accepted belief and practice of the Church; and where I found the whole Church had definitely spoken, or that this or that was the generally accepted rule of the Church, *there*, as far as I was concerned, the matter ended.[4]

In view of this confession of faith, we can well understand not only Lord Halifax's strong commitment to the cause of Christian unity but the fact that at the beginning of the

---

4 From a letter to Lord Wolmer of March 1919 reproduced in J. G. Lockhart, *Charles Lindley, Viscount Halifax* (London: Geoffrey Bles, 1935), Vol. 1, p. 82.

twentieth century he became President of one of the earliest Marian societies in the Church of England and much later, in his extreme old age, a Guardian of the restored Shrine of Our Lady of Walsingham.

3 The growth of interest in the Breviary was not unconnected with the restoration of the Religious Life for men and women in the Church of England, strongly encouraged by the early Tractarians, notably by Newman and Pusey. The development of community life always involved a strong liturgical life and the corporate recitation of the Office, with the Anglican offices of Morning and Evening Prayer either replaced or supplemented by the Breviary offices. It is no accident, I believe, that one of the earliest sisterhoods (and one still surviving today), founded in 1848, took the title of 'The Community of St Mary the Virgin'.

4 The early Tractarians were not particularly interested in ceremonial development, were very reserved in their attitude to the revival of eucharistic vestments and were opposed to going beyond what was provided in the *Book of Common Prayer*. Their successors, however, often called the 'Ritualists', took things many steps further. In most cases they were zealous and hard-working parish priests, often working in the poorest districts of the great cities, and they felt it pastorally essential to translate Tractarian teaching, for example on the Eucharist, into outward and visible expression. They also began to restore the daily celebration of the Eucharist and so came up against the need to find propers for use on those black-letter saints' days (including the Visitation, Nativity and Conception of our Lady) which were to be found in the Prayer Book Calendar but for which no liturgical provision had been made. Their solution was either to 'borrow' material from mediaeval or modern Latin rites or, at a later stage, to persuade some of the more sympathetic bishops to authorize collects and readings for use in their diocese.

5 At first the Tractarians were equally reticent about the use of hymns, but in a relatively short time they found themselves

captivated by the beauty and richness of the Latin sequences and breviary hymns and even Newman tried his hand at translating some of them. In the sixteenth century Cranmer had confessed that he had no gift for translating poetry, though we now honour him as a brilliant translator of Latin prose, and this may explain why only one verse hymn, the *Veni Creator*, is found in the Prayer Book. What Cranmer was for Latin prose, John Mason Neale (1818–66), the leading Cambridge figure in the Oxford Movement, was to become for Latin poetry and even for Greek, and today our hymn books are full of his translations of Greek and Latin hymns. Most of these found their way into *The Hymnal Noted* of 1852 and the more celebrated *Hymns Ancient and Modern*, first published in 1861. But it was the publication of *The English Hymnal* in 1906 which was to provoke the fiercest controversy, for it was in this book that appeared for the first time an English translation of *Ave maris stella*. This hymn book and its successor *The New English Hymnal*, first published in 1986, contain not only *Ave maris stella*; *Quem terra, pontus, aethera*; *O gloriosa femina* and *Stabat mater dolorosa* but also a number of more modern hymns composed in English and a striking hymn composed by Bishop Thomas Ken in the seventeenth century, containing a verse which points towards the Assumption:

> Heaven with transcendent joys her entrance graced,
> Next to his throne her Son his Mother placed;
> And here below, now she's of heaven possest,
> All generations are to call her blest.[5]

The Church of England, unlike some other churches of the Anglican Communion, has never officially authorized any

---

5 A remarkable verse in the same poem (not printed in any of our hymn books) seems to echo the doctrine of the Immaculate Conception:

The Holy Ghost his Temple in her built,
Cleansed from congenial, kept from mortal guilt,
And from the moment that her blood was fired
Into her heart celestial love inspired.

hymn book or hymn books, but there is no doubt that the singing of hymns at liturgical services makes a profound impression (as great, if not greater, than the words of the liturgy itself) on those who sing them.

The 1928 Prayer Book

Early in the twentieth century it had become clear that the old wineskins of the 1662 Prayer Book were bursting under the influence of so much new wine and that some liturgical revision was necessary. The Tractarian influence was not the only one at work here; nearly everyone felt the need for some shortening of the services and some adaptation to the changed situation of the twentieth century, while more liberal Anglicans wanted, for example, to drop the compulsory use of the *Quicunque vult*. The process of revision culminated in the Proposed Prayer Book of 1928, but, largely, under the pressure of protestant hostility, the British Parliament refused to give it legal authorization, although most of the bishops condoned or even actively encouraged its use. This Prayer Book did authorize propers for 2 July (The Visitation), 8 September (The Nativity) and 8 December (The Conception of the Blessed Virgin Mary) and included a fuller thanksgiving for the saints (but without naming any of them, even Our Lady, in the eucharistic liturgy). However, a revision of the Scottish Prayer Book, authorized in 1929 (and, since the Anglican Church in Scotland was not the 'established' Church of that country, it did not require parliamentary sanction), did include a prayer which gave thanks 'for The Blessed Virgin Mary, for the holy Patriarchs, Prophets, Apostles, and Martyrs, and for all other thy righteous servants' and went on to ask that we might be 'encouraged by their example, strengthened by their fellowship, and [this is the important phrase] aided by their prayers'.

The 1958 Lambeth Conference

I would exhaust both your patience and the time allotted me if I tried to describe all the liturgical revisions that have taken place in all the churches of the Anglican Communion since that time. Before I move on to describe those liturgies at present in use or about to be authorized in the Anglican Communion (and you will, I hope, forgive me if I concentrate on the Church to which I belong, the Church of England), I must briefly report on the Lambeth Conference (the meeting of all the bishops of the Anglican Communion) of 1958, which, at the beginning of the present round of liturgical revision, listed first a number of features in the official liturgical texts felt to be 'essential to the safeguarding of the unity of the Anglican Communion' and then a number of features in those same texts felt to be 'most effective in maintaining the traditional doctrinal emphasis of the worship and witness of the Anglican Communion'. One item in this second list is, I quote, 'the honouring of the Saints without invocation', meaning by 'invocation' in this context a direct address to the saints.

Other Churches of the Anglican Communion

Let me now attempt a brief analysis of the place of Our Lady in the liturgies of the other churches of the Anglican Communion before returning in my final section to the present position in the Church of England.

There are listed in the 1996 edition of *The Church of England Year Book* thirty-seven self-governing churches and provinces of the Anglican Communion. As far as I can ascertain, 15 August is to be found in the calendars of Scotland, Wales, the United States, Australia, Canada, the West Indies, Brazil and Papua New Guinea, though with a variety of titles and degrees of solemnity. It is not found in the present calendars of Ireland, South Africa or North India (and 15 August is India's National Day). Most of the churches which do not observe 15 August keep 8 September as the principal feast of Our Lady. Many churches have a proper preface of the Blessed Virgin Mary in the Order for the Eucharist, but there will in any case always be a preface of Christmas or of the Incarnation which can be used on her days. There is specific provision for mentioning Our Lady in the Eucharistic Prayers in use in some of these churches and, although there is almost universally great flexibility about the forms used for the Prayers of the Faithful, it is specifically provided for in many of these that they should end with a thanksgiving for the saints, who may, of course, be named. One of the most uniformly catholic-minded churches in the Communion is the Anglican Church of Papua New Guinea. Its official Prayer Book (published in 1991) contains the texts of the *Hail Mary*, the *Angelus* and the *Regina Coeli* and its Collect for the Falling Asleep of the Blessed Virgin Mary (15 August) runs as follows:

> Lord God, we rejoice today in the festival of blessed Mary. She is the pattern of your Church, and obeyed your call and carried Christ for the world's salvation. May her prayers support us, and may we share with her the glory of your heavenly Kingdom where Jesus reigns with you and the Holy Spirit now and for ever.

The Church of England

In the Church of England the process of trial use for authorized experimental liturgical rites culminated in the publication in 1980 of the *Alternative Service Book* (ASB), so called because it did not replace the 1662 Prayer Book but co-existed with it. In this way more conservative congregations were allowed to retain the old rites for some or all of their services and, since the Prayer Book itself was not altered, the need for parliamentary approval of the new rites was avoided. The *Alternative Service Book* endorses the principle, generally accepted throughout the Anglican Communion, that the Presentation of Christ (2 February) and the Annunciation (25 March) are really feasts of Our Lord and that therefore some other day has to be found to serve as the principal festival of our Lady. In the *Alternative Service Book* this is located on 8 September and there is no place for 15 August; place, however, is found for the Visitation on 31 May, and Mary is also honoured on the Fourth Sunday of Advent. A fine proper preface is provided for use on days when she is commemorated; it runs as follows:

> And now we give you thanks because in choosing the blessed Virgin Mary to be the mother of your Son you have exalted the humble and meek. Your angel hailed her as most highly favoured; with all generations we call her blessed, and with her we rejoice and magnify your holy name.

Since the authorization of the ASB in 1980 a great deal of optional supplementary material has been published; most of these texts are 'commended' by the House of Bishops of the Church of England, which gives them authority, but not the same degree of authority as the official liturgical books. One of these books is called *The Promise of His Glory*;[6] it contains seasonal material from All Saints to Candlemas. There is particularly rich provision for Candlemas, but I would like to draw your attention to two other texts which are to be found in it.

The first of these is a form for use at the *Lucernarium* (The Service of Light) which may precede the office of Evening Prayer. Here is the text provided for the Blessed Virgin Mary:

> Blessed are you, Lord our God, King of the universe:
> to you be glory and praise for ever!
> In the greatness of your mercy you chose the Virgin Mary
> to be the mother of your only Son.
> In her obedience the day of our redemption dawned

---

6 *The Promise of His Glory: Services and Prayers for the Season from All Saints to Candlemas, commended by the House of Bishops of the General Synod of the Church of England* (London: Church House Publishing, 1991).

when by the overshadowing of your Holy Spirit
he took our flesh and dwelt in the darkness of her womb.
In her your glory shines as in the burning bush,
and so we call her blessed with every generation.
With her we rejoice in your salvation
and ponder in our hearts the mystery of your love.
May we bear with her the piercing sword of sorrow
in the hope that we like her may share the joy of heaven.
As now we join our praise with hers, blessed among all women,
create in us a heart of love obedient to your will,
for you are Lord and you are our God for ever. *Amen.*

The second is a text for use on the fourth Sunday of Advent at the lighting of the fourth candle on the Advent Wreath. The introduction into our churches of the Advent Wreath is a custom that has come to us from Scandinavia and Germany through the Lutheran tradition. The text is as follows:

Lord Jesus, light of the world,
blessed is Gabriel, who brought good news;
blessed is Mary, your mother and ours.
Bless your Church preparing for Christmas;
and bless us your children, who long for your coming.[7]

These words are, I believe, of particular significance. They are meant to be said by the whole congregation and they do very clearly affirm that Mary is not only Christ's mother but ours as well.

Another volume which has been published recently and is of an experimental character is a book for the Divine Office called *Celebrating Common Prayer*. It came out in 1992 and carries a foreword by the Archbishop of Canterbury. Although it has no formal authorization, many bishops are encouraging

---

7 *Editor's note*: this text is now included in the Common Worship prayers for use at the Advent Wreath: *Common Worship: Times and Seasons* (London: Church House Publishing, 2006), p. 54.

its use for the Daily Office. It provides a number of interesting Marian texts, including the *Angelus*, the *Regina Coeli* and the *Salve Regina*.

Meanwhile, the official work of revising the Liturgy is being done by means of texts prepared by the Liturgical Commission of the Church of England, which are being submitted for approval to the General Synod of the Church. In July of this year [1996] a new Calendar, new Lectionary and new Collects were approved. It is important to note the implications of this decision for the place of our Lady. Her principal Festival now becomes 15 August, but the day is simply called 'The Blessed Virgin Mary', with no mention of Assumption or Dormition. The Collect, however, does allude to Mary's entry into glory:

> Almighty and everlasting God,
> who looked upon the lowliness of the Blessed Virgin Mary
> and chose her to be the mother of your only Son:
> grant that we who are redeemed by his blood
> may share with her in the glory of your eternal kingdom;
> through Jesus Christ your Son our Lord,
> who is alive and reigns with you,
> in the unity of the Holy Spirit,
> one God, now and for ever.

Our Lady has one other festival of major rank, The Visit of the Blessed Virgin Mary to Elizabeth on 31 May and two lesser festivals, her Birth (8 September) and her Conception (8 December).[8]

The subject given to me concerns liturgical texts, but you will not need me to remind you that liturgy is not exclusively a matter of texts: it is equally a matter of performance – or, more properly, of celebration – and this is deeply affected by the con-

---

8 *Editor's note*: *Common Worship: Festivals* (London: Church House Publishing, 2008) includes a full set of propers for 31 May (pp. 69–73), the Collect (quoted above) and readings for 15 August and, in the Common of the Saints, a full set of propers for use on 15 August and at any other Eucharist in honour of Our Lady – including on 8 September and 8 December where these days are celebrated (pp. 268–76).

text in which it occurs. The advance which is demonstrated by these new texts has been made possible by the following factors (among others):

1. The changed ecumenical climate and the greater exposure of Anglicanism not only to the doctrinal and liturgical tradition of the Eastern Churches but to Roman Catholicism renewed (not least in its Mariology) by the Second Vatican Council. The foundation in the United Kingdom in 1967 of the Ecumenical Society of the Blessed Virgin Mary has transformed attitudes – and not only those of Anglicans. It is important to note the influential place in the work of this society of scholars from the churches of the Reformation and it would have astonished Christians of an earlier generation to learn that one of the best recent books on the Rosary in English, *Five for Sorrow, Ten for Joy* (published in 1971), was written by a Methodist minister, Neville Ward.
2. The restoration of the mediaeval Shrine of Our Lady of Walsingham in Norfolk between the two world wars was viewed at the time as a phenomenon that would appeal only to the most extreme Anglo-Catholics. The popularity of Walsingham today – a place of pilgrimage that attracts Roman Catholics, Orthodox and Anglicans – has done much to further Anglican devotion to Mary in parishes all over England.
3. The increased interest in and appreciation of sacred art, accompanied by the virtual disappearance of the former hostility to images, has done much to further the visual presence of our Lady in the churches and cathedrals of our land. It is exceptional to find a chapel of Our Lady in any of our cathedrals, for example, that does not contain a fairly prominent statue or icon of the Blessed Virgin.
4. Our Lady has come back into our churches not only through the visual arts but through music. There has been a re-discovery of the rich heritage of Marian music to be found in both the English and the wider European repertoire, especially in plainchant and in renaissance polyphony.

In many cathedrals it is easier to introduce the *Hail Mary* as an anthem, sung (in Latin!) and set to music by one of our great composers, than as a prayer. However, there is also music by some leading composers of the present day, such as Benjamin Britten and John Tavener, that has been inspired by Marian texts, Latin, Byzantine and English.[9]

5 Lastly, there is the not inconsiderable influence exerted by Christian feminists. Some of this has been hostile to traditional Mariology, but a lot of it has been positive and has led many, who do not in any way belong to the Catholic tradition in Anglicanism, to explore more sympathetically the place of Mary in Christian theology and worship.

Conclusion

If the phenomenon of contemporary Anglicanism is confusing for those on the *outside*, I have to tell you that it is almost equally confusing for those on the *inside*. In particular, it is difficult for those who stand firmly within the catholic tradition in Anglicanism to discern the future direction of Anglicanism and so to perceive precisely where their own duty lies.

The story I have been telling has been one, on the whole, of real progress. But you will be aware that other developments within Anglicanism, such as the ordination of women to the priesthood and the episcopate in so many churches of the Anglican Communion, an increasing liberalism on doctrinal and moral issues, which means that one can no longer take for granted the Trinitarian and Christological orthodoxy of all our leaders and theologians, and an increasing liturgical diversity – in places amounting to lawlessness, have led to a crisis of Anglican identity within our Communion and a serious lack of confidence on the part of our partners in ecumenical dialogue.

---

[9] A particularly striking example is the Magnificat (Collegium Regale) of 1986 by the Orthodox composer John Tavener, written for use at Evensong in King's College Chapel, Cambridge. The Byzantine refrain 'Greater in honour than the cherubim' is interpolated between the verses.

If the advances I have tried to catalogue are seen as merely permissive ('We will allow the Anglo-Catholics to believe and do what they want if *they* will let us believe and do what *we* want'), then such advances are merely delusions, even dangerous delusions. For those of us in the Catholic tradition who still remain (but not without difficulty) *inside* Anglicanism, the continuing task of discernment is both painful and difficult. We ask for your prayers and for those of the Mother of all Christians.

PART 4

The Blessed Virgin Mary in Ecumenical Dialogue

15

Mary and the Church: The Ecumenical Dialogue and Our Lady (1964)[1]

At the second session of the Second Vatican Council one of the most controversial decisions (passed by a narrow margin of forty votes) was the abandonment of the idea of a separate *schema* on Our Lady and the adoption of the suggestion that there should instead be a chapter devoted to her in the *schema* on the Church. It might not be immediately apparent why such a suggestion and such a decision should seem so controversial and arouse in some circles so many heated and passionate arguments; to understand the situation it is necessary to take a look at the background of recent theological thinking about the Blessed Virgin and its relation to the ecumenical movement.

It used to be thought that here in the sphere of Mariology the boundary walls between Catholic and Protestant could be seen at their most massive and clearly defined. In fact even here positions have been changing, both from the Catholic and the Protestant side. What are the changes apparent in the Roman Catholic approach? First of all, the increasing dialogue with Protestants has helped Roman Catholics to be very sensitive to exaggerations or deformations in language and devotional practice that not only give offence to the most sympathetic of Protestants but endanger the purity of the faith of Catholics themselves. Writers like Père Bouyer and Père Villain have been

[1] First published as 'The Ecumenical Dialogue and Our Lady', *Walsingham Review*, 13 (Sept. 1964), pp. 6–10.

prominent in this work but the best known example to most people is Professor Hans Küng's *The Council and Reunion*, where there is a very frank and honest examination of Protestant charges of exaggeration and superstition.[2] Even John XXIII found it necessary to utter a warning: 'The Madonna is not pleased when she is put above her Son.' Secondly, Roman Catholic theologians are aware of and concerned about an apparent clash and a real tension between the movement of biblical and liturgical renewal and the so-called 'Marian Movement', both of them movements of vitality in the Church today but seemingly pulling in opposite directions. Liturgical piety is essentially objective, sacramental and communal; Marian piety seems to be essentially subjective and individualistic. The solution these theologians are seeking to develop and work out is a union of the two movements by a clear demonstration of the fact that the mystery of the Church and the mystery of Mary are inseparably bound up together. Thirdly (and in a sense following on from this second point), there has been an increasing awareness of the danger of a Mariology evolving as it were in a vacuum in isolation from the mainstream of theological, biblical and liturgical thinking. A distinguished Marian theologian, Padre J. A. de Aldama, SJ, has admitted that Mariology is 'a theological subject which lends itself more than many others to exaggerations and deviations'; it is realized that a healthy Mariology must constantly refer itself to two essential poles, the theology of Christ and the theology of the Church. An important influence here has been the contact with Eastern Orthodoxy, which has always given a very high place in theology and devotion to the *Theotokos* (Mother of God) but has had better success in avoiding distortions.

Alongside this re-appraisal of Mariology in the Roman Catholic Church – and it would be wrong to interpret this as a retreat, except perhaps in the resolve to avoid further Marian definitions for the sake of unity – there has been a corresponding re-appraisal in some circles in the Protestant churches, partly in

2 Hans Küng, *The Council and Reunion* (London: Sheed and Ward, 1961), pp. 182–7.

the form of a response to the 'new look' on the Roman side and to the challenge so well expressed by Hans Küng:

> But even in Mariology and Marian devotion, *peccatum per excessum*, the sin of excess, is not the only possible one: there is a *peccatum per defectum*, a sin by neglect, as well. And as we do not spare ourselves in our examination of conscience, so our Protestant brethren cannot spare themselves either ... Once again, it is only reform from *both* sides that can help us.[3]

In this gradual change of approach from the Protestant side three factors can be discerned. First of all, there is the realization that Mariology is not a purely 'Roman' phenomenon: it has been encountered in the Ecumenical Movement first of all among the Orthodox and then among Anglicans. What is more, historical studies have revealed that the sixteenth-century Reformers said some quite 'extreme' things about Our Lady. Secondly, the recovery of the sense of the Church and of the Christian life as essentially (to borrow Fr Thornton's phrase) 'the common life in the Body of Christ'[4] has made Protestants aware of the need to give fuller and more explicit expression to the doctrine of the Communion of Saints. Thirdly, Protestants have been able to see that to pay some attention to Mary does not involve withdrawing attention from Christ; that it is possible to have a strong and biblically-fed evangelical faith centred unwaveringly on the Person of Christ and to find that this includes, rather than excludes, a devotion to Mary, the Mother of Christ.

One must not exaggerate the strength of this 'new look' in Protestantism: though it has found some expression among Scandinavian and German Lutherans, it is principally associated with the *Communauté de Taizé* in France. It is interesting to note first of all the place of Our Lady in the Taizé liturgy. In the calendar 15 August is called the 'Memorial of the Virgin

---

[3] Küng, *The Council and Reunion*, pp. 186–7.
[4] L. S. Thornton, *The Common Life in the Body of Christ* (London: Dacre Press, 1941).

Mary, Mother of the Lord', while the Wednesday and Friday of the Ember Week in Advent are treated as memorials of the Annunciation and Visitation respectively (cf. the masses for those days in the Roman Missal). In the eucharistic liturgy there is a commemoration of Mary and the saints in the Intercession which concludes, 'united with their faith, their lives and their prayer, we beseech thee to grant unto us at all times the help of thy strength and thy protection'; there is also a proper preface of the Virgin Mary, a shortened and slightly weakened version of the Roman one, and a preface of the saints, borrowed from the rite of Lyon, which recounts how God bestows on us, through the saints, 'an example of godly life, a share in their fellowship, and the aid of their prayers'. The style is sober and discreet, but while direct invocation is excluded there is explicit appeal to the intercession of the saints. One or two members of the Taizé Community have written about the Communion of Saints in general, but there is now accessible in an English translation a book by the Sub-prior, Frère Max Thurian, specifically on Our Lady. It is called *Mary, Mother of the Lord, Figure of the Church* (Faith Press, 1963), and the very title gives expression to the double polarity (Christ and the Church) of the best theological thinking about Our Lady today. The book is not an easy one to read, but those who tackle it will find it a rewarding though demanding exercise. It is warmly recommended to the Priests-Associate of Walsingham and to all lay pilgrims who can feed and inform their devotion with fairly solid works of theology.

The book has two interests. The first is that it is written by a Protestant (who has, however, drunk deeply of the living waters of Catholic tradition) and the second that is basically concerned with the same problem as the best of modern Catholic writing, the relation between Mary and the Church.

As far as the author's Protestantism is concerned, it will be noted that he deliberately refrains from discussing the dogmas of the Immaculate Conception and the Assumption since he does not wish in this book to indulge in controversy but to point out the extent to which even in this field so much is held in common. For the same reason he does not discuss or comment on the practice of direct invocation of Our Lady, though he stresses the importance of the liturgical commemoration of Mary and the saints since we are united with them in a single stream of worship and intercession. Another valuable element is the frequent reference to and quotation from the Reformers. There are to be found in this book some impressive and astonishing extracts from the writings and sermons of Luther, Zwingli, Bullinger, Calvin and (in some ways the most attractive of all) Charles Drelincourt, a seventeenth-century French Reformed pastor. Lastly, it is clear that Frère Max Thurian always begins and ends with scriptural revelation. He quotes the Fathers, the liturgies and mediaeval Catholic theologians in rich abundance but his thinking is rooted in the Bible and soaked in the feel and spirit of the Bible.

In tracing the relation between Mary and the Church Pasteur Thurian is suggestive and illuminating, though he does not always present us with clear and easily grasped conclusions. We are shown a number of parallels that help us to see Mary as a type or figure or image of the Church. Both Our Lady and the Church share the same fundamental vocation of motherhood (Mother of Christ; Mother of the faithful), while they share also in the vocation of virginity (for the Church is the Bride of Christ awaiting her consummation in the marriage feast of the Lamb). Some biblical images, notably the 'Heavenly Woman' of Revelation 12, apply first of all to Israel, the Church of the Old Testament, then to Mary, then to the Church of Christ, while a number of titles apply both to Mary and the Church: Daughter of Sion, Dwelling Place of God, Second Eve, Mother of the Faithful, Bearer of the Word of God, Faithful Servant and Handmaid of the Lord. Our Lady is in fact the personal embodiment of the old Israel, the 'incarnation' of the faithful remnant: she is also the first of the redeemed, the model and example of faith, present in the Church from the beginning. What does all this add up to? It can sound like mere theologizing, mere playing about with words and ideas, without any practical reference, unless we take it a stage further, as Frère Max Thurian does in fact, and say that *because* Mary is both Mother of God and Type of the Church she is also a Mother in the Church, the Mother of all the Faithful. This is of course the crucial development, for once we admit a certain relation between all Christians and Our Lady, based on her spiritual motherhood of all believers at the foot of the Cross, then there is bound to grow up some expression of this relationship in liturgy and devotion. When we see signs that this relationship is being recognized and affirmed by Protestants (even if as yet by only a few) then we may dare to hope that the gulf between Catholics and Protestants is not as unbridgeable as we had feared.

Meanwhile on the Catholic side, in view of what some Roman writers have not hesitated to call the 'crisis' of contemporary Mariology, there is the double necessity of scrutinizing and purifying all existing Marian devotions and of trying to embody the new insights into expressions of devotion that will be fully in harmony with the movements of renewal in the Church. We can do no better than to end, where we began, with the Second Vatican Council. The Constitution on the Sacred Liturgy which was solemnly promulgated on 4 December 1963 is a magnificent document (which Anglicans should find very profitable and edifying to study) and it contains some extremely significant sections on the liturgical *cultus* of Our Lady and the saints. Paragraph 103 is concerned entirely with Our Lady and it incorporates in a lucid, sober and concise fashion the emphases of the best of recent Mariology:

> In celebrating this annual cycle of Christ's mysteries, holy Church honours with especial love the Blessed Mary, Mother of God, who is joined by an inseparable bond to the saving work of her Son. In her the Church holds up and admires the most excellent fruit of the redemption, and joyfully contemplates, as in a faultless image, that which she herself desires and hopes wholly to be.[5]

---

5 Constitution on the Sacred Liturgy (*Sacrosanctum Concilium*), para. 103: W. M. Abbott (ed.), *The Documents of Vatican II* (London: Geoffrey Chapman, 1967), p. 168.

16

Mother of All Christians (1998)[1]

These days my memory is always letting me down, but there is one memory from the year 1962, when I was an Anglican priest studying at Louvain, that is still crystal clear. One of our professors had just returned from a meeting of a preparatory commission for the Second Vatican Council in Rome, and he was profoundly disturbed. Talking of a draft *schema* that at that point bore the title *De Duobus Fontibus Revelationis* (On the Two Sources of Revelation), he said emphatically: 'If this goes through, it will be the end of ecumenism for the Catholic Church.' He was right, of course: any such constitution with such a title would have killed off for good the budding dialogue of the Roman Catholic Church with the ecumenical movement. But, as we know, the bishops at the Council had a mind of their own, and the constitution which they enacted, *De Divina Revelatione*, bore no trace either of its former title or of the theology that undergirded it.

'If this goes through, it will be the end of ecumenism for the Catholic Church.' Thirty-five years on, I can apply this comment with no less emphasis to the proposal that Pope John Paul II should infallibly proclaim Mary to be 'Co-Redeemer', 'Mediator of all Graces', and 'Advocate'. But what right have I,

---

[1] This article first appeared in *The Tablet* for 24 January 1998 as the second of a series of four articles on the proposal, vigorously pursued by some Roman Catholics at that time, that the new millennium should be marked by the formal definition of a doctrine that Mary is the Co-Redemptrix of mankind. The articles were reprinted by the Ecumenical Society of the Blessed Virgin Mary in a pamphlet entitled *The Place of Mary in the Church: Mariologists on Mary – Co-Redeemer?*

as an Anglican, to comment on this proposal? At least, I think, two.

In the first place, I was an invited guest at the 1996 International Mariological Congress held at Czestochowa, Poland, and delivered a lecture on the place of Mary in the liturgies of the Anglican Communion.[2] A commission was set up at the congress (*The Tablet*, 6 September 1997) in direct response to the Holy See's request that it should study 'whether it was possible and opportune to define the Marian titles of Mediator, Co-Redeemer and Advocate' and five non-Roman Catholic participants, of whom I was one, were added to the commission. It was significant that we were asked and even more significant that the commission was unanimous in advising strongly against any such definition.

The conclusion was in fact a double one. It noted in the first place that it would be inherently difficult to define such ambiguous titles, when the scriptural references to Redeemer and Mediator all point to Christ, and those to Advocate all point to the Holy Spirit. Moreover, to do so would reverse the theological line taken by the Second Vatican Council, which set itself against any further mariological definitions and put all its thinking about Mary very firmly in the context of its reflection on Christ and on the Church. The commission noted in the second place that any such definition would run counter to the priority given to ecumenical dialogue by the present Pope in his encyclicals *Tertio Millennio Adveniente* and *Ut Unum Sint*.

I have, as an Anglican, a second right to speak. Commitment to ecumenism implies that all Christians – and the churches to which they belong – are, by virtue of a common baptism, members of one body, the Body of Christ. This means that, although a properly sensitive discretion will hold us back from intervening directly in the strictly internal affairs of other denominations, nothing that takes place in another church is in the last resort outside our concern.

As a non-Roman Catholic I hope there are three reflections which I can usefully contribute.

---

2 Chapter 13 of the present volume.

First, the last few decades have seen remarkable signs of a new openness to Marian theology and spirituality, not only within Anglicanism but within churches more fully identified with the Reformation. We must not forget the pioneering work in this and many other countries of the Ecumenical Society of the Blessed Virgin Mary nor the liberating effect on ecumenical dialogue of the Second Vatican Council's declaration in its constitution on the Church, *Lumen Gentium*, that 'the Church does not hesitate to profess this subordinate role of Mary'. In the Church of England the popularity of the shrine at Walsingham has increased enormously in the past few decades, the General Synod has recently restored 15 August to our calendar as the principal feast of the Blessed Virgin, and an unofficial and experimental office book, *Celebrating Common Prayer*, published with an *imprimatur* from the Archbishop of Canterbury, even contains the *Salve Regina*, which addresses our Lady as *advocata nostra*. Do the promoters of this new definition realize that if they get their way they will (not to put it more strongly) severely inhibit this new Marian openness in other churches?

Secondly, many Anglicans have been opposing the ordination of women to the priesthood and the episcopate in their communion precisely on ecumenical grounds, since they believe it has proved to be a new and serious obstacle to reconciliation with the Roman Catholic and Eastern Orthodox Churches. Many people in the Anglican tradition have been sincerely pursuing two quite separate aims, the ordination of women and unity with Rome and Constantinople, while failing to perceive the degree to which they are incompatible. Is not the same true of those who are promoting this definition, if – that is – they are seriously concerned about Christian unity at all?

Thirdly, one of the most moving and most promising documents to come from Rome in a long time has been Pope John Paul II's encyclical *Ut Unum Sint* of 1995. In it the Pope not only solemnly reaffirms that the ecumenical task is 'one of the pastoral priorities' of his pontificate, but also declares his readiness to heed the request made to him of finding new ways to exercise his ministry, expressing his conviction that he cannot do this alone but needs to engage in dialogue with the leaders of other churches and their theologians. Such a conviction is incompatible with any willingness even to contemplate the proposed new Marian definition, not only on the diplomatic ground that it would cancel out any prospect of the dialogue he so clearly desires but, more fundamentally, because it would destroy the vision of a universal primacy whose principal care is to serve, promote and safeguard the unity and communion of all the churches. Personally, I am not too anxious. I think it is extremely unlikely that Rome will accede to the request of those who are campaigning for the definition, for in the end nobody would gain from it. For those who so earnestly desire it, it would be a Pyrrhic victory, for any eventual definition would have to deny and limit more than it could affirm; it would certainly polarize to a point of almost unbearable tension the already acute divisions within the Roman Catholic Church; it would be 'the end of ecumenism' for the Roman Catholic Church, not only for the more hard-line Protestants but also for those in the Eastern and Anglican traditions who are sensitive both to the place of Mary in the Church and to the need to give to the universal ministry of the Bishop of Rome greater recognition and a more widely acceptable form.

17

An Ecumenical Pilgrimage in Honour of Mary, Mother of Our Lord (1998)

Sermon preached at an ecumenical pilgrimage in Durham Cathedral, 16 May 1998

As I prepared myself to come on a very long pilgrimage (for Chichester is quite a distance from Durham) to this lovely and hallowed Cathedral Church of Christ and Blessed Mary the Virgin, I could not help recalling a notorious and bitter row (one would like to be able to add that such rows never happen in the Church today) that broke out in this Cathedral in the year 1628. One of the prebendaries, called Peter Smart, mounted the pulpit to denounce another of the prebendaries, John Cosin (later to become Bishop of Durham; the author of the prayer on page 4 of our service booklet).[1] To make matters worse he published his sermon, and in his introduction made an inventory of those practices of John Cosin which he was condemning and refuting.

'Fourthly,' he writes, 'on Candlemas Day last past Mr Cosens, in renewing that Popish ceremony of burning candles

---

1 'Almighty God, we offer you most high praise and hearty thanks for the wonders of your grace and virtue, which you have declared in all your saints, and which you have bestowed on your holy Church from the beginning of the world; but chiefly in the glorious and most blessed Virgin Mary, the Mother of your Son, Jesus Christ our Lord; as also in the blessed Angels in heaven and in all other holy persons who, in their lives and labours, have shone forth as lights to the world in their own generations. Amen.'

to the honour of Our Lady, busied himself from 2 of the clock in the afternoon till 4 in climbing long ladders to stick up wax candles in the said Cathedral Church. The number of all the candles burnt that evening was 220, besides 16 torches, 60 of those burning tapers and torches standing upon and near the High Altar (as he calls it), where no man came nigh.'[2]

John Cosin, however, was not without friends and allies; one such was a neighbour of his in Cambridge, another great seventeenth-century Anglican divine called Mark Frank. We have come today on pilgrimage to the House of Christ and Blessed Mary the Virgin. Perhaps the first such pilgrimage was that of the Magi, recounted in the second chapter of St Matthew's Gospel and brilliantly evoked in an Epiphany Day sermon by Mark Frank.[3]

First, he describes the journey:

Many a weary step had they trod, many a fruitless question had they asked, many an unprofitable search had they made to find him; and, behold, yet they will not give over. Twelve days it had cost them to come to Jerusalem, through the Arabian deserts, over the Arabian mountains ...: the difficulty of the way, through sands and rocks – the danger of the passages, being infamous for robbers – the cold and hardness of a deep winter season – the hazard and inconvenience of so long, so hard, so unseasonable, so dangerous, and I may say so uncertain a journey, could no whit deter them from their purpose: to Jerusalem they will, through all these difficulties. But after all this pains, to lose the star that guided them, – to hear nothing at Jerusalem of him they sought, – to be left, after all this, at a loss in that very place they only could

---

[2] P. Smart, *The Vanity and Downfall of Superstitious Popish Ceremonies; ... A Sermon Preached in the Cathedral Church of Durham* (Edinburgh, 1628), quoted in P. E. Moore and F. L. Cross (eds), *Anglicanism: The Thought and Practice of the Church of England, Illustrated from the Religious Literature of the Seventeenth Century* (London: SPCK, 1951), p. 551.

[3] M. Frank, *Sermons by Mark Frank, D.D.* (Oxford: John Henry Parker, 1849), Vol. 1: The First Sermon on the Epiphany, pp. 273–80, the extracts quoted are on pp. 277–80.

expect to find him, and hear nothing there but a piece of an obscure prophecy, without date or time, – to be left now to a mere wild-goose search, or a new knight-errantry, and yet still to continue in their search, – is an extreme high piece both of faith and love, that considers no difficulties ...; that will be overcome with nothing; is resolved, come what will, to find what they believe and desire; such a piece of faith and love that we, later Christians, cannot parallel.

He then goes on to ask his hearers about their own commitment to the pilgrim quest, which is the Christian life, and their own readiness to persevere in that quest:

How would a winter journey scare us from our faith! A cold or rainy morning will do it; a little snow, or wind, or rain, or cold, will easily keep us from coming to the house where Jesus is, from coming out to worship him ...

The truth is, if our coming to Christ, if our religion, may cost us nothing – nor pains, nor cost, nor cold, nor heat, nor labour, nor time, nor hurt, nor hazard, nor enquiry, nor search, – then it may be we will be content to give Christ a visit, and entertain his faith and worship, but not else; if it may not be had, nor Christ come to, without so much ado, let him go – let all go: so we may sit at ease and quiet in our warm nests, come of Christ's worship and of his house what will.

Next he describes the arrival of the Magi at the house in Bethlehem (that first House of Christ and Blessed Mary the Virgin):

I do not wonder interpreters make this house the church of God. It is the gate and court of heaven, now Christ is here; angels sing round about it, all holiness is in it, now Christ is in it: here all the creatures, reasonable and unreasonable, come to pay their homage to their Creator; hither they come, even from the ends of the earth, to their devotions; 'a house of prayer' it is 'for all people,' Gentiles and all; hither they come to worship, hither they come to pay their offerings and their vows; here is the shrine and altar, the glorious Virgin's lap, where the Saviour of the world is laid to be adored and worshipped; here stands the star for tapers to give it light; and here the wise men this day become the priests – worship and offer, present prayers and praises, for themselves and the whole world besides; all people of the world, high and low, learned and ignorant, represented by them.

And he concludes this section of his sermon with the words: 'This house, then, is a place well worth the coming to.'

And now it is no longer Mark Frank who speaks but myself: I hope you will agree that your journey today, less hazardous than that of the Magi, has been time well spent and this house 'a place well worth the coming to'. For a pilgrimage is no aimless ramble; rather it is a journey consciously undertaken with a particular end in view, an end which colours and motivates the whole journey. But the journey itself is an essential part of the pilgrimage: it expresses the nature of the Church as the pilgrim people of God; it binds us together as fellow-travellers and fellow-seekers; it is an appropriate image of our divided Christian communities travelling together on the long, hard, uphill road to unity.

An ecumenical pilgrimage in honour of Mary, Mother of our Lord and God Jesus Christ, is a tremendous risk; so the courage and faith of those who conceived and planned it and those who are taking part in it need to be acknowledged and saluted. It could so easily become an exercise in accentuating our divisions and in hardening our conviction that our own tradition is on the right lines and all the others on the wrong lines. Today's pilgrimage has demanded – and demands – from all of us who take part in it at least three things:

- First, sorrow that the figure of one whom our Lord and Master Jesus Christ loved and revered as his Mother has been allowed to become the focus of controversy and division, and penitence for our own complicity in this

tragic confrontation, in which Catholics have used their rosaries to flog the backs of Protestants and Protestants their Bibles to bash the heads of Catholics.
- ❖ Second, sensitivity to the convictions of our fellow Christians and an awareness of those points in our own tradition that can scandalize and hurt our fellow-Christians.
- ❖ Third, a conviction that we and the churches to which we belong are called, in this domain as in so many others, to a real conversion as we try to confess together with one voice the Faith of the Scriptures and of the Creeds and as we seek for the right language in which – in obedience to her own Magnificat – to call Mary blessed.

We are not starting from cold; our presence together here this morning speaks of a pilgrimage begun by others before us. There are a number of factors which have contributed to a real change of attitude on this question and so made today possible:

1. The Ecumenical Movement has taught us all to look behind and beyond what divides us to a shared faith and a common tradition; not to allow what still divides us to obscure what we can gladly confess together; to recognize that each tradition has developed its own language and that what divides us is often more a question of vocabulary than of substance, so that what we *hear* others say is not always what they *intend* to say.
2. Inextricably bound up with the Ecumenical Movement have been movements of renewal in the common study of the Scriptures, of the Fathers of the Early Church and of the Liturgy, all of which have led to a growing convergence on the place of Mary in the Scriptures and in the Church.
3. Until the Second Vatican Council those in the churches of the Reformation who wanted to engage in theological dialogue with those in the Catholic tradition on the role of Mary had, almost exclusively, to do so with those in the Eastern Orthodox and Anglican Churches, and it was from them that they learned to question their own deeply rooted

antagonism to all Marian devotion as essentially Roman. The Second Vatican Council radically changed all this, and it is difficult to over-estimate the influence of a single phrase in the Council's most important doctrinal text, the Constitution on the Church (*Lumen Gentium*): 'The Church does not hesitate to profess this subordinate role of Mary.' There are words and there are gestures which have a crucial role in removing obstacles to unity; this has been one of them.

4 The comparatively recent consciousness of the role of women in the Church has led to a new interest in the role of Mary; along with some criticism of traditional Marian devotion, seen as an exercise in reinforcing male supremacy, has come the awareness of Mary as the greatest of all the great heroines of the Bible and as a role model for women and for men.

I want to conclude by sharing with you very briefly some conclusions from the latest publications of a French ecumenical group of Catholic and Protestant (Lutheran and Reformed) theologians, *Le Groupe des Dombes*, although in doing this I am not undervaluing the work that has been done in the English-speaking world, notably under the auspices of the Ecumenical Society of the Blessed Virgin Mary. [*This section of the sermon was included in the address which forms Chapter 18 of this volume and is therefore omitted here.*] Their common conviction is that Mary must *never* be separated from her Son either in our thinking or our praying, and it is that conviction which is so well expressed in the lines of an anonymous nineteenth-century or early twentieth-century English-speaking author with which I myself now conclude:

Mary the Dawn, Christ the perfect Day:
Mary the Gate, Christ the heavenly Way.

Mary the Root, Christ the mystic Vine:
Mary the Grape, Christ the sacred Wine.

Mary the Corn-sheaf, Christ the living Bread:
Mary the Rose-tree, Christ the Rose blood-red.

Mary the Fount, Christ the cleansing Flood:
Mary the Chalice, Christ the saving Blood.

Mary the Temple, Christ the temple's Lord:
Mary the Shrine, Christ its God adored.

Mary the Beacon, Christ the Heaven's Rest
Mary the Mirror, Christ the Vision blest.

18

Our Lady, Chosen by God (1999)

The *Groupe des Dombes* on 'Mary in God's Plan
and in the Communion of Saints':
Address to the Society of Our Lady of Pew,
Westminster Abbey, 26 February 1999

Introduction

Although I am not complaining (well, not really), I have really an impossible task this evening. In about twenty minutes I have to try to do three things: to tell you about the *Groupe des Dombes*; to give you an overview of their latest two-volume report (not yet translated into English) on *Marie dans le Dessein de Dieu et la Communion des Saints* (Mary in God's plan and in the Communion of Saints); and to introduce the first of its three main themes: 'Our Lady, Chosen by God'.

The *Groupe des Dombes*

The *Groupe des Dombes* is an unofficial group of theologians, about forty in number, half of them Roman Catholic and half Protestant, from the Reformed and Lutheran churches, coming either from France itself or from the French-speaking areas of Switzerland. Its life began in 1937 (so it is now sixty-two years old) with a very discreet meeting of priests from Lyon and pastors from Switzerland; it was only after the Second World War that pastors from France itself joined the group, which at first alternated its meetings between the Trappist Abbey of Les Dombes (north east of Lyon) and a Protestant retreat house near Geneva, but which now meets every year at Les Dombes (hence the name *Groupe des Dombes*). The moving spirit from the Catholic side in the early days was the Abbé Paul Couturier (the founder, or strictly perhaps the re-founder, of the Week of Prayer for Christian Unity), and one of the best known participants from the Protestant side was Frère Max Thurian of Taizé.

Though it is an unofficial group it carries great weight and its members are respected for their theological seriousness, their loyalty to their own tradition and their ecumenical commitment. Their work – often in the form of a set of theses for the consideration of the Churches, followed by a theological commentary – has had a profound influence at an ecumenical and international level. Their agreed statements on the Eucharist and on the Ordained Ministry were being hammered out at the same time as the texts of ARCIC and of Faith and Order (*Baptism, Eucharist and Ministry*, 1982) and there is much evidence of convergence and mutual influence in these texts. On the whole, Anglican and English-speaking participation has been absent, but I was privileged to take part (together with an Orthodox observer) in one meeting of the *Groupe des Dombes* in September 1974 and to present a paper on the doctrine and practice of episcopacy in Anglicanism to a meeting engaged in preparing an Agreement on Episcopal Ministry (1976).

Mary in God's Plan and in the Communion of Saints

The *Groupe des Dombes*' two volumes on Mary were published in 1997 and 1998 and follow a number of important texts devoted to such questions as the Eucharist; the Reconciliation of Ministries; Episcopal Ministry; and the Petrine Ministry. I am not sure whether there is any conscious and explicit connection with Pope John Paul II's Encyclical of May 1995, *Ut Unum Sint*, but it is worth noting that in his list of five areas 'in need of fuller study before a true consensus of faith can be achieved' the Pope includes (as number 5) 'the Virgin Mary, as Mother of God and icon of the Church, the spiritual Mother who intercedes for Christ's disciples and for all humanity' (paragraph 79). It is also worth noting – particularly in view of the fact that there is no reference to Anglicanism in the *Dombes* text and, as far as I can judge, no Anglican input – that the House of Bishops of the Church of England in its response to the Pope of 1997 feels able to affirm that 'Anglicans acclaim Mary as Theotokos and honour her place in the economy of salvation ... she was prepared by divine grace for her role as mother of our Redeemer, by whom she was herself redeemed and received in glory in the communion of saints'. I mention this not in order to say that the *Dombes* text has no relevance to the English-speaking ecumenical world; on the contrary I am convinced that it has an immense amount to teach us all, and I look forward to seeing it translated into English.

The *Groupe* begins by pointing out that Mary has never been a cause of separation between the churches but rather the victim, and that to date she has not been the main focus of any official international ecumenical theological dialogue. The first volume consists of a common re-reading of the evidence of history and Scripture and stresses the fact that the sixteenth-century Reformers themselves had a much more positive attitude to Mary than the later silence of the Protestant churches – itself largely produced by the polemics of the post-Reformation period – would have led us to suppose. Before we return briefly to the final section of the first volume – 'The Witness of Scripture and the Confession of Faith' – I need to say something about the second volume, *Controverse et Conversion* (Controversy and Conversion). It consists of a careful scrutiny of the four main points of controversy which are seen to remain:

1 Is it proper to speak of Mary as 'co-operating' in the work of salvation?
2 Can we affirm her perpetual virginity?

3 To what extent are the Roman Catholic dogmas of the Immaculate Conception (defined in 1854) and the Assumption of Our Lady (defined in 1950) obstacles to unity?
4 Is it legitimate to invoke Mary and the saints, to ask them to pray for us?

The last chapter of the second volume is entitled 'Towards the Conversion of our Churches' and follows a method that has characterized the *Groupe des Dombes* for many years. First of all, the Catholic members of the group write of Catholic conversion, enumerating a number of unhealthy exaggerations and dangerous deviations and giving guidelines for the reform and purification of Catholic thinking and practice. Then the Protestant members make their self-examination and go so far as to pose the challenge, 'Protestants must ask themselves whether their too frequent silence about Mary does not prejudice their relation to Jesus Christ?' Together Catholics and Protestants conclude that the real and serious divergences that remain are not so fundamental that they justify continued separation.

Our Lady, Chosen by God

And now a final word (necessarily rather brief, not to say breathless) about 'Our Lady, Chosen by God'. The biblical and doctrinal section of volume one is organized around the three articles of the Nicene and Apostles' Creeds: belief in God the Father, in his Son Jesus Christ and in the Holy Spirit and the Church (the Communion of Saints) which he sanctifies. And so reflection on Mary centred on the first article (God the Father, Creator of heaven and earth) is given the title 'Mary as creature, as woman and as daughter of Israel'. She is indeed a creature, and here I quote the text: 'She is neither outside nor above humanity but belongs totally to that humanity with which God has willed to crown his creation.' Important things are said about Mary as a woman and as a daughter of Israel, the last in a long line of heroic women of the Old Testament who embody the image of the Virgin Daughter of Sion. All I have time in conclusion to do is to pass on to you one theme which I am sure is very much in tune with the preoccupations of contemporary society. The text tackles head-on certain false images of Mary as woman – an idealized woman for those who cannot cope with real women or with the realities of human sexuality, a submissive woman for those who want to use Our Lady as a model for women's submission to male domination. Feminists are right in condemning these false stereotypes: all reflection on Mary as creature, as woman, as daughter of Israel must take seriously the reality of her creatureliness, her Jewishness, and above all, perhaps, the reality of her condition as a woman. Let me end with one final quote from the text:

> Above all, Mary is that woman towards whom great numbers of the poor have turned, seeking in her comfort and consolation. People have been sensitive to her human and maternal proximity, have spontaneously recognized her face of tenderness and compassion, and have remembered her in the midst of the joys and of the sorrows of our existence.

19

Mary: Grace and Hope in Christ (2005)[1]

My task is both simple and complicated at the same time. It is simple in the sense that I am not presenting my own ideas to you but rather an official text, the most recent text of the Second Anglican–Roman Catholic International Commission, published in May 2005: *Mary: Grace and Hope in Christ*. It is complicated in the sense that, before presenting and summarizing it, I need to put it in the historical context of the dialogue between the Anglican Communion and the Roman Catholic Church. I am therefore going to divide my remarks into three sections. In the first part I will sketch the background to this agreed statement in order to help you to understand why the decision was taken to prepare a text on Mary at this stage in the dialogue. The second part will examine the agreed statement itself and, in particular – without losing sight of the overall text – what it says about the theme of this conference, the Immaculate Conception. Finally, the third part – and inevitably at that point it will be a question of personal analysis – will try to assess the importance of this agreed statement and the weight of its influence on the dialogue between our two churches.

---

[1] The paper which forms this chapter was given at a conference at Lourdes in 2005. It first appeared in *Je suis l'Immaculée: Colloque organise par les Sanctuaires Notre-Dame de Lourdes et la Société Française d'Études Mariales* (Editions Parole et Silence, 2006), pp. 173–89. The translation and footnotes are by the present editor.

I: Historical Context

The official dialogue between our two churches goes back to the official visit which the then Archbishop of Canterbury, Michael Ramsey, paid to Pope Paul VI in Rome in 1966 after the Second Vatican Council had concluded. In their Common Declaration they affirmed that they intended

> to inaugurate between the Roman Catholic Church and the Anglican Communion a serious dialogue which, founded on the Gospels and on the ancient common traditions, may lead to that unity in truth, for which Christ prayed ... a restoration of complete communion of faith and sacramental life.[2]

That Common Declaration opened the way for this dialogue and, after the report of a Preparatory Commission which had the task of preparing a list of the questions to be examined, ARCIC (the Anglican–Roman Catholic International Commission) was established in 1967 and very swiftly began its work. The members of the Commission had been appointed by the Pope and the Archbishop of Canterbury, and they took care to give it an international character. The Commission's task was to examine – and, if possible, to resolve – the three major problems that constituted an obstacle to the restoration of a 'complete communion of faith and sacramental life': that is to say, the doctrine of the Eucharist, the doctrine of ministry and ordination, and the nature of authority in the Church. One may note in passing that the substantial agreement on the Eucharist, signed by the Commission and confirmed by the churches of the Anglican Communion, was the decisive factor which permitted catholic bishops, for example in France, to offer eucharistic hospitality to Anglicans living at a distance from any Anglican church. It is in the fourth ARCIC text, the second agreed statement on Authority in the Church (signed at Windsor in 1981), and in the context of reflection on papal infallibility, that the Commission touched for the first time on

---

[2] Quoted in Anglican–Roman Catholic International Commission, *The Final Report* (London, 1982), p. 118.

Mariology, but from this particular angle, because of 'the reaction of many Anglicans to the Marian definitions, which are the only examples of such dogmas promulgated by the bishop of Rome apart from a synod since the separation of our two communions'.[3]

I will continue the quotation:

> Anglicans and Roman Catholics can agree in much of the truth that these two dogmas are designed to affirm. We agree that there can be but one mediator between God and man, Jesus Christ, and reject any interpretation of the role of Mary which obscures this affirmation. We agree in recognizing that Christian understanding of Mary is inseparably linked with the doctrines of Christ and of the Church. We agree in recognizing the grace and unique vocation of Mary, Mother of God Incarnate (*Theotokos*), in observing her festivals, and in according her honour in the communion of saints. We agree that she was prepared by divine grace to be the mother of our Redeemer, by whom she herself was redeemed and received into glory. We further agree in recognizing in Mary a model of holiness, obedience and faith for all Christians. We accept that it is possible to regard her as a prophetic figure of the Church of God before as well as after the Incarnation.[4]

At this point a footnote is added – a footnote, because it is a comment by the Roman Catholic members of the Commission:

> The affirmation of the Roman Catholic Church that Mary was conceived without original sin is based on recognition of her unique role within the mystery of the Incarnation. By being thus prepared to be the mother of our Redeemer, she also becomes a sign that the salvation won by Christ was operative among all mankind before his birth. The affirm-

---

3 'Authority in the Church, II': *Final Report*, p. 95, para. 30.
4 'Authority in the Church, II': *Final Report*, pp. 95–6, para. 30.

ation that her glory in heaven involves full participation in the fruits of salvation expresses and reinforces our faith that the life of the world to come has already broken into the life of our world. It is the conviction of Roman Catholics that the Marian dogmas formulate a faith consonant with Scripture.

Three things can easily be understood. First, if on the questions of the Eucharist and ministry the Commission believed that it had arrived at a 'substantial agreement', on the question of authority in the Church it could only register a convergence. Second, the first Commission (ARCIC I), having reached the end of its mandate, published its report – entitled *The Final Report* – but that ambiguous and even perhaps unhappy title has given rise to not a few misunderstandings. Finally, in May 1982 Pope John Paul II and the then Archbishop of Canterbury, Robert Runcie, decided to appoint a second Commission (ARCIC II) to continue the work of the first Commission and evaluate the reception of its report.

It took a good deal of time for the work on authority to be taken up again, but in 1995 Pope John Paul II published his encyclical letter *Ut unum sint*. In this letter, addressed to all Christians, the Pope listed five themes which needed to be examined in ecumenical dialogue, of which the last was Marian doctrine and piety. In their response, the bishops of the Church of England took note of this conviction expressed by the Pope, affirming afresh that Anglicans honour Mary as *Theotokos*; at the same time they argued for a certain diversity of expression in Marian devotion.

In 1999 – at last – ARCIC II published a text of the highest importance on the Gift of Authority (which is also referred to as Authority III, because ARCIC I had published two texts on authority). This text does not discuss Mariology, but it does speak about the infallibility of the Bishop of Rome, going much further than the text of 1981. The Commission affirmed without ambiguity that it is the faith of the whole Church, which the Bishop of Rome in certain circumstances has a duty to discern and make explicit ... The reception of the primacy of the Bishop of Rome entails the recognition of this specific ministry of the universal primate. We believe that this is a gift to be received by all the churches.[5]

Given that ARCIC did not choose its own programme of work but applied itself to the subjects that were given to it by the authorities of the two churches, it is important to understand the reasons why the subject of Mary was given to the Commission. This is the first time – if I am not mistaken – that Mariology has been the subject of an official dialogue between two churches at the international level. The text of the *Groupe des Dombes* – so important and so influential – '*Marie dans le dessein de Dieu et la communion des Saints*' ('Mary in God's Plan and in the Communion of Saints'), which came out in 1997 and 1998, was produced by a group of French-speaking priests and pastors. The historical summary that I have sought to give you in this first section of my lecture, will, I hope, help you to appreciate why the choice of this subject is the natural, if not the inevitable, consequence of the work that had preceded it.

II: The Agreed Statement

I turn now to the second section of my presentation, an examination of this ARCIC document. Before I give you a summary of its contents, there are some points to note. The text is 32 pages long in the French translation[6] and it has the status of an 'Agreed Statement', that is to say, a common declaration endorsed by all the members of the Commission. Its publication has been authorized by the authorities of the two churches, who must

---

[5] Anglican–Roman Catholic International Commission, *Mary: Grace and Hope in Christ, An Agreed Statement* (Harrisburg and London: Morehouse, 2005), para. 47.

[6] *La Documentation Catholique*, no. 2341 (August 2005).

examine and evaluate it in due time. The Commission worked on this text over a period of five years in an atmosphere of fraternal prayer and friendship. It follows ARCIC's customary method: the starting point is not the period of divisions and controversies, but rather the Commission tries first to go back to Scripture, to the ancient common traditions of the two churches, to the period before our divisions, before formulating conclusions in a new and common language. 'The more one goes back to the source', an eastern patriarch has said, 'the clearer the water is.'

The text is divided into four chapters, together with an introduction and a conclusion. The first chapter (A) is devoted to Scripture, Chapter B to Christian tradition, Chapter C to the themes of grace and hope and Chapter D to Mary in the life of the Church. Let us examine these four chapters briefly, one by one.

The Introduction sets out the historical context that I have already tried to describe and repeats the affirmations of the Final Report: Christ is the only mediator between God and mankind and Mariology must always situate itself between the two poles of Christology and ecclesiology.

Chapter A: Mary According to the Scriptures

Throughout the Old and New Testaments, men and women were prepared by God to accomplish particular and important tasks. It is God who gives them the grace necessary for their mission, and those who are called have to give a response to that call. In the same way, the Blessed Virgin Mary was prepared by the grace of God to become the Mother of the Saviour and she gives a response of free and unreserved consent in giving herself completely and in trust. In the witness of the New Testament we find a solid basis for Marian devotion; in each generation the faithful are to call her 'blessed'.

Chapter B: Mary in the Christian Tradition

According to the Fathers, the virgin birth of Christ underlined both the humanity and the divinity of Jesus. Mary was proclaimed *Theotokos* first and foremost in order to safeguard the orthodox doctrine of the unity of the person of Christ. It was in the first seven centuries that the essential outlines of Marian doctrine, devotion and liturgy were established.

In the latter part of the Middle Ages Mariological speculation became less scriptural and more and more detached from its Christological and ecclesiological context; moreover, theology and devotion developed separately, and popular religion began to regard the Virgin Mary as an independent intermediary between God and man. This explains the severe reaction of the Reformers against 'real and perceived abuses surrounding devotion to Mary' (para. 44). The Church of England retained five Marian feasts, including that of the Conception, though it suppressed that of the Assumption (restored at the end of the twentieth century). A certain renaissance of Marian thought and devotion is seen, above all in the seventeenth century, without – before the Oxford Movement of the nineteenth century – going as far as direct invocation of the Blessed Virgin.

With the Counter-Reformation, Roman Catholic identity came to be linked increasingly to the cult of Our Lady. The intensity and popularity of Marian piety contributed to the definitions of the Immaculate Conception in 1854 and the Assumption in 1950. But with the ecumenical movement and the Second Vatican Council a phenomenon which ARCIC calls 're-reception' can be seen in our two communions. Re-reception is a way of being both aware of the necessity to correct some exaggerations of the past and at the same time aware of the need to re-locate the traditional teaching in a more biblical and a more ecumenical climate, and thus to renew it and give it a new point of departure. Re-reception is thus both an act of faithfulness and an act of liberty. This process encourages a very positive evolution in our two churches, which are now closer to each other – at least, as far as Marian theology devotion are concerned.

Chapter C: Mary within the Pattern of Grace and Hope

It is the theology of St Paul that is the key to this chapter and the key to the Commission's approach to the two definitions of 1854 and 1950. For St Paul, one must begin at the end: one cannot understand rightly what it means to be fully human without seeing it in the light of what we are to become in Christ, the 'last Adam', without seeing it in an eschatological perspective. Paul speaks as it were from the future retrospectively, when he says, 'those whom God predestined he also called; those whom he called he also justified; and those whom he justified he also glorified' (Romans 8.30). Viewed eschatologically, Mary embodies the 'elect Israel' of whom Paul speaks – glorified, justified, called, predestined. It is in following this paradigm of anticipated eschatology that one can see Mary as 'the faithful disciple fully present with God in Christ. In this way, she is a sign of hope for all humanity' (para. 56). This is how ARCIC tries to present to us its 're-reception' of the doctrine of the Assumption.

As for the Immaculate Conception, the fact that this conference is being held here in Lourdes itself and is devoted to the theme of the Immaculate Conception almost requires me to read you paragraph 59 of the Agreed Statement in its entirety:

> Roman Catholics are also bound to believe that 'the most blessed Virgin Mary was, from the first moment of her conception, by a singular grace and privilege of almighty God and in view of the merits of Christ Jesus the Saviour of the human race, preserved immune from all stain of original sin' (Dogma of the Immaculate Conception of Mary, defined by Pope Pius IX, 1854). The definition teaches that Mary, like all other human beings, has need of Christ as her Saviour and Redeemer (cf. *Lumen Gentium* 53; *Catechism of the Catholic Church* 491). The negative notion of 'sinlessness' runs the risk of obscuring the fullness of Christ's saving work. It is not so much that Mary lacks something which other human beings 'have', namely sin, but that the glorious

grace of God filled her life from the beginning. The holiness which is our end in Christ (cf. 1 John 3.2–3) was seen, by unmerited grace, in Mary, who is the prototype of the hope of grace for humankind as a whole. According to the New Testament, being 'graced' has the connotation of being freed from sin through Christ's blood (Ephesians 1.6–7). The Scriptures point to the efficacy of Christ's atoning sacrifice even for those who preceded him in time (cf. 1 Peter 3.19, John 8.56, 1 Corinthians 10.4). Here again the eschatological perspective illuminates our understanding of Mary's person and calling. In view of her vocation to be the mother of the Holy One (Luke 1.35), we can affirm together that Christ's redeeming work reached 'back' in Mary to the depths of her being, and to her earliest beginnings. This is not contrary to the teaching of Scripture, and can only be understood in the light of Scripture. Roman Catholics can recognize in this what is affirmed by the dogma – namely 'preserved from all stain of original sin' and 'from the first moment of her conception'.

Two footnotes are appended to this paragraph. The first explains that the definition of Pius IX addresses and resolves an old controversy about the exact timing of Mary's sanctification; then second directs itself to the assertion of St Paul in Romans 3.23 that 'all have sinned and fall short of the glory of God', which seems to admit of no exception, not even Mary. 'However' (I quote), 'it is important to note the rhetorical-apologetic context of the general argument of Romans 1–3, which is concerned to show the equal sinfulness of Jews and Gentiles (3.9). Romans 3.23 has a quite specific purpose in context which is unrelated to the issue of the "sinlessness" or otherwise of Mary.'

The members of the Commission record that they 'have agreed together that the teaching about Mary in the two definitions of 1854 and 1950 ... can be said to be consonant with the teaching of the Scriptures and the ancient common traditions' (para. 60). That is very good, but evidently it does not suffice. The Roman Catholic Church goes much further; it affirms that the dogmas are revealed by God and consequently must be believed 'firmly and constantly' by all the faithful – in effect, they are *de fide*. This position is not easy to reconcile with Article VI of the Thirty-nine Articles of the Church of England, which says,

> Holy Scripture containeth all things necessary to salvation: so that whatsoever is not read therein, nor may be proved thereby, is not to be required of any man, that it should be believed as an article of the Faith ...

ARCIC proposes three ways of trying to get out of this impasse. First, it offers a clarification:

When the Roman Catholic Church affirms that a truth is 'revealed by God', there is no suggestion of new revelation. Rather, the definitions are understood to bear witness to what has been revealed from the beginning. (para. 61)

Secondly, here and later on ARCIC refers to its previous text *The Gift of Authority*, which affirms the legitimacy under certain conditions of a papal definition made independently of a council.

Thirdly, the Anglicans asked whether it would be a condition of the future restoration of full communion that they should be required to accept the definitions of 1854 and 1950. The response of the Catholics is nuanced. They find it 'hard to envisage a restoration of communion in which acceptance of certain doctrines would be requisite for some and not for others' (para. 63). On the contrary, the hope is expressed that the two churches

> will recognize a common faith in the agreement ... which we here offer. Such a re-reception would mean the Marian teaching and devotion within our respective communities, including differences of emphasis, would be seen to be authentic expressions of Christian belief.

Furthermore, certain common declarations between the Roman Catholic Church and other churches are evoked, such as the Christological definitions with the non-Chalcedonian or even non-Ephesian Oriental churches or the Lutheran-Catholic declaration on justification, which show that if the Roman Catholic Church has to satisfy itself that it is the same faith, its partners are not always required to express it in the same language.

Chapter D: Mary in the Life of the Church

The most thorny questions have been grappled with in Chapter C and have required quite detailed attention. In turning to this last chapter, I must therefore be briefer!

If the Church of England's sixteenth-century Articles had sharply criticized the Roman doctrine of that time about the invocation of saints, ARCIC can affirm today that 'asking the saints to pray for us is not to be excluded as unscriptural, though it is not directly taught by the Scriptures to be a required element of life in Christ' (para. 70). Going further, the Commission declares in para. 75,

> Affirming together unambiguously Christ's unique mediation, which bears fruit in the life of the Church, we do not consider the practice of asking Mary and the saints to pray for us as communion dividing. Since obstacles of the past have been removed ... we believe that there is no continuing theological reason for ecclesial division on these matters.

The **Conclusion**, after re-affirming the agreements reached previously by ARCIC, the Commission offers five 'agreements, which we believe significantly advance our consensus' (para. 78):

1 that the teaching that God has taken the Blessed Virgin Mary in the fullness of her person into his glory is consonant with Scripture, and is only to be understood in the light of Scripture;

2 that in view of her vocation to be the mother of the Holy One, Christ's redeeming work reached 'back' in Mary to the depths of her being and to her earliest beginnings;
3 that the teaching about Mary in the two definitions of the Assumption and the Immaculate Conception, understood within the biblical pattern of the economy of hope and grace, can be said to be consonant with the teaching of the Scriptures and the ancient common traditions;
4 that this agreement, when accepted by our two Communions, would place the questions about authority which arise from the two definitions of 1854 and 1950 in a new ecumenical context;
5 that Mary has a continuing ministry which serves the ministry of Christ, our unique mediator, that Mary and the saints pray for the whole Church and that the practice of asking Mary and the saints to pray for us is not communion-dividing.

And to conclude this second section of my presentation of the ARCIC text, I shall quote the Commission's final aspiration, in para. 80:

> Our hope is that, as we share in the one Spirit by which Mary was prepared and sanctified for her unique vocation, we may together participate with her and all the saints in the unending praise of God.

III: Assessment

In this third section I promised to try to assess the importance of this agreement and the chances of it being accepted by our churches. My analysis will consist of some positive elements, followed by some negative elements, and a conclusion.

First, the positive elements:

1 If this agreement can succeed in being accepted by our two churches after a period of evaluation and consultation, it

will be possible to consider that the Marian question in itself is no longer a divisive factor. If very serious differences persist – and no one can deny that – they are in the area of the Church's magisterium and its authority.

2 One of the members of the Commission, an Anglican theologian brought up in the evangelical tradition, has acknowledged that this work on Mary was for him a veritable voyage of discovery. Let us hope that his experience will also be that of many others.

3 The report has succeeded in introducing a new vocabulary that is very often rich, beautiful, powerful and promising, which can help us to escape from certain impasses. I am thinking above all about Chapter C on grace and hope.

4 The text does not mention it explicitly, but there was none the less an Eastern and Orthodox influence. One of the ARCIC sessions was held at Chevetogne in Belgium and Dom Emmanuel Lanne was the 'consultant' to the Commission. I regret that there has been no Orthodox voice here to witness to the Orthodox tradition, but you will know that the Orthodox Church does not accept the dogma of the Immaculate Conception (a) because it was proclaimed unilaterally and (b) because the Catholic doctrine has come out of an Augustinian theology of original sin that has never been part of the Eastern tradition. The Orthodox Church proclaims Mary as '*Panagia*' (all-holy), and it is this same positive approach that has been adopted by ARCIC.

And now the negative elements.

First, there is inevitably a sizeable gap between the members of the Commission who have prayed and worked together for five years and the other members of our two communions – both the hierarchies and the faithful at large. My fear is that the Commission will neither be heard nor understood and that its report will not be read, above all – where the Anglicans are concerned – by liberals and evangelicals, who are in danger of responding with indifference and hostility respectively.

Secondly, there are words and phrases in the Agreed Statement which are not without ambiguity, notably the phrase 'consonant with Scripture'. What does that mean exactly? In conformity, in harmony with Scripture? The only legitimate interpretation of Scripture, or simply one interpretation (among others)? Compatible with Scripture? I cannot prevent myself from recalling a certain Anglican bishop[7] affirming in the General Synod in London that the ordination of women to the priesthood was 'consonant with Scripture'!

Finally, one cannot deny that the context for the dialogue between our two churches has changed radically since it began and that the climate has become more gloomy; that questions such as the ordination of women to the priesthood and episcopate and ethical questions, for example homosexuality, have at the same time both made the reconciliation of our two communions more difficult and also introduced a very grave crisis within Anglicanism, bringing it almost to breaking point.

When I was a child, I often played a game called 'Snakes and Ladders'. If your dice bring you to the bottom of a ladder you go to the top, but if your dice bring you to the head of a snake you go down to the tail. I fear that in our relationship today there are more snakes than ladders.

But this Agreed Statement is certainly a ladder. I would like to conclude with the analysis of Cardinal Cormac Murphy-O'Connor, Archbishop of Westminster and a former Co-Chairman of ARCIC. In these Agreed Statements, he said, ARCIC has been able to build firm columns across the chasm which separate our two communions. Nothing can destroy these columns, even if the day has not yet come to construct on these columns the viaduct which will reunite us in full communion.

---

7 The Rt Revd Michael Adie (then Bishop of Guildford) in the General Synod's debate on the final approval of the legislation for the ordination of women to the priesthood on 11 November 1992.

Publications by Roger Greenacre: A Select Bibliography

1955–74

'By Bicycle to the Shrine of Our Lady', *Church Observer*, 115 (July 1957), p. 5.

'The Real Presence: The Barrier of the Rejection of Localization', in M. Bruce (ed.), *Barriers to Unity* (London: The Faith Press, 1959), pp. 61–5.

'An Anglican Considers the Council', *Old Palace*, 31 (1962), pp. 248–50.

'Ourselves as Others See Us' [recent literature on Anglicanism by French and Belgian Roman Catholics], *Faith and Unity*, 7 (1963), pp. 25–9.

'Sanctification and Unity: Some Impressions of the Second Faith and Order Conference', *Faith and Unity*, 7 (1963), pp. 90–1.

'A Preface of the Saints', *Faith and Unity*, 7 (1963), p. 111.

'Die Beziehungen zwischen der anglikanischen und der römisch-katholischen Kirche in England seit der Ankündigung des Zweiten Vatikanischen Konzils', *Una Sancta* (2/1964), pp. 173–8.

'The Ecumenical Dialogue and Our Lady' [review article], *Walsingham Review*, 13 (Sept. 1964), pp. 6–10. See Chapter 15 of this volume.

'Unity and Worship: The Convergence of Traditions' [review article], *Faith and Unity*, 8 (1964), pp. 92–4.

'The Constitution on the Sacred Liturgy: Reflections of an Anglican', *The Eastern Churches Quarterly*, 16 (1964), pp. 338–44.

'The Anglican Church and the Ecumenical Movement', *Catholic Gazette* (January 1965), pp. 6–7, p. 13.

'Schism in the Church', *Faith and Unity*, 9 (1965), pp. 11–12.

The Sacrament of Easter: An Introduction to the Liturgy of Holy Week (London: The Faith Press, 1965); [later editions with Jeremy Haselock in 1989, 1991 and 1995].

'En guise de conclusion' and 'Les ordinations anglicanes', *Unité des Chrétiens*, 5 (January 1972), pp. 29–30, p. 35.

1975-89

'Le Père Portal, serviteur de l'Unité', *Unité des Chrétiens*, 22 (April 1976), p. 27.

'Si le grain ne meurt ...' [on Mercier and Portal], *Faith and Unity*, 20 (1976), pp. 42-6.

'Fernand Portal: An Anglican Tribute', *One in Christ*, 12 (1976), pp. 400-2.

'Dom Lambert Beauduin', *One in Christ*, 13 (1977), pp. 173-4.

'Père Maurice Villain, S. M.', *Faith and Unity*, 21 (1977), p. 26.

'Unité et Pluralisme dans la Liturgie anglicane', *Amitié: Rencontre entre Chrétiens*, 1 (January 1978), pp. 17-21; reprinted in *La Maison-Dieu: Revue de Pastorale Liturgique*, 134 (1978), pp. 10-18.

'Homélie prononcée le 31 août 1976 sur Actes 20,17-38', in *Veilleur avant l'aurore: Colloque Lambert Beauduin* (Chevetogne, 1978), pp. 27-9.

Christian Unity and the Ordination of Women: A Statement to the Loughborough Conference (London: Church Literature Association, 1978).

'Signification de la participation anglicane à l'I.S.E.O.' [Institut supérieur d'études œcumeniques], *Unité des Chrétiens*, 31 (July 1978), p. 12.

'Liturgical Prayer and Personal Prayer', *Quarterly Paper, Confraternity of the Blessed Sacrament* (December 1979-February 1980; March-May 1980).

'Benedictines and Christian Unity', in *Journey to God: Anglican Essays on the Benedictine Way* (Malling Abbey, 1980), pp. 105-45; reprinted in *One in Christ*, 16 (1980), pp. 283-98.

'Ordination, Recognition and Incorporation', in *Proposals for Covenanting: Some Considerations from the Church Union Theological Committee* (2nd edn, London: Church Literature Association, 1981), pp. 9-11.

'One Day in July' [Speech to the Cardinal Legate at Lourdes], *Church Observer*, 1981, no. 3.

'Papal Visit: Anglican Hopes and Responses', *Church Observer*, 1982, no. 1, pp. 13-14.

[with Dennis Corbishley] English Anglican-Roman Catholic Committee, *Study Guide to the Final Report of the Anglican-Roman Catholic International Commission* (London: CTS/SPCK, 1982).

Lord Halifax (Oxford Prophets, 3: London: Church Literature Association, 1983).

'Les dialogues bilatéraux dans lesquels la Communion anglicane est engagée', *Irénikon*, 56 (1983), pp. 34-45

A SELECT BIBLIOGRAPHY

'The Great Fifty Days: A Sermon for Pentecost (1983)', *Kairos*, 9 (Easter 1984), pp. 13–16.

'Celebration at St Peter's Church, London, 19 January 1984' [Sermon preached at a commemorative solemn requiem mass for the Second Viscount Halifax with 'The Franco-Belgian Connection: A Postscript'], *One in Christ*, 20 (1984), pp. 135–43.

'L'identité confessionelle et les "traditions" de la Communion anglicane dans la quête de l'unité de tous', *Irénikon*, 57 (1984), pp. 163–75. [For English translation, see below.]

'Theotokos' [Sermon preached at Chichester Cathedral], *Studies and Commentaries 1984* (Society of Mary/American Region), pp. 1–4.

'The Kingship of Christ' [Sermon preached at St Mary's, Bourne Street], *Kairos*, 10 (Advent 1984), pp. 15–20.

'L'anglicanisme devant la crise actuelle de l'œcumenisme', *Les quatre fleuves: Cahiers de recherché et de reflexion religieuses*, 20 (1984), pp. 69–74.

'Anglicanism and Confessional Identity', *One in Christ*, 21 (1985), pp. 121–30.

'La reception des textes des dialogues et la reception de la doctrine: deux problèmes pour les Anglicans', *Irénikon*, 58 (1985), pp. 471–91.

'Homélie de Mr Le Chanoine Roger Greenacre' [Sermon at Solemn Evensong in the Cathedral of Notre-Dame de Paris], *Oecumenisme Informations*, 163 (March 1986), pp. 8–11; reprinted in *Amitié: Rencontre entre Chrétiens*, 2 (1986), pp. 7–10.

'Rome et Cantorbéry: contradiction ou complémentarité', *La Foi et le Temps: Revue des dioceses francophones de Belgique*, 16 (1986), pp. 140–55.

'Prestige and Patrimony' [interview by Jeremy Haselock about the importance of the words and actions of Pope Paul VI in relation to the Anglican Communion], *The Messenger of the Catholic League*, 229 (May 1986), pp. 17–21.

'La Mére cachée aux regards', *Réforme*, 16 May 1987, p. 6. See Chapter 10 of this volume.

'Seeing and Hearing', *The Friends of Cathedral Music: Thirtieth Annual Report* (1987), pp. 9–12.

[with John Stott] Preface [as consultant editors] in C. Baxter (ed.), *Stepping Stones* (London: Hodder & Stoughton, 1987), pp. ix–xiii.

'Two Aspects of Reception' in G. R. Evans (ed.), *Christian Authority: Essays in Honour of Henry Chadwick* (Oxford: Clarendon Press, 1988), pp. 40–58.

'Causa Nostra Agitur? An Anglican Response', in H. Legrand, J. Manzanares and A. García y García (eds), *The Nature and Future of Episcopal Conferences*: *The Jurist*, 48 (1988), pp. 384–96. [The volume also appeared in Spanish, French and Italian editions.]

'Tenir le cap, sous un ciel changeant', *Unité des Chrétiens*, 71 (15 October 1989), pp. 36–40.

'An Open Letter from Roger Greenacre', in J. M. R. Tillard and R. Greenacre, *Lost in the Fog? The Lesson for Ecumenism of Lambeth* (Church Union Theological Committee Occasional Paper no. 3: London: Church Literature Association, 1989), pp. 7–9.

[with Jeremy Haselock] *The Sacrament of Easter* (Leominster: Gracewing, 1989); revised edn: 1991; 3rd edn: 1995.

1990–2000

Preface in M. Dudley and G. Rowell (eds), *Confession and Absolution* (London: SPCK, 1990), pp. viii–xii.

[with Jeremy Haselock], 'Ordination and Pastoral Care', J. Greenhalgh and E. Russell (eds), *Building in Love: The Vocation of the Church* (London: St Mary's, Bourne Street, 1990), pp. 60–8.

'Le dialogue Anglican-catholique', *Unité Chrétienne*, 97–98 (1990), pp. 7–43.

Mother Out of Sight: A paper delivered to the East Sussex, West Sussex and Canterbury branches of the Ecumenical Society of the Blessed Virgin Mary during 1989 (ESBVM pamphlet, 1990). See Chapter 12 of this volume.

[with Suzanne Martineau] Introduction in *Twinnings and Exchanges: Guidelines proposed by the Anglican–Roman Catholic Committees of France and England* (London, 1990), pp. 4–7.

'Diversity in Unity: A Problem for Anglicans', in *Centro Pro Unione*, 39 (Spring 1991), pp. 4–10.

'Subsidiarity' in *Aambit* (Newsletter of the Association for Apostolic Ministry), 9 (February 1992).

'Il problema liturgico in ambito anglicano tra XIX e XX secolo', in C. Alzati (ed.), *L'anglicanismo: Dalla Chiesa d'Inghilterra alla Comunione Anglicana* (Genoa: Marietti, 1992), pp. 163–76.

'Subsidiarity in Church and State', *Contemporary Review*, 260, issue 1517 (June 1992), p. 287.

'I Sing of a Maiden', Southern Cathedrals Festival 1992 programme brochure, pp. 63–5; reprinted in the Newsletter of the Ecumenical Society of the Blessed Virgin Mary, 51 (October 1992). See Chapter 11 of this volume.

'An Amber Light: A speech to the Convocation of Canterbury in July 1993', *The Messenger of the Catholic League*, 248 (October 1992), pp. 2–5.

A SELECT BIBLIOGRAPHY

'La signification des Églises orientales catholiques au sein de la communion romaine dans la perspective de "l'Église anglicane unie non absorbée"', *Irénikon*, 65 (1992), pp. 339–51.

'*Epistola ad Romanos*: an open letter to some Roman Catholic friends', *The Month*, 254 (March 1993), pp. 88–96; abbreviated version in *The Tablet* (20 March 1993), pp. 366–7; French translation in *Istina*, 38 (1993), pp. 117–33.

'Le credo: L'Europe et la foi', in A. Compagnon and J. Seebacher (eds*)*, *L'Esprit de l'Europe, 2 – Mots et Choses* (Paris: Flammarion, 1993), pp. 73–85; English translation: 'Europe and the Faith', *Contemporary Review*, 263 no. 1531 (August 1993), pp. 57–65.

Introduction in M. Dudley and G. Rowell (eds), *The Oil of Gladness: Anointing in the Christian Tradition* (London: SPCK, 1993), pp. 1–6.

'The Place of Reception: An Open Letter to the Archbishop of York', *Church of England Newspaper* (8 October 1993), p. 7; French translation in *Istina*, 39 (1994), pp. 117–21.

General Synod speech on the Episcopal Ministry Act of Synod 1993 in *Unity Digest*, 9 (February 1994), pp. 5–6; French translation in *Istina*, 39 (1994), pp. 192–3.

'Autumn Festival Sermon', *The Server: Quarterly Magazine of the Guild of the Servants of the Sanctuary*, 16, no. 9 (Spring 1994), pp. 18–19.

'Eucharist and Evangelization: Ecumenical collaboration in the Mission ad gentes' in *Christus Lumen Gentium: Eucharistia et Evangelizatio: XLV Conventus Eucharisticus Internationalis – Sevilla 1993* (Vatican City, 1994), pp. 933–8.

'Homélie prononcée à la celebration œcumenique du 27 janvier 1994' and 'Relations entre anglicans et catholiques', in C. Perreau and B. Poirier (eds), *Un Chemin d'Unité: Hommage au Père Jacques Élisée Desseaux* (Paris: Les Éditions du Cerf, 1994), pp. 38–41, pp. 132–9.

Mark Frank (1613–1664): A Caroline Preacher: an edited version of a talk given at the Annual General Meeting of the Society on 5th March, 1994 (Ecumenical Society of the Blessed Virgin Mary pamphlet, January 1995). See Chapter 13 of this volume.

'La communion entre nos Églises: l'experience anglicane de sa fragilité', *Unité des Chrétiens*, 99 (July 1995), pp. 11–17.

'The Liturgy: Past, Present and Future' [interview], *Cathedral Music* (November 1995), pp. 23–7.

The Catholic Church in France: An Introduction (CCU Occasional Paper no. 4: London, 1996 – reprinted with corrections, 1998).

[with Cecily Boulding, John Muddiman and Edward Yarnold at the request of the English Anglican–Roman Catholic Committee] 'Apostolicae Curae: A Hundred Years On', *One in Christ*, 32 (1996), pp. 295–309.

'The Malines Conversations: a significant milestone in the history of Anglican–Roman Catholic dialogue', in W. McLoughlin and J. Pinnock (eds), *Mary is for Everyone: Essays on Mary and Ecumenism* (Leominster: Gracewing, 1997), pp. 128–45.

'The Chancellors of Chichester Cathedral', *Chichester Cathedral Journal* (1997), pp. 9–14.

'Mother of All Christians', *The Tablet* (24 January 1998). See Chapter 16 of this volume.

'Fury at the Abbey: A Controversial Sermon at a Royal Funeral', *Chichester Cathedral Journal* (1998), pp. 4–12.

'Anglican Identity and the Caroline Divines', *Tufton Review*, 2.2 (1998), pp. 26–45.

'The Virgin Mary in the Liturgical Texts of the Anglican Communion', *De Cultu Mariano Saeculo XX: Acta of the International Mariological-Marian Congress, Częstochowa, 1996* (Vatican City: Pontificia Academia Mariana Internationalis, 1999), pp. 213–30. See Chapter 14 of this volume. Italian translation in *La 'Theotokos' nel dialogo ecumenico: Rivista Liturgica*, 85 (1998), pp. 221–40.

'Démocratie dans les Églises: témoignage d'un Anglican', in J. Baubérot, J. Famerée, R. T. Greenacre and J. Gueit, *Démocratie dans les Églises* (Brussels: Lumen Vitae, 1999), pp. 10–28.

'The Precentors of Chichester Cathedral', *Chichester Cathedral Journal* (2000), pp. 20–35.

'Le don de l'autorité', *Les Amis du Bec-Hellouin*, 130 (June 2000), pp. 6–24.

2001–10

'Un Anglican témoigne', *Marie, signe pour les croyants: Les actes du colloque marial de Lourdes: Lourdes Magazine*, 109 (March–April 2002), pp. 15–17. See Chapter 10 of this volume.

'Trying to be Honest: Witnessing to the Place of Mary in the Life and Worship of Anglicanism', *Walsingham Review*, 130 (Assumptiontide 2002), pp. 6–8. See Chapter 10 of this volume.

'L'Eucharistie, sacrement d'unité: reflexions sur un texte récent de l'épiscopat de l'Église d'Angleterre', *La Maison-Dieu*, 235 (2003): *Baptême unique, Églises divisées*, pp. 125–35.

'L'Abbé Couturier en Angleterre' in *L'Œcuménisme Spirituel de Paul Couturier aux Défis Actuels: Actes du colloque universitaire interconfessionnel Lyon et Franchevile, 8–10 Novembre 2002* (Lyon: Profac, [2003]), pp. 45–57.

A SELECT BIBLIOGRAPHY

'Le Débat dans l'Anglicanisme au sujet du mariage, du divorce et de la sexualité humaine', *Revue d'éthique et de théologie morale ('Le Supplément': Religions et Nations)*, 228 (2004), pp. 263–74.

'L'amitié de Lord Halifax et de Monsieur Portal', *Église en Savoie – numéro spécial* (June 2006), pp. 9–11.

'Marie: grâce et espérance dans le Christ' in *Je suis l'Immaculée: Colloque organise par les Sanctuaires Notre-Dame de Lourdes et la Société Française d'Études Mariales* (Editions Parole et Silence, 2006), pp. 173–89. See Chapter 19 of this volume.

'Homélie pour la fête de saint Joseph, donnée par le chanoine Roger Greenacre à l'occasion des 25 ans de son oblation au Bec', *Les Amis du Bec-Hellouin*, 157 (April 2007), pp. 35–7. See Chapter 9 of this volume.

'Introduction' in D. Kennedy with J. Haselock, *Using Common Worship: Times and Seasons, Lent to Embertide: A Practical Guide* (London: Church House Publishing, 2008), pp. 1–11.

C. Aubé-Elie, 'Le chanoine Roger Greenacre' [interview], *Unité des Chrétiens*, 152 (October 2008), pp. 29–31.

'Cranmer et la liturgie anglicane' in *La Bible lue au temps des Réformes (xvie siècle): Supplément Cahiers Evangile*, 146 (December 2008), pp. 55–8.

'Père Philibert et l'œcuménisme: Témoignage d'un ami anglican', *Les Amis du Bec-Hellouin*, 164 (December 2008), pp. 8–11; reprinted in *Chrétiens en Marche*, 102 (April–June 2009), p. 6.

'Les racines d'une tradition catholique dans l'anglicanisme', *Unité des Chrétiens*, 155 (July 2009), pp. 14–16.

Presentation of the Anglican tradition and selection and translation of Anglican texts in M. de La Roncière (ed.), *Trésors de la Prière des Chrétiens d'Orient et d'Occident* (2009).

'Dr Eric Kemp', *New Directions*, 13, no. 176 (January 2010), p. 23.

2011

'Un souvenir personnel du Père Abbé Paul Grammont', *Les Amis du Bec-Hellouin*, 173 (March 2011), pp. 54–5.

'A Dinner in Paris' [account of a dinner with the Duke and Duchess of Windsor in 1970], *The Charterhouse Magazine*, 28 (July 2011), pp. 11–12.

Index

Adam 59, 212
Adie, Michael 218
Aldenham School, Herts 3-4
Allchin, A. M. (Donald) xv, 125, 127, 134, 139, 155n, 156
Altar 7, 41, 46-7, 53, 110, 126n, 142, 146, 147, 149, 153, 155, 194, 195
Alternative Service Book 1980 174-5
Ambrose of Milan 48, 137
Andrewes, Lancelot xvi, xvii, 111-12, 125, 135, 136, 164
Angel(s) 42, 44, 51, 53, 56, 57, 58, 59, 60, 63, 67, 70, 83, 88, 90, 92, 113, 118, 128, 130, 144, 147, 148, 150, 151, 152, 154, 158, 175, 193n, 195, *see also* Gabriel
Angelus 54-7, 104, 174, 177, *see also* Hail Mary
Anglican-Roman Catholic International Commission (ARCIC) xviii, 4, 10, 12, 27, 39, 127n, 206,
Final Report 9, 77, 99-101, 102, 206-8, 210, 220
Mary, Grace and Hope in Christ xvi-xviii, 61, 84-7, 99n, 205-18
The Gift of Authority 208-9, 214
Anselm of Bec and Canterbury 109, 110
Ark of the Covenant 42, 55
Ave 53, 98, 112, 116, 131, 151, 153, 168, *see also* Angelus, Hail Mary, Marian antiphons
Ave maris stella 107-8, 171
Augustine of Canterbury 41
Augustine of Hippo 34, 137

Beauduin, Lambert 5, 6, 10, 220
Bec xiii, 5, 9-10, 15, 19, 90, 109
Bede 137, 153
Belloc, Hilaire 66-7
Benedict 135
Benedictus 69, 138

INDEX

Benedikte of Denmark, Princess 14
Bernard of Clairvaux 58–9, 109, 137, 149
Bethlehem 48–9, 54, 83, 147, 148, 195
Bonaparte, Napoleon 57–8
Book of Common Prayer xvi, 39, 82, 87, 91, 111, 115, 117, 118–19, 158–60, 165, 166, 167–8, 170, 171, 172, 174
Bouyer, Louis 5, 111, 183
Breviary 107, 129, 158, 168, 170–1
Britten, Benjamin 104, 179
Brooks, Phillips 48
Bullinger, Heinrich 187

Calendar xv, xvi, 60, 76n, 91, 111, 117, 118, 158, 160–1, 166, 170, 173, 177, 185, 191
Calvin, Jean 120, 122, 187
Calvinism, Calvinists 122n, 123, 124, 135, 155, 162
Candlemas 69, 136, 139, 147, 148–50, 175, 193–4, *see also* Christ, presentation of
Carey, George xi, 24
Caroline Divines 115, 124, 162–4, 167, 168, 224
Carver, Elizabeth 14
Celebrating Common Prayer 176, 191
Chadwick, Henry 4, 221

Charles I 134, 165
Charterhouse, London xi, xiii, 17–18, 21, 30, 37, 225
Chartres 5, 8, 41, 43, 110
Chevetogne 6, 18, 62–3, 217, 220
Chichester Roundel 110
Chichester Theological College xix, 8
Christ 29, 33, 40, 42, 43, 48, 49, 50, 52, 53, 54, 55, 56, 64, 70, 71, 72, 73, 74, 75, 79, 80, 81, 83, 84, 85, 87, 88, 89, 90, 100, 101, 102, 103, 107, 108, 109, 111, 113, 117, 118, 119, 120, 121, 128, 137, 139, 140, 142, 143, 144, 145, 146, 147, 149, 151, 174, 184, 185, 186, 187, 188, 190, 195, 196, 198–9, 203, 206, 207, 210, 211, 212, 213, 215, 216, 221, *see also* Jesus
  ascension of 73, 79, 80
  as mediator 85, 100, 101, 111, 120, 128, 140, 190, 207, 210, 216
  incarnation of 43, 50, 52, 55, 56, 57, 60, 73, 73, 74, 79, 87, 96, 100, 102, 107, 150, 163, 166, 174, 207
  passion/crucifixion of 18, 56, 57, 109
  presentation of 75, 147, 174, *see also* Candlemas

resurrection of 28, 56, 57, 72, 79
sacrifice of 26, 142, 213
transfiguration of 79
Church ix, xix, 3, 11–12, 23, 25, 29, 31–2, 44, 47, 50, 51, 53, 57, 63, 64, 69, 70, 71, 72, 73, 74, 80, 85, 86, 91, 92, 99, 100, 101, 102, 103, 107, 109, 111, 118–19, 120, 126, 127, 128, 131, 138, 139, 140, 141–2, 146, 150, 152n, 153, 164, 169, 174, 176, 183, 184, 185, 186, 187, 188, 190, 191, 192, 193, 196, 197, 198, 202, 203, 206, 207, 208, 210, 215, 216, 217
Church Union Theological Committee 9, 15, 19, 220, 222
Churches
 Bath, Holy Trinity 78
 Beaulieu-sur-Mer, St Michael's xiii, 13–14, 15, 16, 17, 20, 22, 28, 37, 51, 54, 57, 69, 87
 Bourne Street, St Mary's 6, 221, 222
 Boxgrove Priory 41, 42n, 48n, 69n
 Cambridge, Little St Mary's 62, 64
 Chant D'Oiseau, Brussels, Notre-Dame-des-Grâces 62, 64
 Chartres Cathedral 41, 43
 Chichester Cathedral ix, xiii, xix, 8, 9, 12, 14, 18, 22, 26, 27, 30, 41, 45, 48n, 49, 69n, 82, 91, 106, 110, 221, 224
 Chichester, St John's 45, 46
 Chichester, SS Peter and Paul 75
 Clerkenwell, Our Most Holy Redeemer 38, 45, 46, 71
 Durham Cathedral 136, 193
 Hanworth, All Saints xii, 5
 Marble Arch, The Annunciation 6
 Margaret Street, All Saints 18
 North Audley Street, St Mark's 6
 Oxford, University Church of St Mary the Virgin 83, 115, 163
 Paris, St George's 7, 21–2, 23, 24, 31, 37, 62
 Ufford, The Assumption 84
 Westminster Abbey 65–6, 68, 200
Cinderella 82, 84
Cîteaux 58
Clairvaux 58
Clare College, Cambridge 4, 62, 126n
Coles, Stuckey 88
College of the Resurrection: *see* Mirfield

INDEX

Common Worship xv, 7, 52, 76n, 176n, 177n
Community of the Resurrection: *see* Mirfield
Connaught, Prince Arthur, Duke of 13–14
Corinthians, First Letter to 80
Cosin, John 136, 193–4
Cost of Conscience 79
Councils 43, 100, 141–2, 163, 214
  Chalcedon 169
  Ephesus 43, 50, 72, 101, 107
  Trent 123
  see also Second Vatican Council
Courtesy 63, 66–7, 68, 73
Couturier, Paul 201, 224
Cranmer, Thomas 69n, 157, 158, 159, 171
Creeds 55, 86, 87, 89, 130, 163, 166, 197, 203
Cwiertniak, Stanislas 132–3
Czestochowa 95, 190

Discretion 66, 91–2, 98, 190
Dix, Gregory 39, 78, 82
Donne, John 39, 49, 52, 124, 136, 163
Drelincourt, Charles 187

Easter, The Sacrament of xii, 6–7, 23, 28
Ecumenical movement 12, 183, 185, 189, 197, 211, 219

Ecumenical Society of the Blessed Virgin Mary vii, xiv, 9, 76, 103, 106, 115n, 120, 124n, 132n, 178, 189n, 191, 198
Edinburgh, Prince Philip, Duke of 17–18, 91
Egypt 82, 92
Elizabeth 48, 52, 57, 63, 64, 67, 68, 70, 71, 76n, 80, 89, 91, 154, 177
Elizabeth I 160
English ARC 9, 12
Emmanuel Community 47
Erasmus, Desiderius 120, 157
Eve 53, 108, 113, 125, 131, 187
Evensong (Evening Prayer) xvi, xvii, 69, 89, 106, 111, 117, 147, 159, 160, 162, 170, 175, 179n

Faith and Order Advisory Group xviii
Fathers 38, 44, 63, 67, 73, 137, 142, 153, 163, 187, 197
Fauré, Gabriel 84
Feminists 104, 179, 204
Ferrar, Nicholas 139
Font, baptismal 14, 44, 48, 148
Forbes, Alexander Penrose 129
Forbes, George 129
Forbes, William 97, 127, 129, 164

Fountains 58
France, The Catholic Church in xii, 9, 23, 31
Francis of Assisi 109
Frank, Mark xiv–xv, xvii, 97, 125, 132–56, 164, 194–6
French ARC 8, 12
Frere, Walter 5

Gabriel 42, 52, 67, 70, 108, 112, 176, *see also* Angel(s)
Gillett, Martin 103
Goodall, Jonathan 31
Gore, Charles 5
Grammont, Paul 5, 225
Greenacre, Roger ix–x, xi–xvi, xix, 3–20, 21–34, 37–40
  and Bec xiii, 5, 9–10, 15, 19
  and Belgium 3, 6, 12, 19, 22, 23, 39
  and France 3, 5, 7–8, 9, 10, 12, 13–14, 15, 19, 23, 39
  and monasticism 5, 9–10, 19
  and Walsingham xii–xiii, 5–6, 14–15, 87, 95
  and women's ordination 10–13, *see also* Women, ordination of
  death, funeral and requiems (2011) xi, 12, 18–19, 21–34, 37
  early life (1930–49) 3–4
  in Cambridge (1949–52) 4, 62, 126n
  in Mirfield (1952–54) 4, 5
  in Hanworth (1954–59) xii–xiii, 5
  in Louvain (1961–62) 6, 22, 62–3, 85, 189
  in Central London (1962–65) 6
  in Paris (1965–75) 7–8, 12, 15, 20, 21–2, 24, 31, 37
  in Chichester (1975–2000) xiii, 8–9, 13, 20, 22, 24, 91, 106
  in Beaulieu-sur-Mer (2000–10) xiii, 13–14, 16, 20, 22, 28, 37
  in Charterhouse (2010–11) xi, 17–18, 25, 30, 33
Gregory I (the Great) 41, 135, 137, 138
Groupe des Dombes 198, 200–4, 209

Haddington 104
Hail Mary 56–7, 104, 107, 118, 131, 159, 161, 164, 168, 174, 179, *see also Angelus*
Halifax, Earl of 169, 220, 221, 225
Halliburton, John 6
Haselock, Jeremy xii, xiii, 6, 8, 18, 20, 21, 23, 37, 38, 39
Hebrews, Letter to 89
Henry VIII 87, 117, 120, 157–8, 161
Herbert, George xvii, 124–5, 126, 136, 163

INDEX

Hester, John 45n
Hickes, George xvii
Hind, John ix, 12, 14, 18, 26, 28n
Holy Spirit x, 29, 42, 44, 48, 51, 53, 57, 58, 63, 73–4, 142, 176, 190, 203, 216
Hooker, Richard 163
Hope, David 13
House of Bishops 50, 101–2, 175, 202
Hughes, Anselm 45
Hume, Basil 103
Hymns 39, 43, 48, 76, 79, 83, 86, 88, 98, 104, 107, 109, 122n, 125, 167, 170–2
Hymns Ancient and Modern 79n, 125n, 171

'I sing of a maiden' 66, 106,
Institut catholique de Paris, 8
Israel 42–3, 47, 50, 52, 56, 60, 67–8, 70, 187, 203, 204

James I xvii, 165
Jennings, Derek 21, 23
Jesus 28, 29, 32, 48, 51, 53, 54, 64, 70–1, 72, 73, 79, 89, 91, 92, 109, 114, 130, 143, 149 *see also* Christ
John, First Letter of 34
John, Gospel according to 52
John the Baptist 47, 52, 54, 56, 60, 69, 75, 121
John XXIII 111, 184

John Paul II 12n, 101, 103, 189, 191, 201, 208
Joseph 51, 52, 90–2, 148
Julian of Norwich 109

Kasper, Walter 16, 27n
Keble, John xvii, 96, 98, 115–16, 117, 129, 162, 168
Kemp, Eric 8, 16, 225
Ken, Thomas xvi, xvii, 39, 76, 78–9, 83, 98, 125, 171
Knock 65
Küng, Hans 184–5

Lady Chapels xiv, 104, 106, 110, 178
Lady Day 42, 55, 56, 60, 150
Lambeth Conference (1958) 173
Lanne, Emmanuel 217
Laski, John 160
Laud, William 39, 46, 83, 117, 135, 163
Leonard, Graham 31
Lérins 58
Liberalism 179
Liddon House 6
Litany, English 118, 158, 159
Lourdes xvi, 95, 205n, 212, 220
Louvain 6, 22, 62–3, 85, 189
Lubac, Henri de 5
Luke, Gospel according to 57, 60, 64, 69, 71, 90, 92, 107, 213

Luther, Martin 88, 89, 120, 157, 187

Magnificat xvi, xvii, 14, 64, 69, 78, 82, 88, 89, 101, 111, 117, 159, 162, 179n, 197
Malines Conversations 5, 224
Marian antiphons (final anthems) 110–11, 112–14
  Alma redemptoris Mater 110, 112
  Ave Regina Caelorum 113
  Regina caeli laetare 110, 113, 174, 177
  Salve Regina 111, 113, 177, 191
Marian dogmas xviii, 100–1, 102, 208
  Assumption (dogma/definition of 1950) 75n, 77, 100, 186, 203, 211, 216
  Immaculate Conception (dogma/definition of 1854) 100, 186, 203, 211, 212, 216, 217
Martineau, Suzanne 9
Mary viii, 96
 and the Church 44, 47–8, 53, 71, 73–4, 80, 85–6, 100–1, 103, 131, 183, 184, 186, 187–8, 190, 202, 207
  Annunciation to 42, 44, 49, 52, 53, 55–7, 58–60, 67, 70, 75, 83, 117, 118, 126n, 150–4, 158, 162, 163, 166, 175, 186
  Assumption of 75–8, 78–81, 83–4, 84–7, 98, 100, 103, 118, 158, 161, 171, 177, 186, 203, 211, 212, 216
  as ark 42, 55
  as blessed 44, 48, 53, 56, 62, 63–4, 67, 68, 69, 70–1, 76, 80–1, 83, 89, 144, 150–1, 152, 154, 175, 176, 197, 210
  as Daughter of Zion 47, 64, 68, 70
  as ever-virgin (perpetual virginity of) xvi, 75n, 108, 112, 123, 125, 163, 164, 202
  as full of grace 56, 60, 125, 131
  as gate of heaven 108, 112, 144,
  as model (example) ix, 63, 68, 71, 73, 80–1, 83, 89, 100, 101, 125, 163, 187, 198, 204, 207
  as mother 15, 42, 44, 46, 49, 50, 51, 52, 53, 54, 55, 66, 67, 70, 74, 75, 75, 76, 77, 78, 79, 80, 85, 88, 89, 91, 92, 106, 108, 115, 119, 120
  as 'Our Lady' 106, 117, 123, 153, 163, 166
  as *Panagia* 217

INDEX

as predestined/prepared 60–1, 75, 84, 86, 100, 101, 202, 207, 210, 212–3, 216
as Queen of Heaven 64, 82–4, 113, 144
as second Eve 53, 125, 163, 187
as star of the sea 107n, 108, 112, 125, 153, 163
as tabernacle 52, 53
as *Theotokos* 43, 44, 50, 52, 63, 67, 70, 71, 72, 81, 83, 84, 100, 101, 107, 110, 184, 202, 207, 208, 211, 221
as virgin 41, 42, 43, 44, 47, 48, 50, 51, 59, 76, 80, 82, 84, 108, 110, 112, 117, 123–4, 144, 145, 148, 152, 163, 164, 187, 202
as woman clothed with the sun / heavenly woman 82, 144, 187
at Cana 68, 81, 85
at Pentecost 73–4
at the Cross 61, 73, 188
birth (nativity) of 75, 76n, 89, 117, 161, 170, 172, 177
Conception of 75, 76n, 100, 117, 161, 170, 171n, 172, 177, 186, 203, 205, 211–13, 216, 217
invocation of xviii, 86, 88, 99, 107, 153, 164, 187, 203, 211

pregnancy of 42, 48, 50, 52, 53, 63, 73, 92
statues of 83, 85, 97, 104, 106, 117, 126, 161, 163, 178
Visitation of 52, 67–8, 76n, 117, 161, 170, 172, 175, 177, 186
Yes of 53, 57, 66, 70, 73
Mascall, Eric 6, 23, 39, 43, 50
Matthew, Gospel according to 90, 194
Matins 69
Maycock, Hugh 62
Millet, Jean-François 55
Mirfield 4, 5, 22
Mo(u)ntagu(e), Richard 126n, 135–6
Montauroux 24
Moule, Charles 4
Murphy-O'Connor, Cormac 218

Nashdom 5
Nathan 42
Nazareth 66, 78, 82, 84, 92
Nazir-Ali, Michael xvii
Neale, John Mason xvii, 39, 43n, 135n, 171
Neile, Richard 135
New English Hymnal 39, 43n, 76, 88n, 107n, 122n, 171
Newman, John Henry xvii, 33, 99, 115, 129, 133, 168, 170, 171

233

Nonjurors 97–8, 115, 167
Nunc dimittis 69

Orthodox, Eastern ix, 39, 49, 52, 53, 71, 77, 87, 104, 107, 111, 178, 179n, 184, 185, 191, 197, 201, 217
Overall, John 135
Oxford Movement xvii, 46, 96, 97, 98, 99, 102, 115, 129, 135, 162, 167, 171, 211, *see also* Tractarians

Patten, Alfred Hope xiii, xvii, 5–6
Paul 25, 60–1, 79, 80, 142, 212, 213
Paul VI 206, 221
Pearson, John xvii
Peck, Arthur 62
Pentecost 71, 73–4, 111, 221
Peterhouse, Cambridge 136
Pew, Society of Our Lady of 65, 68, 200
Pilgrimage ix, xii, xvii, 5, 24, 27, 33, 41, 64, 65, 87, 102, 104, 110, 118, 161, 178, 193, 194, 196, 197
Pius IX 212, 213
Pius XII 75n, 77
Platytera ton Ouranon 39, 49, 50
Podmore, Colin x, xi, 3, 23, 37
Prayer Book: *see* Book of Common Prayer

Prestige, G. L. 109
Primacy 192, 209
Promise of His Glory 175
Pulpit 45, 46, 47, 136, 193
Pusey, Edward 133, 170
Pusey House 62n, 88, 133, 134

Quarr 5

Ramsey, Michael 4, 8, 62, 206
Reardon, Martin 6
Redemptoris Mater 95, 103
Reformation, English xvi, 85, 88, 96, 97, 106, 111, 116, 119, 121, 157, 166, 178, 191, 197, 202
Resurrection of the body (general resurrection) 77, 79, 86, 87, 89, 159
Revelation to John 82, 187
Richard of Chichester 84, 110
Rievaulx 58
Ritualists 99, 170
Romans, Letter to 60, 79, 212, 213
Root, Howard 134, 153
Rosary 110, 178
Routledge, Patricia 15
Rowell, Geoffrey 15
Runcie, Robert 12n, 103, 208

Sagovsky, Nicholas xvii
St John's Hospice, St John's Wood 18

INDEX

Saints
 communion of 59, 76, 93, 94, 106, 108, 109
 invocation of xvii, 91, 93–4, 98, 103
Scotland 104, 128, 165, 172, 173
Second Vatican Council 6, 7, 12, 22, 27, 62–3, 85, 103, 111, 178, 183, 188, 189, 190, 191, 198, 206, 211, 219
Sexuality 204, 218
Simeon 69, 90, 143, 148
Sisterhoods 170
Snakes and Ladders 85, 218
Solesmes 5
Southern, Richard 109
Stephenson, Colin xiii, 6
Stevenson, Kenneth xv, 134n, 155n, 156
Sweet, Mervyn 3–4

Tabernacle 46, 51, 52–3, 142
Tablet 65, 189n, 190, 223
Taizé 185–6, 201
Tavener, John 14–15, 104, 179
Tauran, Jean-Louis ix, 14, 18, 27, 28, 30
Taylor, Jeremy xvi, xvii, 39, 44–5, 48, 51, 125, 136
Thirty-nine Articles 122–3, 214, 215
Thomson, James 17–18
Thorndike, Herbert 126–7, 135, 164

Thornton, L. S. 185
Thurian, Max 186–7, 201
Timms, George 39, 76
Tractarians 116, 129, 133, 135, 167, 168–9, 170, 172, *see also* Oxford Movement
Tschann, Jean-Marie 13, 15

Upper Room 73
Ut unum sint 50, 101, 102, 190, 191, 201, 208

Venantius Fortunatus 43n
Villain, Maurice 132, 183, 220
Virgo orans (praying virgin/woman) 47, 52, 53
Virgo paritura 41, 43

Walsingham ix, xii–xiii, xvii, 5, 15, 65, 87, 95, 104, 110, 117, 157, 170, 178, 183n, 186, 191
Wake, William 29
Ward, Neville 178
Wessex, Earl and Countess of 13
William Temple Association 6
Williams, Rowan 15, 19, 30
Wirgman, Theodore 133
womb 42, 43, 44, 47, 48, 49, 50, 51, 52, 55, 56, 60, 63, 64, 67, 70, 71, 73, 75, 79, 80, 81, 83, 114, 124, 176

womb-community ix, 42, 44, 47, 50–1, 57, 67–8, 70
women, ordination of 10–13, 16–7, 78, 79n, 85, 179, 191, 218, 220
Wren, Matthew 136
Wybrew, Hugh 6

Zechariah 60, 63, 67, 69, 91
Zobel, Philibert 5
Zwingli, Huldrych 120, 187